MW00990646

THE FOURTH DIMENSION

To my Beloved Father
on Christmas, 1996.

Pano

Princeton Modern Greek Studies

This series is sponsored by the Princeton University Program in Hellenic Studies under the auspices of the Stanley J. Seeger Hellenic Fund.

Firewalking and Religious Healing: The Anastenaria of Greece and the American Firewalking Movement *by Loring M. Danforth*

Kazantzakis: Politics of the Spirit *by Peter Bien*

Dance and the Body Politic in Northern Greece *by Jane K. Cowan*

Yannis Ritsos: Repetitions, Testimonies, Parentheses *edited and translated by Edmund Keeley*

Contested Identities: Gender and Kinship in Modern Greece *edited by Peter Loizos and Evthymios Papataxiarchis*

A Place in History: Social and Monumental Time in a Cretan Town *by Michael Herzfeld*

Demons and the Devil: Moral Imagination in Modern Greek Culture *by Charles Stewart*

The Enlightenment as Social Criticism: Iosipos Moisiodax and Greek Culture in the Eighteenth Century *by Paschalis M. Kitromilides*

C. P. Cavafy: Collected Poems *translated by Edmund Keeley and Philip Sherrard; edited by George Savidis*

George Seferis: Complete Poems *translated, edited, and introduced by Edmund Keeley and Philip Sherrard*

The Fourth Dimension *by Yannis Ritsos; translated by Peter Green and Beverly Bardsley*

THE FOURTH DIMENSION

· YANNIS RITSOS ·

TRANSLATED BY

PETER GREEN

AND

BEVERLY BARDSLEY

PRINCETON UNIVERSITY PRESS · PRINCETON NEW JERSEY

Copyright © 1993 by Peter Green and Beverly Bardsley
Published by Princeton University Press, 41 William Street,
Princeton, New Jersey 08540

Translated from the Greek edition of Yannis Ritsos, Tetartē Diastasē (Poiēmata
1956–1972) (Athens: Kedros, 1st ed., December 1972; 6th ed. [including "Phae-
dra"], June 1978).

All Rights Reserved

Library of Congress Cataloging-in-Publication Data

Ritsos, Giannēs, 1909–
  [Tetartē diastasē, English]
  The fourth dimension / Yannis Ritsos ; translated by Peter Green
and Beverly Bardsley.
    p. cm. — (Princeton modern Greek studies)
    ISBN 0-691-06940-9. — ISBN 0-691-02465-0
    I. Title. II. Series.
PA5629.I7T4313   1993
889'.132—dc20   92-27141
                                                          CIP

Publication of this book has been aided by the Princeton University Program in
Hellenic Studies under the auspices of the Stanley J. Seeger Hellenic Fund

This book has been composed in Sabon typeface and designed by Frank Mahood

Princeton University Press books are printed on acid-free paper and meet the guide-
lines for permanence and durability of the Committee on Production Guidelines for
Book Longevity of the Council on Library Resources

Printed in the United States of America

10 9 8 7 6 5 4 3 2 1
10 9 8 7 6 5 4 3 2 1
(Pbk.)

C O N T E N T S

• A C K N O W L E D G M E N T S •

We would like to thank Professor A.P.D. Mourelatos, Professor Edmund Keeley, and Ms. Catherine Makrinikola of Kedros Publishers for much generous and useful help and advice.

Earlier versions of four of the poems in this volume were published in *Southern Humanities Review, Grand Street,* and *Southeastern Review.*

It is a pleasure to make available for the first time to English-speaking readers the complete text of Yannis Ritsos' *The Fourth Dimension*. This collection of seventeen sustained dramatic soliloquies constitutes—in Ritsos' own opinion and that of many others—his finest and most powerful work.

Ritsos has been gracefully and ably introduced to English readers primarily through selections from his shorter poems, including *Yannis Ritsos: Selected Poems* (Kedros, Penguin), translated by Nikos Stangos with an introduction by Peter Bien, and *Yannis Ritsos: Repetitions, Testimonies, Parentheses*, translated and introduced by Edmund Keeley and published by Princeton University Press. The result of this concentration on Ritsos' shorter poems has been to present a fascinating yet narrow glimpse into the vast and various oeuvre of this major figure of the twentieth–century Greek literary renaissance. A more generous and catholic choice is now available in *Yannis Ritsos: Selected Poems 1938–1988*, edited by Kimon Friar and Kostas Myrsiades (BOA Editions), but the individual poems still lack that coherent organic context which Ritsos himself always gave them.

As with all human relationships that are worth pursuing, there comes a time when the introductions have been made and the acquaintance must be allowed to grow deeper and more wide-ranging. Translation inevitably to some extent places the sensibility of the translators between reader and writer, but in presenting this complete volume as Ritsos wrote and published it for his Greek readers, we have tried as far as possible to let the poet speak here as he speaks at home, keeping the translators' role as mediator between poet and audience to a minimum, without the additional intrusion inherent in any attempt at excerption, selection, or rearrangement. Our explanatory Notes to the Poems have been gathered separately at the end of the book, keyed to the pages on which the references occur.

The Fourth Dimension was first published in 1972 as the fifth volume of Ritsos' collected works, with only sixteen poems included. "Phaedra", written in 1974–75, was added in the sixth and subsequent editions. The soliloquies fall into two clearly distinguished groups, the first with modern, the second with mythical settings. In chronological order, which is not the order in which Ritsos carefully arranged them for publication, the earlier group comprises the following: "Moonlight Sonata" (1956), which won the National Poetry Prize of Greece, was translated into French by Louis Aragon, and introduced Ritsos to literary Europe; "Winter Clarity" (1957); "Chronicle" (1957); "When the Stranger Comes" (1957); and "The Window" (1959). These poems represent the genre in its formative stages.

The composition of the second, mythic cycle began with "The Dead House" (1959), followed by "Under the Shadow of the Mountain" (1960), "Orestes" (1962–66), "Ismene" (1966–71), "Ajax" (1967–69), "Chrysothemis" (1967–70), "Helen" (1970), "The Return of Iphigenia" (1971–72), and "Phaedra" (1974–75). Again, the order of composition is not the order of the poems' arrangement for publication.

We plan to discuss elsewhere the autobiographical elements and the political context of these poems, in particular the pressures in Ritsos' personal and intellectual life that forced him to turn to legendary personae, to establish an "elsewhere" that allowed him to explore problems he could not, or dared not, confront more directly. Here we consider the implications of Ritsos' reordering of the poems, his structuring of *The Fourth Dimension* into an organic whole, including what is perhaps the most intriguing and significant decision, to place "When the Stranger Comes" (1957) as the final poem in the collection—a position that it retained even after "Phaedra" (1974–75) was added.

We begin with "The Window", a cinematographic choice for the opening poem, like the initial tracking shot at the start of a film. For the speaker the window is a way out, opening a prospect on a lively world in which he half fears, half longs to participate. For the reader the window is a way in—a first statement of many of Ritsos' central themes and an adumbration of the poetic strategies he will use to explore those themes.

The speaker in "The Window" is a man about whom we know nothing. Unlike the towering ancient figures whose soliloquies form the heart of the collection and who come to us barnacled with centuries of accreted history, myth, and legend, our first speaker is, like his window, transparent. He is a pure voice. We know him only through what he says. Ritsos thus begins to teach us to listen to the many voices in *The Fourth Dimension* by giving us an apparently easy case to start on.

By day, the speaker at his window resembles the figure in "a silent photograph, in its old-fashioned frame." This photograph is our first glimpse of the crowding presence of the dead in the pages to come. At twilight and at night, the speaker becomes, like the poet, an observer, who looks out on the world and can see without being seen. He observes freely, but he cannot move, can make no real contact with other people, or with things. "If I tried / to touch something, my elbow / could shatter the glass, leaving / a hole in my side, exposed to rain and to observation." Our journey into the fourth dimension begins, then, in two dimensions, and the initial problem is how, or whether, to move from two to three. It poses neatly one of the central dilemmas explored in these poems—on the one hand the lure of withdrawal, detachment, observation, the poet's stance; on the other, the pressure toward involvement, connection, and action.

Immobility and silence would let the speaker keep his integrity, leave him unexposed, with no "hole in his side", no pain inflicted by others, no Christlike martyrdoms. Inaction also lets possibilities remain unlimited, while to act is to define, to limit—and perhaps to falsify. Immobility thus retains transparency, but it is a "suffocating transparency", and one feels the pressure on the speaker, and the poet, to find some way to break out of immobility and silence, as fish "forced by pressure of water come up to the surface, mouths open like little triangles / to take a deep breath." Silence, too, can be a kind of hypocrisy: "How many crucified cries, / how many kneeling gestures lodge / behind this sheer crystalline brightness?" Yet speech can also be mere obfuscation: "If I start to talk, the breath from my voice / clouds the windowpane . . . and I no longer / see the thing I wanted to talk about. . . ."

A poem, especially a short poem, can be a sort of verbal photograph. Indeed, one of Ritsos' strengths in many of his shorter poems is precisely his ability to capture one moment, one image, with heart-stopping rightness, to fix what Pindar called a "moment of brightness". But, as the speaker in "The Window" says, the figures in photographs "can't stand it behind their glass, / in whatever pose, no matter how beautiful. . . ." They too need a breathing space. "The whole span of time lies in wait for them, before and beyond their beautiful moment, / and they want it completely, their time." The frame-frozen perfection of certain shorter poetic forms is seen here as another sort of falsification. Trying to capture life it manages only to stop it in its tracks.

"Each of us is two people," says the speaker, again introducing in a simplified and, as it were, two-dimensional form, the many voices that will speak to us in *The Fourth Dimension*. We are divided and "only by being torn to pieces can we ever hope to become whole." The collection is an exploration, then, for Ritsos and for us, of controlled and creative psychic fragmentation. The contending voices within the poet are each in their turn permitted to be heard unhindered; at the same time, the careful organization of the poems themselves sets up the dialogue among the voices that is a necessary step in the process of psychic integration.

In a lovely geometrical progression, the window becomes, as the poems will become, a frame for photographs (of ourselves, of our dead), a mirror (to see ourselves, to see the world), and the prescribed rectangle of a coffin—a coffin that we ourselves bury and from which rises, resurrected, a mysterious figure—Christlike, wandering, rejected, redemptive: a stranger who may at the same time also be a part of ourselves. This stranger recurs throughout the collection, reappearing as the central figure in the last poem, "When the Stranger Comes".

Like Plato, who wrote dialogues to avoid what he took to be dangerous shortcomings in other forms of writing, Ritsos turned to the extended dramatic soliloquy as a poetic form that offered a way out of immobility and silence. Like Plato, he does not speak in these poems in his own name. The use of multiple voices allows him to explore themes at a remove and to experiment with various forms of self-definition, testing the possibilities and limits of each, while retaining the freedom to move among them, to be both defined and protean. Those poems set in the remote past (yet always with links to the present) provide an additional distancing device that, like the window-as-mirror, allows Ritsos to look at and explore real scenes "in a deeper, more permanent setting", and to look at himself and others "as in a distant, magical mirror".

By constructing each soliloquy through the counterpointing of images, building small parts—many of which could stand on their own as shorter poems—into a larger architectural whole, Ritsos creates a "breathing space", both for his characters and for himself. Indeed, the long, natural lines of the verse have the rhythm of deep, easy breathing. The second-order counterpointing of one soliloquy against another sets the speakers' varying points of view in dialectical tension, again not unlike that in a Platonic dialogue. Finally, and perhaps most importantly, through the dramatic settings and the extended soliloquy—with its interwoven threads of memory, anticipation, and acute perception of the present moment—Ritsos enables the speakers, like the figures in the photographs, to come down from their frames, move around, have "their time". The form is as close as Ritsos could come to writing poems in the fourth dimension.

In the dramatic soliloquy form Ritsos found his solution to the problem posed in "The Window", found a way to give his characters "their time". "Winter Clarity" is a meditation on the meaning of such a gift. We are thus introduced at the outset to that dialectical destabilization Ritsos has created by his ordering of the poems, as "Winter Clarity" asks us to question what "The Window" asked us to value.

"Winter Clarity" is set in a notary's house, filled with old photographs that have lost their force, their color, their meaning. "What will you do with them?" asks the speaker. "What will you do with time?" Should one let go of the past, leaving the house, and the self, "all open to the world, with nothing of its own to hold on to"? Should one preserve what one can, and if so, is poetry, too, mere preservation, like putting blankets in mothballs, "burying something you loved in order to keep it safe"? The present and the future are as problematic as the past. In the face of mortality, what can you do with time? On the other hand, "what can you do with immortality? You cannot purchase / one single Sunday breakfast in the winter sunshine. . . ." The poem ends with a celebratory telescoping of all meaning into a delightfully timeless present. The speaker insists on "moving, living, acting", in an affirmation that betrays none of the ambivalence of "The Window". The family photographs twitch their nostrils as if they were sniffing hot bread, the "good here-and-now"—the dead are beginning to stir, but here they are harmless and hunger only for bread. The poet's benign function is to guard "the deeds of men, their little actions, / . . . their big innocent eyes, confused and eager, their enormous hands, / . . . life with its kitchen apron, its little songs in season". It is a charming and seductively inadequate intimation of the poems to come.

Ritsos follows this paean to the "good here-and-now" with "Chronicle", in which the good here-and-now is seen to be not good enough, and the speaker struggles to make some sense of his relation to history and to that larger fourth-dimensional extension of time into which the Mycenean soliloquies will shortly take us. In "Chronicle" we experience the bleakness of the loss of historical continuity. Ancient figures appear, but they are awkward and artificial, sharing little with their mythic prototypes except a famous name. The "hero" of the poem, the Treasurer of the Pythagoras Club, combines the features of Christ, Pythagoras, and the poet, but does so in such a modest and ineffectual fashion that he makes us smile. The poem evokes in the reader a longing for some richer connection with these past figures, a longing to meet, perhaps even to be, human beings who live life on a larger scale. *The Fourth Dimension* gives us both, and forces us to confront the implications of, the authenticity of, those longings. It is no accident that the complete collection has never appeared in English, that the temptation to present fragments, to excerpt, to dilute its impact has been too strong to resist. The book's overwhelming impact is deliberate. At moments we will feel—as we are meant to do—that there are too many dead, that they are too large, that they go on too long. *The Fourth Dimension* challenges us to confront our own ambivalence toward the Other and toward the past, to ask how many of those who pray for the resurrection of the dead would truly welcome it.

"Moonlight Sonata", by both placement and form, is the poem that looks forward most directly to the great mythic soliloquies that follow. The scene is one of those dark, decaying, haunted family mansions, full of memories and dusty bric-a-brac, which the phrase "the dead house" captures with such horrifying appropriateness. The speaker is a Woman in Black who, in her gnawing loneliness and losing battle against age and death, is an early version of Ismene or Electra, even as in her uneasy yet acute erotic awareness of her young male visitor she prefigures the more intense eroticism of Phaedra. She is the contemporary pole of that stunning fusion of present and past that Ritsos will achieve most fully in "The Dead House" and "Under the Shadow of the Mountain". The woman is trapped in the strangling embrace of her house; she longs both for escape and for some human connection. "Let me come with you" becomes her desperately reiterated refrain. Ritsos' implicit reply to the Woman in Black is that no real human connections can be rooted in denial of the connections one has already. There is no simple escape from the past, no way out but through. Instead of the easy flight the woman longs for, Ritsos takes us deep into an exploration of the "house" in its richest and most terrible meanings (as physical setting, as entangled, tormented family—human connections, one might say, with a vengeance) as he confronts us with the tragic House of Atreus, in all its full-blown horror.

The order of composition of the mythic poems began with the house itself, first "The Dead House", then "Under the Shadow of the Mountain", in both of which Ritsos fused the archetypal story of the House of Atreus with the story of his own unhappy family, living under the shadow of the great limestone mountain of Monemvasia. Ritsos followed these with "Orestes" and "Philoctetes" (in which the speaker is Neoptolemus, Achilles' son)—continued, that is, with the voices of sons, struggling under the weight of their fathers' deeds and their family past. Next to be written was "Persephone", in which, again, the voice is that of a young person, trying to integrate warring and terrifyingly disparate selves.

In *The Fourth Dimension*, however, Ritsos presents the Atreid poems in their *dramatic* order, allowing the reader to experience in turn the overwhelming pressure that drives Clytemnestra to kill Agamemnon; the conflicting forces that both impel Orestes toward and pull him back from the murder of Clytemnestra; and the later reflections on these events by Electra, Iphigenia, and Chrysothemis, through whom Ritsos explores the healing powers of compassion, oblivion, memory, and poetry.

The technique of the mythic soliloquies seems to be stated at the start of "The Dead House": "she mixed up mythology, history, and her own private life, past and present. . . ." This fusion of past and present is, on one level, the poet's deliberate achievement. Ritsos blended the story of the House of Atreus with his own autobiography, even adding to the story a second brother, who is the poet himself. There are carefully placed anachronisms: phone numbers, an ashtray, a firing squad, a tourist bus.

But on a deeper level the fusion of past and present is not so much achieved as revealed. The domestic and particular "good here-and-now" is not made to be, but *found* to be, resonant with deep significance, rooted often in ancient magic and tradition: the big family kitchen in "The Dead House" (both Mycenae and Monemvasia) is a Delphic shrine or Sibyl's cave, where the ghosts of Iphigenia, Homer, and Agememnon form in the cauldrons' curling smoke. Surrealist techniques, too, are used to draw, not merely on the poet's own private and overcharged subconscious, but on the deep well of Greek philosophy, poetry, and religious and popular belief and practice. In "Winter Clarity" the dome of the church that was "a great egg beneath the six mighty wings of the sun" takes us straight back to Orphic cosmology, while the red eggs that mysteriously appear in "Chrysothemis" are the same red eggs so lovingly prepared for every Greek Easter. Thus surrealism, too, becomes an instrument of timeless synchronicity.

The many masks that begin to appear—Orestes' funeral urn or Iphigenia's deer mask from which she can utter "thunderstruck truths"—are similar to the distancing device that Ritsos has found in the dramatic soliloquy. But as with the fusion of past and present, so the willed identification of self and Other behind these dramatic masks gives way to a deeper sense in which that fusion too is not willed but acknowledged. Like the existentialists, Ritsos explores the shift in consciousness that accompanies our confrontation with our own mortality. But he also explores what we might call an *existentialisme de l'au delà*, in which the dead seem to have as much vividness, presence, "being", as the living. They may not speak, but that, as Iphigenia observes, merely serves to "thicken the silence". More important, it is in part in relation to the dead—our ability to love, to feel loss, to remember—that the living have their own being. Says Iphigenia: "We confirm . . . our own existence in the dumb crush of those who are absent, / who miss us, whom we miss."

For Ritsos, purely personal consciousness must be enriched and extended by memory, by some connection to a larger whole to which the individual belongs.

The Atreid soliloquies are followed by "Persephone". Like the eleventh book of Homer's *Odyssey*, the eleventh poem of our journey through the fourth dimension takes us on a descent into Hades. Here the various tensions and antitheses of the earlier poems—between speech and silence, involvement and withdrawal—are explored at their most fundamental level as the choice between Eros and Thanatos. In Persephone's complex character we confront most starkly the problem of a divided self and the desire to resolve the conflict by simply opting to come down on one side or the other: " 'Keep me,' I said to him— / 'let me be only one—even half—the whole half (whichever it is), / not two, separate and unmingled. . . .' " The poem ends in an unexpected gesture of affirmation, as Persephone flings open her shutters and accepts life and the light. It is, however, a qualified acceptance, and Ritsos' choice of an archetypal year-myth as the image of the self divided hints that doubts and the lure of the dark remain potent, and will return. With Persephone's opened window we also emerge from under the shadow of the House of Atreus to explore and embrace a wider mythic heritage, as if—what the Woman in Black longed to do—we have come to some terms with the enclosed world of the "house" and can now make broader human connections.

Again the themes of action and nonaction, involvement and withdrawal, masks and authenticity are central, and again Ritsos has arranged the poems so that each comments on the implicit conclusion of the one preceding it. Thus "Ismene" explores the implications of Persephone's choice, contrasting the narrow carnality of Ismene herself with the more principled life of her sister Antigone. "Ajax" explores Antigone's choice of principled action and ends with Ajax's own withdrawal in suicide. "Philoctetes" begins in withdrawal but ends with a complex affirmation of the indomitable resilience of the human spirit that permits a fusion of action and withdrawal, makes possible both clarity and participation, and lets Neoptolemus see even "behind or among the shields and the spears / a bit of sea, a little twilight, a beautiful knee. . . ."

In "Helen" we meet the casus belli of that terrible ten-year war that dominated and broke up the lives of most of the characters we have encountered in *The Fourth Dimension*. Helen could not care less about any of them. Ghosts fill her house, but they are unwelcome: "I don't know why the dead stay here when no one pities them; I can't think what they want," she says testily. In a break with the past worse even than that in

"Chronicle", the famous names—Paris, Achilles, Menelaus—are "sounds, mere sounds". The ultimate polarities of Eros and Thanatos have been reduced to the meaningless symbols E and Θ scrawled in cold cream on a windowpane. Like the photographs at the start of "Winter Clarity", Helen's memories are without force or power to move. Only one remains vivid: the memory of her own triumphant moment on the walls of Troy. "Everything else is gone as though it had never existed."

But having come this far with Ritsos, for the reader too Helen's memories function as old photographs, as reminders of our own memories of earlier poems. We too remember that orange and black butterfly, which carried off Clytemnestra's coffin in "Chrysothemis" and perched on dead Haemon's sex in "Ismene". We too remember that necklace of gold masks first encountered in "The Return of Iphigenia". For us the names are now far more than "sounds, mere sounds". As at the start of the collection Ritsos taught us to listen, so now he begins to teach us to remember, to find our own relation to these tormented figures, a relation more generous and compassionate than Helen's.

Originally "Helen" was followed by "When the Stranger Comes", in which the vital and sustaining importance of memory is affirmed. The addition of "Phaedra" not only contributed one of the most powerful figures in *The Fourth Dimension*, but provided an additional perspective on themes already explored and an intriguing challenge to the point of view in the final poem. Phaedra is the victim of Eros transformed from a life force to an all-consuming passion. Her masks hide not a purer, more authentic self, but a hunger as insatiable as it is ugly. Even the house, elsewhere so capacious a symbol for the past, is for Phaedra reduced to body, "your body and mine, together". Like Milton's Satan, she is both terrible and magnificent, and her compelling power is in disturbing contrast to the benign sweetness of the Stranger in the final poem.

In "When the Stranger Comes" the mysterious redemptive figure of "The Window", who has been glimpsed also in "Chronicle" and "The Dead House", takes center stage. The scene is set in a house of mourning, with veiled mirrors, a setting that also recalls the rituals of Holy Week before Greek Easter. To the bereaved there appears, without explanation, a Stranger, a spiritual healer whose magic reveals the coexistence of past and future in the present, stills the fear of death, and opens the mourners' hearts with words "like a row of small pitchers in island windows". The Stranger breaks the "siege of the moment" with a timeless sense of the rare loveliness of natural and human things—the steps of the lamb, the shepherd's pipe, even the hunter's snare. "When we have remembered," says the Stranger, "the moment of that we remember has never passed." The dead are carried within us, we continue their life, as others will continue ours. "There is always a birth," says the Stranger, "and death is an addition, not a subtraction. Nothing is lost."

Nothing is lost, provided we *do* remember—as *The Fourth Dimension* has progressively taught us to do. We leave the Stranger, shaving, in a house of mourning no longer, its mirrors now uncovered. The poem serves as a fitting envoi to the collection, a requiem for the dead who have crowded its pages, an affirmation of hope, and a declaration of belief in the immortalizing and redemptive power of poetry.

THE FOURTH DIMENSION

· THE WINDOW ·

Two men are sitting beside the window of a room overlooking the sea.
They seem to be old friends, who have not met for some time. One of
them looks like a seaman. The other—the one speaking—does not.
Dusk is falling slowly—a peaceful spring evening, violet and purple. The
sea before them is like oil, its striped and undulating reflections lighting
up the sides of boats, ropes, masts, houses. Simply and somewhat
wearily at the beginning:

I sit here, at the window; I watch the passers-by
and see myself through their eyes. I feel as if I am
a silent photograph, in its old-fashioned frame,
hanging outside the house, on the west wall,
I and my window.
                Now and then I myself look at
this photograph with its amorous, tired eyes—
a shadow hides the mouth; the flat gleam from the glass in the frame,
at certain moments, when facing the sinking sun, or moonlight,
covers the whole face, and I am hidden
behind a square light, pallid or silver or rose,
and I can look freely at the world
without anyone seeing me. Freely—what can one say?
I can't move; at my back
the damp or burning wall; on my chest
the cold windowpane; the small veins of my eyes
reticulate in the glass. And pressed this way
between wall and windowpane, I dare not move my hand
to lift my palm to my brow when the sun blazes
like inexorable glory; and I'm forced
to see, to want, yet not to move. If I tried
to touch something, my elbow
could shatter the glass, leaving
a hole in my side, exposed to rain and to observation.

Then again, if I start to talk, the breath from my voice
clouds the windowpane (as now) and I no longer
can see the thing I wanted to talk about.

Silence and immobility, then. You could also say hypocrisy,
since you know, perhaps, how many crucified cries,
how many kneeling gestures lodge

behind this sheer crystalline brightness.
Especially when night falls, now, in springtime, and the harbor
is a distant fire, gold and red,
amid the dark forest of masts, and you're aware
of the fish, forced by pressure of water, coming up
to the surface, mouths open like little triangles
to take a deep breath—have you noticed that?
At such times the water's dense light is splintered
by a thousand open mouths of tiny fish. No one can stand
to be under the water's mass without respite, in these
     mysterious, maritime forests,
in that suffocating transparency, with the infinite, dangerous view.

In the same way, I think that photographs can't stand it behind their
     glass,
in whatever pose, no matter how beautiful, at whatever moment of their
     lives,
frame-frozen in their prime, at a moment of proud innocence,
one splendid young hand resting on the stylish studio table
or on their knee, with a fresh flower (naturally) in their lapel,
with an imperceptible, triumphant smile on their lips,
neither over-broad, which would reveal arrogance,
nor altogether closed, which would reveal submissiveness to fate.
Yet the whole span of time lies in wait for them, before and beyond their
     beautiful moment,
and they want it completely, their time, even if they lose
this petrified respectability of theirs, this
superior pose, premeditated or not—it makes no difference,
even if their upright legend melts like white wax beneath the fire of their
     eyes,
even if their youth, starting out from the light of the crystal, should be
     belied.

But then again, fear seems greater than their desire
or exactly its equal; and then their smile
is like a silver fish, stretched out and still
between two rocks on the sea bottom—or like a
gray bird with motionless wings, poised in the air,
immobile amid its own motion. And the photographs remain
shut away there, with all their remorse or repentance, their hatred too,

without stirring from their frames, from their longing and their fear,
face to face with imperious heaven and the boundless sea.

Because of this we often choose a narrow space that will protect us
from our own boundlessness. And perhaps that's why
I sit here, at this window, watching
the fresh footprints from the boatman's soles
on the flagstones of the jetty fade, little by little,
like a row of small, oblong moons in a fairy tale.

And I no longer understand anything, or try to understand.
A woman fresh from the bath leans over on the next balcony,
singing softly to dry her hair with her song. A sailor
stands uncertainly, legs apart,
before his enormous afternoon shadow, as if he were
upright at the prow of a ship in a strange harbor
and didn't know the waters or where to drop anchor.
Later, as dusk slowly falls, as the sunset's still violet heartbeat
fades on the walls and yards, before they have lit
the street lamps, there comes a sudden warmth—and then
the faces are more surmised than actually there;
you see the shadow merge into sweaty armpits;
the sound of a fugitive dress stirs the leaves of a tree;
the young men's white shirts take on a distant blue color and steam,
and everything's so lonely, bewitched and elusive, that maybe this is
    why
they turn every light on at once, to disperse it all, positively, at their
    command.

Inside the houses, the sheets are like drooping flags
in an inexplicable sea-calm, when all have abandoned ship
and the flags have no more reason to wave and hang in the evening air
warmed by the sun, forgotten, slack,
like flayed skins of huge beasts they slaughtered
on a national holiday with parades, music, dancing, feasting.
The holiday's over. The streets are deserted. On the sidewalks
oily bits of paper, crushed rosettes, bread crusts, bones—
yet no one's gone home, as if they'd thought better of it,
as if they'd all taken a break they didn't need.

The rooms remain dark and depressing, lit only
by the multicolored lights from the street and the ships or by a few
        absent-minded stars
or the sudden headlights of a passing truck, loaded
with drunken soldiers, shouts and songs,
and the headlights nail the window's shadow inside the house,
silently and discreetly, as if it were a great plank coffin
being carried by two mysterious sailors to a deserted shore.

Some strange ideas come to you then—doesn't that happen to you
        too?—
as that each of us may be two people
with muffled faces, and both of them vindictive,
at loggerheads with each other, who only this minute have agreed
to move that coffin, to dig with their nails
a little further up on the beach, and to bury it.

And you too know, just as they do, for all their secretiveness,
that in the coffin lies a dismembered body,
a young body, much beloved; and it is
their own one body, which they themselves killed and buried
as though they were two strangers.
                                    That coffin
with its impeccable shape, the prescribed rectangle,
resembles a closed door,
resembles those framed photographs we were talking about,
resembles this window from which we watch the pleasant activity on the
        springtime street.

I have often encountered this body, this face,
especially on nights when there is a moon, strolling
—somewhat pale, but always young—along the quayside
or on the upper street with the filthy brothels,
the painted women, ravenous dogs, rusty corrugated iron,
unshaven sailors, rotten fruit, curses, bits of lemon peel,
green washbasins, toilet bowls, candles, acetylene lamps.
Once I even saw him haggling with a woman,
but she didn't agree since he offered her too much. "No, no," she told
        him,
"It won't do. No," in a hoarse voice, and her hand

with its red nails shook a little. She was afraid
they might involve her in something to do with robbery, perversion,
    skeleton keys,
with great iron-barred doors like those that fortune-tellers are always
    foreseeing
and which, in fact, are never lacking. What did she want with such
    things?
Her price was fixed—not, of course, any less, but not any more either.

Unfathomable man, with such eyes—
huge and vacant in the pallor of his face
like burning coals. They could actually set her on fire,
could even melt her hairpins, make
the molten iron run hot from her waved hair down into her eyes.
He always seemed sad—perhaps because of his strength
which he never succeeded in killing—a beautiful sadness
like the broad, afternoon melancholy of spring. And it suited him,
and was almost a necessity for him. He never was,
to the best of our knowledge, dismembered. He'd open the coffin,
    calmly,
as though he were opening a door, and emerge whole beneath the moon
with the veins outlined vividly on his hands,
red, so red—strange in such moonlight—
beneath his pale, Christlike skin.

Truly, I sometimes think that only being torn to pieces
can keep us whole—it is enough that we know it.
And how can we not know it, since it is our knowledge
that tears us apart and reunites us with that which we have denied.

On that upper street I told you about, it's delightful—
the most improbable shops in the world—secondhand shops, coal
    merchants', groceries,
barbershops with old lithographs and heavy, conspiratorial armchairs,
butcher shops with huge mirrors that reflect, multiplied
into a red procession, slaughtered lambs and oxen;
greengrocers' shops and fish markets mingling the odors of fish and
    fruit—
a suspicious, wordless din outside the doors,
a mute illumination like the reflection from sheets of tin

or from large yellow, planed planks leaning
upright against the front of the carpenter's shop. On sale up there in
    confusion,
raincoats, poultry, clothespins, bottles, combs,
empty biscuit tins, cheap coffins, perfumed soaps,
rusty cabins from wrecked ships that they'd put up for auction
and hauled off later, bit by bit,
duty-free silks imported from all over, with all sorts of patterns and
    colors,
Japanese dinner sets, hashish and tablecloths
and some strange cages, vaulted like half-completed churches
and in them a few red-golden, unfamiliar birds, watching
the activity in the street with strange, unfathomable eyes
like two yellow-black gemstones, stolen at night from the fingers of the
    dead.

Barefoot children play dice in the middle of the street,
women bed sailors in low-ceilinged rooms with open windows,
sunburnt itinerant peddlers piss in a row in the yard;
fish in their creels glint fitfully like huge, bloody knives
and, sometimes, a straying bee
buzzes around out there in great confusion,
leaving in the air the golden, wiry coils of its whirling
like little springs from some gutted children's toy.

A cloud of dust stirs slowly at nightfall among the faces
like a purple secret of breath, sweat, self-interest, and crimes,
a deep secret of inexhaustible hunger, hastily nourished,
endless coming and going, endless haggling, endless spending
that sustains commerce, ambition, the clever, and life itself, of course,
so that sometimes you see a beautiful girl wearing a clean, flowered
    dress,
in the coal alley, by the pistachio seller's cart and the sacks of coal,
all lit up by the sea,
smiling, with two rows of perfect teeth, at the sound of a ship's siren.

Around her, rotting lemon peels shine like little suns;
a chintz curtain drawn back slantwise in a low window
is like a dog-eared page of a much-loved book
reminding you to come back one day and read it again.

No humiliation, then, in that place where life insists upon living,
where the dogs search with well-bred gestures in the garbage heap
and the girls hold smooth foreheads high, under loads of luxuriant hair
as though balancing black jugs of still water
that they fear might fall. I have seen many girls
in this posture, yes, on that very street,
and swarthy hirsute youths, with fleshy mouths,
always enraged (as the very sad tend to be),
who never manage to be as coarse as they would like
and so they curse still more, in a more forceful voice. If you pay
    attention
you will understand. Their voices are
a wide palm stroking the ship's black cat
settled warily on their knees—at night, of course,
so neither the hand nor the cat can be seen. Only the cat's eyes—their
    phosphorous glow
like two sidelights on a small boat circling an island thick with flowers.

If you go a little further up that street, to St. Basil's hill,
you can see the whole harbor beneath your gaze,
and, shining in the dark water, at the very edge of the boundless sea,
large golden-green, iridescent slicks of oil or petroleum,
gleaming slicks, immaculate, you might say, like bright moving islets of
    calm indifference
amid the dead dogs, rotting potatoes, straw, pine cones, and boats.

So, you see, you can watch without any hesitation from this window,
or even go out in the street. A quiet sanctity
underlies the doings of men. A violet shadow
rests silently on the left shoulder of a woman tired from love
who turned on her other side and fell asleep alone. You can see
the large boxer shorts in the next door courtyard stained from wet
    dreams
or unrolled condoms under park benches
or buttons from women's corsets, fallen on the ground
like little ivory flowers, slightly embittered,
since they no longer have anything else to offer—scent, pollen, seeds.
    Nothing.

I too once thought of going out on that same street
to sell this window and the big coffin,
for no other reason but to get free of responsibility for them,
so that I too could have a part in buying and selling,
could hear my voice speaking a strange language. I very soon realized
that I had nothing to sell. It was just an ulterior motive:
the quest for some new ordeal, which once again
I could oversee from this window, even without panes.

I never made it in business. Besides I have
nothing worth buying, nothing
that I can pay for. And these old photographs
aren't worth a thing to anyone else, even though their frames, at least,
are solid gold. Still, for me they are indispensable.

And they aren't dead—no. When evening falls
and the chairs outside the cafés are still warm
and everyone (and I, too, perhaps) tries to take refuge in someone else,
they come silently down from their frames as though coming down
a humble wooden staircase, go into the kitchen,
light the lamp, set the table (one can hear
the friendly sound of a fork hitting against a plate),
arrange my few books and even my thoughts
with comparisons and images (old and new), with respectable
        arguments
and sometimes with ancient, unassailable, lived-through proofs.

For this too I hold on to this window with gratitude.
It doesn't in any way prevent me from seeing, or being—indeed, the
        opposite.

As for what I said to you earlier, "pressed this way between wall and
        windowpane,"
it was a springtime hyperbole, a hyperbole
due to the sensuous profusion of green leaves. The window
is a useful rectangle of calmness and clarity.

When the walls grow dim late in the evening, this window
still shines as if by itself; it retains and prolongs
the last glow of the dying sun,

casts its reflection on the shadowy street,
lights up the faces of passers-by as if catching them red-handed
in their most candid moments, lights up the wheels of bicycles
or the gold chain plunged between a woman's breasts
or the odd name of a vessel anchored in the harbor.

Against these panes, in winter, the wind bends its knees
and I see it depart, furious, turning its broad back.
Or again, from this spot I can hear, on spring evenings like tonight,
the conversations of sailors from one boat to another as though
they were revealing to me the reciprocity of the stars, explaining to me
those incomprehensible numbers on the sides of ships. Suddenly
I hear the sound of an anchor falling into the water
like something offered exclusively to me,
like something that empowers me to point it out.

What complaint can I have, then, about this window?
If you want you can open it halfway, and, without looking outside at
        all,
in the panes you can follow, unseen,
real street scenes, in a deeper and more permanent setting,
with the gentle illumination of great remoteness
while everything's acted out right under your eyes, a yard or so away.
If you want to, though, you can open it all the way and look at yourself
        in the pane, as though inside
a distant magical mirror, to comb your thinning hair
or rearrange your smile a little. In these panes
everything seems clearer—quieter, stiller,
consequently both indispensable and ageless.
                                        Did you ever
look through a glass underwater? Beneath the troubled surface
the seabed appears splendid in its stillness,
in a crystalline order, at once undisturbed and vulnerable,
in a silent sanctity—as we were saying. Only
sometimes it takes your breath away if you stay that way too long,
so you lift your head up into the air again
or you open the window (but knowingly now) or go out the door.
And there is nothing further that can force down your life or your eyes,
and there is nothing that you cannot show proudly and sing about,
and there is nothing of which you cannot turn the face toward the sun.

*They close the window and go out into the street. The ships' riding-
lights are already lit. They walk to the end of the jetty, stand, look at the
sea, listen to the interrupted leap of a fish in the shallows and, without
speaking, clasp hands, palm to palm. Then they sit quietly on a damp
coil of cable, light cigarettes, look at each other in the match-flame.
They seem strangely and almost unjustifiably happy, with that
inexplicable happiness that life always has in spring, when all around
the tang of salt mingles with the smell of fried sprats, shredded lettuce,
and vinegar. In a little while they will go to eat at the neighboring
taverna. They are already hungry, and the sound of the gramophone
robustly strengthens this sense of hunger. Near them the harbor patrol
passes, at regulation pace, summer uniforms gleaming white in the late
evening. The two friends rise from the cable and walk on.*

PIRAEUS, APRIL 1959

· WINTER CLARITY ·

Endless Sunday mornings with chill wintry sunshine:
a few children's voices, loitering in the lane
and the province, whitewashed, shining into the void, in that breath-
    catching translucency—

The notary's house with its big windows,
its clean glass panes, all open to the world,
with nothing of its own to hold on to,
completely won over by winter,
with its closets, its hangers, its kitchen,
with the big bronze brazier in the dining room—
and the tangerine peel burning quietly in the brazier, scenting
old pictures, old times, that have lost their force and their color
and little by little have lost their meaning
and after that their suffering and their burden
and after that their nostalgia—

They existed? They didn't exist? When? Where? Why?
And what can you keep of them? What will you do with them?
What will you do with time? To preserve what?

Worrying about carpets, blankets, woolen dresses,
year after year, every year at the coming of spring,
collecting them, shaking them out, brushing them,
folding them away in trunks or cupboards, layered with old newspapers,
as though you were burying something you loved in order to keep it safe
and to bury it brought grief—but what's to be done?
Later comes the spring light, the spring's greenness,
later still the light of summer and the summer sea,
later neither spring nor summer nor greenness nor sea,
only the light and its gestures amid the infinite,
the pure white light in which everything is burnt, suffocated, destroyed,
old, new, and yet to be, hills, trees and marble,
beliefs and feelings, events and resolutions.

Then you too would forget grief, remorse, plans, changes of heart: you'd
    start over
with the same mistakes, the same kisses, just the same well-dressed
    nakedness
till the first rains came,

the first great much-regretted stars,
the silent, wholly miraculous pillage of autumn.

And there came, too, late and noiseless, ungrieving, that other
      intoxication, for setting in order,
gathering what's scattered, forcing
a magical gain from destruction—yet not forcing:
by themselves they made twofold and threefold offering,
gardens and girls' laughter amid the acacias that once blossomed with
      hostility or indifference
and blossomed again—whole white armies, allies now, in the thin
      darkness.

The green bench, where you sat all alone one night, ringed with futile stars,
transferred itself now from the pale fields of desolate autumn
arriving at your door like a country cart: and on it
now two were sitting—both happy, you might say,
because by seeing and acknowledging things you never had, never will
      have,
it's almost as though you do have them—have them for sure. So
      we said, and perhaps we meant it.

Carts overloaded with hay and barrels came downhill
from the villages into wildly strange sunsets
all gold and purple and violet
all a demonstration of vanity
all dying luxury, and the sea knew it, to beyond the horizon: dying,
though the sea had copied it, chronographically, in detail,
clouds, colors, masts, gulls, and even its depths: this precision
was now its life (itself also dying), its only life, that life bestowed on it.

There's nothing all this wealth can achieve; it's superfluous.
There's nothing it can hide. And you should once more be looking after
      your blankets and rugs,
removing them from their trunks and shaking them out—
and your coffee, day by day, becoming utterly and increasingly
      indispensable.

It's snowing mothballs in the desolate rooms,
the smell of them, released, is dazed by its freedom,

and pestle and mortar ring out there just as cinnamon and nutmeg
chime for Christmas and the New Year. Yet despite all these precautions
time and the moth have done their work—
gaps appear here and there in the carpets, the overcoats show holes,
lapels are threadbare, elbows worn.

Next year you won't bother so much about mothballs,
and even less the year after,
and the moth reigns, an unseen monarch, over these old rooms,
king with no kingdom—
what more can a moth eat from what's already eaten?

A peaceful, silent abdication, almost casually optimistic, just as when
you go out in the rain some night, and the rain on the back of your neck
bothers you, mud clogs your feet, yet little by little
the rain takes possession of you, the mud gets into your shoes,
your feet, far from being heavy, grow buoyant,
and you walk free into the night, with no lighted window
hung in the dark like a luminous watch to fix your time
and orient your direction: you walk
happy in no longer fearing mud, rain, nowhereness or night,
not looking for any window, yet indescribably certain
that the lighted window is there, that you'll make it out
however bowed your head, or tight-shut your eyes—and besides
you keep your head held high, exposed to the rain, and your eyes wide
     open.

All the help now comes from you, from you alone—you've learned that:
neurasthenia is neither a way out nor a justification
—the others got used to it, they no longer worry, or search, or criticize:
those with stomach ailments gave up their diets—what was the use?—
and the old contracts, lying heaped up in the storeroom, breached or
     expired,
make food for unhungry mice.

The climacteric period's over for the mistress of the house,
over for her daughters,
over for the trees in her garden. Only the jasmine
snowing its white stars at evening, every summer, on the garden table

has grown rank, unpruned, choking the house in its tendrils, like some
    vast octopus
sapping the house's foundations. So, what can you do with time?

What can you do with immortality? You cannot purchase
one single Sunday breakfast in the winter sunshine
in this house with its old-fashioned brazier and its modern typewriter,
with its antique sideboard, all cups and silver teaspoons and every sort
    of liqueur glass,
with this fruit bowl on the table, the effrontery of its oranges no longer
    offending the silence,
with these family photographs that no one any longer looks at.

The black hole of the chimney extends thousands of miles into the sky,
likewise the hole of the cesspit underground (discharging on the other
    side, perhaps?), and the knife
when you cut bread slices a deep wound
not just in the table or floor—much further down.

Yet you wouldn't change this inexorable beauty and wisdom,
this nobility of age-lines beside the eyes of silence,
for the bliss of youth in any form. You keep still,
you watch and overhear—a nonparticipating participant—
and the ancient lamp with its faded, sacramental air from long-past
    symposia and last suppers,
with its flyblown gilding,
still hangs, obdurate and forgotten,
in the very heart of the void, like an irrevocable seal on a will
that no one read because there remained neither heirs
nor indeed an inheritance. Yet you
read it, and you are making it over,
you bind the eras that did not perceive their bonds,
and still you cannot rid yourself
of the burden and the wealth of even the emptiest day
whether you talk or not, shut your eyes or keep them open.

And this house, lightened of its petty memories and divisions,
in the heart of its great memory, recognized in its full depth,
soars up the sky into that fearful, frozen clarity
silent, weightless, spiritually free,

like a blue balloon held only by a string
in the fist of a child.
                              The child called out
—a quiet, positive, independent voice,
outside of your time abroad or your return,
an imperative, unprotected voice. He called out
and his mother came running in her white blouse
and the houses settled back in the sunlight
like eggs about to be hatched by gigantic chickens
and the dome of the church shone; it too
was a great egg beneath the six mighty wings of the sun.

The cart that passed by on the road—it wasn't going heavenward at all,
        it was carrying fruit to market.
It had its wheels, unsuspecting, laughing, with that noisy country
        cheerfulness of theirs,
and the wheels, every last one of them, had their distinct shadow. You
        watched
the wheels and their shadows—not just their shadows.

The wheels and their shadows were *not* four pairs of zeros,
each circle had its own subdivisions,
regular and independent: they engaged the eye,
engaged one's perceptions and thought—
the new delight, the new complexity that nullifies the void,
that reveals and hides: reveals
the new passion for revelation—lets you see, behind the allotted circles,
the full range of the sky, the sea, the trees,
as though behind the lace curtains of this house
with the eight domestic interwoven circles
that share and beautify the province's Sunday landscape
in the chill sunlight that warms and opens everything.

And the man who was writing the history of a house that had remained
        without history
packed up his papers and the house rediscovered its history.

A child cried,
its mother bent over it,

and he who was striving to set down on paper an age-old burden
understood once more the inexplicable purpose of time,
understood that one cannot understand it,
understood what we call duration—because he
with all his age and experience and the scars of so many wars
was now his child's child, feeling hungry. Already
it was getting on for afternoon. They laid the table nicely with a linen
    tablecloth,
and in the middle set a flower vase with winter roses.

Such a marvelous rich smell from the steaming food on that table,
with the antique brazier, the antique sofa. And all those family
    photographs
twitched their nostrils as though they were sniffing the good hot bread,
    the good here-and-now,
looking as though they were hungry—and in truth, they were.

The sun shone down on the two big windows
and the dog could be heard barking, guarding the house against its
    invisible foes,
this house that contains and raises a child,
this house that a child contains in his closed hand,
and an odd verse, itself, too, like a dog,
opened its mouth, barking the sum of the ages,
guarding the deeds of men, their little actions,
guarding their big innocent eyes, confused and eager, their enormous
    hands,
guarding life with its kitchen apron, its little songs in season.

And this man you speak of
would rather you call him hypocrite, trickster even,
than betray even one of the blood corpuscles
that begged, demanded, insisted on his
moving, living, acting—in song too—
movement inciting the atoms of light and our life to dance,
tuning (so far as he can) houses and trees, thoughts, steps, wood-grain
    and hands.

And the five country folk in their Sunday best who stood
outside the forecourt of the church
were like pruned trees sure to blossom again
and had the appearance of ploughs at rest
that tomorrow will cut their furrows no further than is needed.

SAMOS, JANUARY 1957

· CHRONICLE ·

*Scene: a Greek island, one particular one or any you prefer—not
Samos—with an adequate supply of pine trees, vines, little shops,
Saturday nights, Sundays, Mondays, and local policemen; with the
obligatory mutilated marbles and one complete Ionic column, huge and
towering. Time: winter afternoon to late evening. Characters: you, me,
various Greeks or, more generally, people of our time.*

Ash-gray winter. Gray dominates
the landscape outside and in. Ash-gray houses,
the streets, the mountains ash-gray, the few trees. This caïque
abandoned on land—I remember it from the year before last;
an untalented summer visitor sat in the glorious sunshine
and sketched it—just as it was—forgotten and at odds
with the different light and the bathers' laughter. Now
it has found its spot, settled down; and even though the winds have
        snapped its masts,
amid the gray wastes, the sea's mute roaring,
and though it keeps talking, talking, no one pays attention any longer;
        they've grown used to it
like a huge old pendulum clock forgotten in the void,
like blood circling unnoticed in the veins. It's settled down
next to these houses on the shore, stripped by the nails
of time and wind, of silence and the sea,
next to these abandoned shops with their barely readable signs,
the "General Store" and the "Dream Café".

Here, years ago, trade flourished:
famous tanneries, large companies that made
wine and spirits (the wine here is still excellent); centuries ago
this place was the center of an important civilization; there still remain
the famous ruins of aqueducts, gymnasia, and theaters,
and some temple—of Hera, I think, or Athena. When the moon was up
they did a bit of excavation: found some things, stole others, were told
        about this and that,
carted off two or three Herms and the odd Apollo to a nearby yard.
The rest they buried, concealed, dust, marble pieces, column capitals,
        dedicatory offerings;
some they even sent abroad (the best naturally)
on a mysterious ghost-ship, used for piracy or gunrunning,
one moonless night when the light at the harbor entrance

rose like a cross in midheaven and a few stars
dripped blood on the turbulent sea. And history was forgotten.
(So, when the ghosts come on stage, they supplant all else.) Now
to the ruins of time have been added the ruins of war—these too are
    worth noting. The breeze
nags at the cassock of a priest who's walking alone on the shore
to receive Holy Communion. Helen died day before yesterday
of cancer of the womb with extensive metastasis. Her husband
the electrician, Menelaus, had been hitting the bottle for months. The
    day of the funeral
relatives swarmed in and ransacked the house. In vain
the electrician hunted for her white dress to bury her with dignity;
he cursed, cried out—useless. Besides, he was drunk.
They buried her in a pair of bloomers borrowed from one of the
    neighbors. *Borrowed?*
—You go right now and find her and get them back off her. On the jetty
large stains of rust and urine. If you go for a walk in the afternoon,
the whole length of the beach you'll stumble over
castaways' blackened shoes, cuttlefish bones, pine cones and turds.
In the evenings, the few fishermen left shit freely on the mole (who's to
    see them?)
but they feel the moon's icy fingers on their balls
and for a long time, beneath their shirts, remains
the inexorable breathing of the sea—something unknown
that makes things near remote: home, wife, hearth—something
    unknown,
and so they are like strangers, sometimes, in their own land.

Here, a while back, a few well-meaning attempts were made to revive
the ancient spirit and sense of beauty. In fact, they founded
the "Pythagoras Club". They organized
a few festivals—"Pythagoria" they called them.
They brought in two busloads of young people and flags—
the athletic club, the society of amateur artists—
someone made a speech standing on a chair,
and there was a soccer match.
That evening the fans got into a brawl, split open the referee's head,
and the festival ended on a sour note, with a rock fight,
and we never learned which team won, "Apollo" or "Ares",

"Ploutos" or "Chronos" (which always used to win). We never found
   out.
An ominous silence spread over the sportsfield, and the neighbors
shut their doors and windows tight so as not to hear it.

Later they decided to organize "Venetian Evenings" at the harbor.
They postponed them once or twice, afraid
the same things would happen again. Besides, they were short of cash—
no one paid their subscriptions—so the "Pythagoras Club"
was ingloriously disbanded, leaving printed receipts
for cash that was never collected. They all had the idea they were in debt
and carefully kept out of sight—a great misapprehension and
   misunderstanding prevailed,
so much so that the Treasurer made off one day in a boat,
as if he'd stolen all that nothing in the cash box (his conduct testified to
   something of the sort),
and disappeared as if he himself owed as much as they all owed ,
when neither he nor they owed a thing,
especially since the club was disbanded before he even took office.

All of these things he took on himself, to gloss over
the involvement of the others, to give them an excuse, to take
upon himself the glory of sacrifice. What heroism!—No one saw him.
   His gesture was futile,
like a violet cloud that suddenly covered the sunset,
shading the prows of two boats and one strip of the harbor, emphasizing
the brightness of houses and sea, while the others,
bent over, drew in the trawl and golden water poured from the nets,
golden and powerful and unsuspecting, and there, in the background,
   five historic dolphins
shook their azure glory framed with rosy lightning. Proud,
free dolphins. —His gesture was futile,
things didn't change in the slightest; no relief. It was poverty, you see,
and with poverty what can you see or do?

Children and lambs in the midden. At election time
they sent two or three representatives to Parliament, but these
took their votes and their parliamentary stipend and forgot their
   promises.
What can they, or anyone, do for you in all this misery?

It's not fair to lump it all on their backs. Perhaps they could have
    thought up something to develop
the radioactive waters (since such things had been discovered), put in
    some cheap baths,
boost tourism, improve the place just a little. Half-measures,
half-measures, half-measures—half deeds, half dreams.
Foreigners run everything (said the congressmen, privately)
and it's not in anyone's power to do what's right. When you get down
    to it
let the people look out for themselves
since they're the ones immediately concerned—and don't you worry,
    they will. But what can you do by yourself,
one alone and on the other side power and money
and the "I hold you responsible" of silence and the half-closed eyes, full
    of implications
and guards and exile? Pick up a crumb or two, of course.

Interwoven events, circumstances, interests and perceptions,
and the sky at its widest—abundant blue, nurturing,
and the soul's fathomless depths—blue,
with a way out, with no way out, antinomies. Poverty, poverty,
—it gets along fine with its own concerns, doesn't bother with far-off
    problems,
real oppressions, absolutes, metaphysical certainties. Lucky poverty—
it survives, with the notion of bread, the notion of death and decay.
    Perhaps we should
ration everyone's bread to bring them closer to happiness. Something
    like that was discussed
by two lawyers, a doctor—former leftists—and a lumber merchant.
The branch of a wild olive tree stirred above them—you didn't know
whether in approval or reproach, and the void, higher up, inexhaustible
in its vast tolerance for everyone and everything,
faults and apostasies and crimes
that disappear and are forgotten in midcourse, before death,
before the pain of the one who committed them has abated—not
    infinite,
the infinite's nonexistent—they never saw it,
they were so tyrannized, so entangled in moments and obscure
    memories.

What can you do with yourself here? The library is deserted
—prey to spiders and dust. The local paper
is published monthly, carrying "Graziella" in installments,
and sometimes a few rhymed verses by female graduates of the business
     school. And social style
is not entirely lacking—a dance in the upstairs café, in the dead of
     winter,
with an out-of-tune violin, an accordion, a lute, and garish decorations.
And afterward the wind would drag the paper garlands
back and forth over the prickly grass
and this choking silence would seem to want to speak
and this rock to insist on foundation. One night
the dogs stared upward, baying—a harlequin moon
in a tall cotton cap—a faint jingling in the clouds—
and the young girls, coughing silently, turned over and fell asleep
as in the wall a hole opened like an ancient cave
and from the window the moonlight fell on their marbled left hands.

Consumption, cancer, tonsillitis
made inroads in the district, as did neuroses
—new growths, these, perhaps formerly known by other names,
madness or alienation. Now they've even opened a sort of pharmacy.
     What do they need with drugs?
Eurydice's daughter learned the art of magic spells from her mother.
She does something with a candle, oil, nutmeg—pure alchemy—
and all sickness vanishes down the wind. In her courtyard
winter roses bloom freely, crimson,
unsuited to the season's ash-grayness, like bedbugs squashed
on the filthy sheets of an inn; only someone
took a moment to say: *the roses*
are like knees reddened by kneeling, the roses
are brought to their knees by their beauty, not by the wind,
by their beauty, for no one has seen them. Then he was silent
as if he'd choked down his saliva, or a sob. But all these things,
nutmeg, roses, spells—spoken and unspoken—
could not halt the endless emigration
to here, or there, to Australia, Tanganyika, or even further away,
where you don't know if there are houses, or what they're like;
where you don't know what language they speak, or if they speak at all.

No one was left to plant or to harvest—what was there to harvest? So
      most of the girls
remained unmarried. The island was full
of spinsters, divorcées, bankrupt gentlewomen;
on Sunday they wear their best clothes, wait for
some shipwrecked American retired dishwasher;
while their old nightgowns with the pale ribbons wait too, for them,
and their dresses, which have not been worn in this time of waiting
for a better time—what time?
(the better-than-average time—there is no other)
and the dresses stayed in the dowry chest, faded,
little by little became superfluous, then tragic, in their determined
      waiting,
and then ridiculous, with their old-fashioned bows,
their schoolgirl lace that hasn't kept up with the times—
and those long slender mauve or rose umbrellas,
like hour hands in a cathedral where time has stopped,
like thin fingers pointing to the inevitable that they refuse to see.

Every spring senseless new vegetation runs riot amid the ruins,
without any memory, sheer effrontery.
Other young people couple there—and they too lack memory
(the memory of others—what would they do with it? —useless—
useless even to themselves—a memory that has lost its force
without having become an experience, a differentiated act). They merely
      wander.
And the seagulls spread out in pure white squadrons or in aerial
      gardens,
invisible, as if they'd migrated to other latitudes, like pediments stolen
from vernal temples, that now will languish in foreign museums.

Here, more people go to funerals than to weddings.
Many envied Penelope's dress. At least her last appearance
made a certain impression, and her loom also was talked about,
—magnificent weaving, heavy silk—where can such things be found in
      our day,
and where can such patience be found? And this beat of the loom,
lovely, domestic, rhythmic, transposed far away now, beyond the
      horizon,
behind the mountains, jangled, disordered,

mixed up with thunder or cannon-fire, untranslatable,
amid a dense silence, almost Latinate, untranslatable.

   At night
someone raps the door-knockers, disturbing everyone;
they get up and open the door—no one—only the naked branches of the
    darkness
and the naked sea with the shattered pentagram of a star.
The bells ring true after midnight
and ghosts have finally taken up residence in the old tanneries. The
    mule-drivers
make wide detours to avoid going by there, and yet
there is a freedom in this place, a splendid view,
and the sea—boundless, impartial, without guile,
one sea, pure sea, with its own nobility,
without purpose or thought or interest,
with the nobility of its epic nakedness. An infinity that smells
of bronze and stars and horses. A leonine wind
overmasters it silently, silently, silently.

   But the man
who strolls on the quayside, searching for something,
looking at the waves, the clouds, the wind,
looking fixedly at the silence and the nothingness,
houses unbuilt, half-built, or demolished,
the half-obliterated signs of seaside shops—what is he looking for?
What does he want, all alone in the wind, altogether without hope,
conversing with naked rocks, empty caïques, locked windows,
or sometimes with that prolonged violet that claims a significance it does
    not have,
tranquil, safe, secure,
with his hands in his pockets, with the courage of acceptance,
with the joy of vision, knowledge, and change—Isn't he the Treasurer of
    the Pythagoras Club,
still seeking to pay however much he and they owe (since all of us, no
    matter who, owe something),
to discharge everyone's debts, single-handed?

Perhaps he'd never fled at all. Perhaps he returned
from some Achaian city in southern Italy, from Croton,

and then, from there to Metaponto—exiled,
as the historian says, and then continues: he insists on
always recording sounds in numbers
that correspond to the lengths of a vibrating string (or of the soul)
and—based, somewhat later, on even and odd, on divisible and prime—
on setting himself up as adversary of rumor,
himself the wronged one, separate and exiled;
on setting up in relief, in number and in deed,
the noble ideals of Justice, Unity, and Freedom; on discharging (and I
    hope he knew it himself) those unpaid debts.

At some point the receipts exist signed, the amount left blank,
and someone allots them to poor and rich (where are the rich to be
    found?),
someone allots them like indulgences to win forgiveness,
though he had done nothing, except to make it clear, the trickster,
that not one of them owes him anything, that he alone is indebted—
and it's true that he owes, and whatever he does won't pay it,
and this happiness is left him: to know that he owes, and to say so,
calling to mind—once more by himself—the indebtedness of all.

It was a desire to comfort the others—a desire
to comfort himself. And it was a strength
beyond comfort—disdainful, solitary and total,
devoted solely to its task and its labor, beside the sea,
not calculating the countervailing strength of the sea
or the tireless teeth of salt, deceit, and wind.

The stars watched from on high, testifying with a certain forbearance,
a certain indifferent benevolence, with that freedom born of exhaustion,
a ten-thousand-fold "yes" of stars fine-traced in the void—
and this obstinate repetition of "yes" was in no way doubtful.

And it was, indeed, the Treasurer of the Pythagoras Club
who gazed with such familiarity into the distance,
and who repaid with the gold of the stars, which wasn't even his own,
repaid debts still unknown of men and centuries.

*This poem which, without prejudice to it, we might call a descriptive
tale, concerns itself, as we have seen, with the most ordinary events and*

characters, in particular with the Treasurer of the Pythagoras Club. This hero was passed over in silence at the beginning in order not to exhaust the reader's interest in him—a trivial trick of the trade. But I would like to take this opportunity to make it clear—to avoid inappropriate comparisons and misinterpretations—that the Treasurer of the Pythagoras Club bears no relation to the Pythagoras of antiquity, about whom in any case we know very little, and that at second or third hand. The other day—Wednesday or Thursday, I don't remember which—it was very sunny. The wind had died away entirely. And all these things, shadows and ghosts, had evaporated and been forgotten. People came down to the shore and the harbor: women with babies in their arms, one or two children in strollers, a few fishermen, a photographer, the only bus, and quite a few policemen. In the distance the regular steamer looked so beautiful and light that, surely, this time, it would bring some good fortune along with the mail sacks and the newspapers from the capital. Even the ramshackle seaside houses seemed freshly plastered with sunlight. And the single Ionic column pointed upward with another kind of certainty.

SAMOS, JANUARY 1957

· MOONLIGHT SONATA ·

A spring evening. A large room in an old house. A woman of a certain age, dressed in black, is speaking to a young man. They have not turned on the lights. Through both windows the moonlight shines relentlessly. I forgot to mention that the Woman in Black has published two or three interesting volumes of poetry with a religious flavor. So, the Woman in Black is speaking to the Young Man:

Let me come with you. What a moon there is tonight!
The moon is kind—it won't show
that my hair has turned white. The moon
will turn my hair to gold again. You wouldn't understand.
Let me come with you.

When there's a moon the shadows in the house grow larger,
invisible hands draw the curtains,
a ghostly finger writes forgotten words in the dust
on the piano—I don't want to hear them. Hush.

Let me come with you
a little farther down, as far as the brickyard wall,
to the point where the road turns and the city appears
concrete and airy, whitewashed with moonlight,
so indifferent and insubstantial
so positive, like metaphysics,
that finally you can believe you exist and do not exist,
that you never existed, that time with its destruction never existed.
Let me come with you.

We'll sit for a little on the low wall, up on the hill,
and as the spring breeze blows around us
perhaps we'll even imagine that we are flying,
because, often, and now especially, I hear the sound of my own dress
like the sound of two powerful wings opening and closing,
and when you enclose yourself within the sound of that flight
you feel the tight mesh of your throat, your ribs, your flesh,
and thus constricted amid the muscles of the azure air,
amid the strong nerves of the heavens,
it makes no difference whether you go or return
and it makes no difference that my hair has turned white
(that is not my sorrow—my sorrow is

that my heart too does not turn white).
Let me come with you.

I know that each one of us travels to love alone,
alone to faith and to death.
I know it. I've tried it. It doesn't help.
Let me come with you.

This house is haunted, it preys on me—
what I mean is, it has aged a great deal, the nails are working loose,
the portraits drop as though plunging into the void,
the plaster falls without a sound
as the dead man's hat falls from the peg in the dark hallway
as the worn woolen glove falls from the knee of silence
or as a moonbeam falls on the old, gutted armchair.

Once it too was new—not the photograph that you are staring at so
      dubiously—
I mean the armchair, very comfortable, you could sit in it for hours
with your eyes closed and dream whatever came into your head
—a sandy beach, smooth, wet, shining in the moonlight,
shining more than my old patent leather shoes that I send each month to
      the shoeshine shop on the corner,
or a fishing boat's sail that sinks to the bottom rocked by its own
      breathing,
a three-cornered sail like a handkerchief folded slantwise in half only
as though it had nothing to shut up or hold fast
no reason to flutter open in farewell. I have always had a passion for
      handkerchiefs,
not to keep anything tied in them,
no flower seeds or camomile gathered in the fields at sunset,
nor to tie them with four knots like the caps the workers wear on the
      construction site across the street,
nor to dab my eyes—I've kept my eyesight good;
I've never worn glasses. A harmless idiosyncracy, handkerchiefs.

Now I fold them in quarters, in eighths, in sixteenths
to keep my fingers occupied. And now I remember
that this is how I counted the music when I went to the Odeion

with a blue pinafore and a white collar, with two blond braids
—8, 16, 32, 64—
hand in hand with a small friend of mine, peachy, all light and pink
    flowers,
(forgive me such digressions—a bad habit)—32, 64—and my family
    rested
great hopes on my musical talent. But I was telling you about the
    armchair—
gutted—the rusted springs are showing, the stuffing—
I thought of sending it next door to the furniture shop,
but where's the time and the money and the inclination—what to fix
    first?—
I thought of throwing a sheet over it—I was afraid
of a white sheet in so much moonlight. People sat here
who dreamed great dreams, as you do and I too,
and now they rest under earth untroubled by rain or the moon.
Let me come with you.

We'll pause for a little at the top of St. Nicholas' marble steps,
and afterward you'll descend and I will turn back,
having on my left side the warmth from a casual touch of your jacket
and some squares of light, too, from small neighborhood windows
and this pure white mist from the moon, like a great procession of silver
    swans—
and I do not fear this manifestation, for at another time
on many spring evenings I talked with God who appeared to me
clothed in the haze and glory of such a moonlight—
and many young men, more handsome even than you, I sacrificed to
    him—
I dissolved, so white, so unapproachable, amid my white flame, in the
    whiteness of moonlight,
burnt up by men's voracious eyes and the tentative rapture of youths,
besieged by splendid bronzed bodies,
strong limbs exercising at the pool, with oars, on the track, at soccer (I
    pretended not to see them),
foreheads, lips and throats, knees, fingers and eyes,
chests and arms and thighs (and truly I did not see them)
—you know, sometimes, when you're entranced, you forget what
    entranced you, the entrancement alone is enough—

my God, what star-bright eyes, and I was lifted up to an apotheosis of
  disavowed stars
because, besieged thus from without and from within,
no other road was left me save only the way up or the way down. —No,
  it is not enough.
Let me come with you.

I know it's very late. Let me,
because for so many years—days, nights, and crimson noons—I've
  stayed alone,
unyielding, alone and immaculate,
even in my marriage bed immaculate and alone,
writing glorious verses to lay on the knees of God,
verses that, I assure you, will endure as if chiselled in flawless marble
beyond my life and your life, well beyond. It is not enough.
Let me come with you.

This house can't bear me anymore.
I cannot endure to bear it on my back.
You must always be careful, be careful,
to hold up the wall with the large buffet
to hold up the buffet with the antique carved table
to hold up the table with the chairs
to hold up the chairs with your hands
to place your shoulder under the hanging beam.
And the piano, like a closed black coffin. You do not dare to open it.
You have to be so careful, so careful, lest they fall, lest you fall. I cannot
  bear it.
Let me come with you.

This house, despite all its dead, has no intention of dying.
It insists on living with its dead
on living off its dead
on living off the certainty of its death
and on still keeping house for its dead, the rotting beds and shelves.
Let me come with you.

Here, however quietly I walk through the mist of evening,
whether in slippers or barefoot,
there will be some sound: a pane of glass cracks or a mirror,

some steps are heard—not my own.
Outside, in the street, perhaps these steps are not heard—
repentance, they say, wears wooden shoes—
and if you look into this or that other mirror,
behind the dust and the cracks,
you discern—darker and more fragmented—your face,
your face, which all your life you sought only to keep clean and whole.

The lip of the glass gleams in the moonlight
like a round razor—how can I lift it to *my* lips?
however much I thirst—how can I lift it—Do you see?
I am already in a mood for similes—this at least is left me,
reassuring me still that my wits are not failing.
Let me come with you.

At times, when evening descends, I have the feeling
that outside the window the bear-keeper is going by with his old heavy
    she-bear,
her fur full of burrs and thorns,
stirring dust in the neighborhood street
a desolate cloud of dust that censes the dusk,
and the children have gone home for supper and aren't allowed
    outdoors again,
even though behind the walls they divine the old bear's passing—
and the tired bear passes in the wisdom of her solitude, not knowing
    wherefore and why—
she's grown heavy, can no longer dance on her hind legs,
can't wear her lace cap to amuse the children, the idlers, the
    importunate,
and all she wants is to lie down on the ground
letting them trample on her belly, playing thus her final game,
showing her dreadful power for resignation,
her indifference to the interest of others, to the rings in her lips, the
    compulsion of her teeth,
her indifference to pain and to life
with the sure complicity of death—even a slow death—
her final indifference to death with the continuity and the knowledge of
    life
which transcends her enslavement with knowledge and with action.

But who can play this game to the end?
And the bear gets up again and moves on
obedient to her leash, her rings, her teeth,
smiling with torn lips at the pennies the beautiful and unsuspecting
    children toss
(beautiful precisely because unsuspecting)
and saying thank you. Because bears that have grown old
can say only one thing: thank you; thank you.
Let me come with you.

This house stifles me. The kitchen especially
is like the depths of the sea. The hanging coffeepots gleam
like round, huge eyes of improbable fish,
the plates undulate slowly like medusas,
seaweed and shells catch in my hair—later I can't pull them loose—
I can't get back to the surface—
the tray falls silently from my hands—I sink down
and I see the bubbles from my breath rising, rising
and I try to divert myself watching them
and I wonder what someone would say who happened to be above and
    saw these bubbles,
perhaps that someone was drowning or a diver exploring the depths?

And in fact more than a few times I've discovered there, in the depths of
    drowning,
coral and pearls and treasures of shipwrecked vessels,
unexpected encounters, past, present, and yet to come,
a confirmation almost of eternity,
a certain respite, a certain smile of immortality, as they say,
a happiness, an intoxication, inspiration even,
coral and pearls and sapphires;
only I don't know how to give them—no, I *do* give them;
only I don't know if *they* can take them—but still, I give them.
Let me come with you.

One moment while I get my jacket.
The way this weather's so changeable, I must be careful.
It's damp in the evenings, and doesn't the moon
seem to you, honestly, as if it intensifies the cold?

Let me button your shirt—how strong your chest is
—how strong the moon—the armchair, I mean—and whenever I lift the
    cup from the table
a hole of silence is left underneath. I place my palm over it at once
so as not to see through it—I put the cup back in its place;
and the moon's a hole in the skull of the world—don't look through it,
it's a magnetic force that draws you—don't look, don't any of you look,
listen to what I'm telling you—you'll fall in. This giddiness,
beautiful, ethereal—you will fall in—
the moon's a marble well,
shadows stir and mute wings, mysterious voices—don't you hear them?

Deep, deep the fall,
deep, deep the ascent,
the airy statue enmeshed in its open wings,
deep, deep the inexorable benevolence of the silence—
trembling lights on the opposite shore, so that you sway in your own
    wave,
the breathing of the ocean. Beautiful, ethereal
this giddiness—be careful, you'll fall. Don't look at me,
for me my place is this wavering—this splendid vertigo. And so every
    evening
I have a little headache, some dizzy spells.

Often I slip out to the pharmacy across the street for a few aspirin,
but at times I'm too tired and I stay here with my headache
and listen to the hollow sound the pipes make in the walls,
or drink some coffee, and, absentminded as usual,
I forget and make two—who'll drink the other?
It's really funny, I leave it on the windowsill to cool
or sometimes I drink them both, looking out the window at the bright
    green globe of the pharmacy
that's like the green light of a silent train coming to take me away
with my handkerchiefs, my run-down shoes, my black purse, my verses,
but no suitcases—what would one do with them?
Let me come with you.

Oh, are you going? Goodnight. No, I won't come. Goodnight.
I'll be going myself in a little. Thank you. Because, in the end, I must
get out of this broken-down house.

I must see a bit of the city—no, not the moon—
the city with its calloused hands, the city of daily work,
the city that swears by bread and by its fist,
the city that bears all of us on its back
with our pettiness, sins, and hatreds,
our ambitions, our ignorance and our senility.
I need to hear the great footsteps of the city,
and no longer to hear your footsteps
or God's, or my own. Goodnight.

*The room grows dark. It looks as though a cloud may have covered the
moon. All at once, as if someone had turned up the radio in the nearby
bar, a very familiar musical phrase can be heard. Then I realize that
"The Moonlight Sonata", just the first movement, has been playing very
softly through this entire scene. The Young Man will go down the hill
now with an ironic and perhaps sympathetic smile on his finely chiselled
lips and with a feeling of release. Just as he reaches St. Nicholas', before
he goes down the marble steps, he will laugh—a loud, uncontrollable
laugh. His laughter will not sound at all unseemly beneath the moon.
Perhaps the only unseemly thing will be that nothing is unseemly. Soon
the Young Man will fall silent, become serious, and say: "The decline of
an era." So, thoroughly calm once more, he will unbutton his shirt again
and go on his way. As for the woman in black, I don't know whether
she finally did get out of the house. The moon is shining again. And in
the corners of the room the shadows intensify with an intolerable regret,
almost fury, not so much for the life, as for the useless confession. Can
you hear? The radio plays on:*

ATHENS, JUNE 1956

· AGAMEMNON ·

Once more, from the top of the marble staircase, now completely covered with crimson carpets, the commander greets the cheering crowd, with a gesture almost of nervous impatience. In the crystalline winter sunshine, drums can be heard in the lower square, together with the clatter of horses' hooves, the snapping of flags, and the voices of servants unloading booty from the wagons. Only the guards remain motionless at the gates, as if they belong to another world. An acrid smell drifts in the air from the many bay wreaths trampled underfoot. Every so often, amid the applause and general clamor, one can distinguish the loud prophetic cries of a crazed woman lying in a heap at the bottom of the stairs—incomprehensible utterances in a foreign tongue. The commander and his wife withdraw. They traverse the long corridor and enter the dining room, where the table is set for breakfast. He removes his military uniform, sets the great helmet with its horsetail plume on the side table, in front of the mirror. The mirror reflects the helmet, as if there were two empty, identical metallic companion-helmets. He lies down on a couch and closes his eyes. Outside, the cheering of the crowd and the cries of the foreign woman can still be heard. He covers his ears with his hands. His wife—beautiful, austere, imposing—bends down to unfasten his sandals, showing a humility incompatible with her style. He places his left hand on her hair, careful not to disturb its beautiful styling. She draws back; stands upright, a little away from him. He smiles a distant, tired smile. He speaks to her. You can't tell if she is listening.

You order them to be quiet, I beg you. Why are they still shouting?
For whom are they applauding? What are they cheering for? Their
    executioners, maybe? their corpses?
or perhaps to reassure themselves that they have hands and can clap
    them,
that they have voices and can shout and can hear themselves shouting?

Make them be quiet. Look, there's an ant going down the wall—
how surely and simply it walks on that vertical plane,
no arrogant sense that it may be accomplishing a great feat—perhaps
    because it's alone,
perhaps because it's insignificant, weightless, almost nonexistent—I
    envy it.

Let it be, don't brush it away—it's climbing the table, it's picked up a
    crumb;
its burden is bigger than it is—just look—that's how things always are,
the burdens we all bear are always bigger than we are.

They're not about to be quiet. And the fires on the altars—this smoke
and the smell of roasting meat—nausea—no, not from the storm at all—
something acrid in the mouth, a fear
in the fingers, the skin—as when, one night, in summer,
I started up from sleep, a crawling stickiness over my whole body;
I couldn't find the matches; I stumbled, lit the small lantern:
on the tent, ground, sheets, shield, helmet,
thousands of slugs; I stepped on them barefoot. I went outside. There
    was a faint moonlight,
naked soldiers had started a fight, laughing, fooling
with those hideous crawling creatures—and they were hideous
    themselves, their cocks
shook like slugs. I plunged into the sea; the water did not cleanse me;
the moon dragged at my left cheek, and it too was sticky,
yellow, yellow, viscous. And now, all this cheering—

Prepare me a hot bath, very hot—have you prepared it already?
with leaves of mastic and myrtle? I remember their scent,
pungent, tonic—a release, as if once more you smelled
your childhood, with trees, rivers, cicadas. Our daughters
seemed confused to me—did you notice?—one of them
touched my chin through my beard like a blind girl. You did well
to send them to their rooms—I couldn't look at them.

Keep all the booty, or share it—there's nothing I want.
And that woman howling on the stairs, take her as your slave
or as a nurse for our son (where is he, in fact? —I didn't
see him)—not for my bed, no,
a totally empty bed is what I need now, in which to sink, to be lost, just
    to be,
to have my sleep, at least, unobserved, not to care
if my face is as severe as it should be or if the muscles
in my belly and my arms have gone slack. Now
only the memory of passion works passionately, highlighting

that huge and unseemly disproportion between
the body's decay and the persistence of desire.

And, of course, I relinquish our common bed to you. I would have no
   wish
to witness the changes time's wrought in your beautiful form,
in your thighs and your breasts. I have no hatred to feed
with such an image. On the contrary, indeed, I'd rather
preserve your erotic presence (for my own sake—not yours)
intact, outside time, like a marvellous statue
that somehow also preserves my own youth's wonder and glory.

Only that ashtray with the carved base (if it is still around)
where sometimes, at night, I left my cigar to smoke itself,
like a distant chimney in a tiny Ithaca, or like my
private personal star, while you slept beside me—that I would like.

As for the other things, keep them—including the heavy diamond-
   crusted sceptre—
especially that—it's no use to me—it's so heavy. Today I understand
Achilles' anger—not antagonism between us at all—it was weariness,
a prophetic weariness that equated victory with defeat,
life with death. By himself, down on the shore,
with his companion the black dog—so inexplicably attached to him—
one fall night with a full moon (so they say).

Perhaps he had need of this dumb presence
that doesn't question, doesn't refuse, but believes and approves always
with a wag of the tail, a blink of the eyelids,
or sometimes resting its muzzle gratefully
on its master's sandals, anticipating with the same delight
a caress or a kick; or at other times panting, not from running,
but from its devotion, hanging its red tongue out
as if it held between its teeth a piece bled from its soul
and wanted to offer it. Such boundless devotion, I imagine,
could save a man or even a god. Patroclus was jealous;

maybe that's why he urged him to fight again
and why he was killed. How much blood was shed—
I never learned why—I don't know—some moments I didn't dare

touch bread—the bread was crimson. And that dog,
when Achilles was killed, returned alone to the shore,
stared at the ships, the clouds, sniffed the stones
where its lord's feet had walked, sniffed his clothes in the tent,
wouldn't eat, wouldn't eat at all—who would look after it?—it got in
    our way,
got tangled in our feet; often got kicked; it sat
and watched the soldiers while they ate; it didn't growl.

One day, someone threw it a bone; it didn't eat it,
just took it between its teeth and vanished. In a little while they found it
at Achilles' tomb—the bone was left on the mound
like a small offering; and the dog howled with huge tears
perhaps for the loss of its master, perhaps, too, for shame because it was
    starving.
Later it took back the bone, hid behind some rocks
and began to gnaw on it. With the gnawing came the sound
of its crying—perhaps, too, the lament of eternal hunger.

How strange your eyes look; and your voice was strange, when you
    said:
"Slave-women, why are you standing around like that? Have you
    forgotten my order?
I told you to lay the carpets from carriage to house so the pathway
    would be
all crimson for my lord's passage." Inside your voice
was a deep river, and it was as if I were floating upon it. When I walked
on those purple carpets my knees grew weak. I looked behind me
and saw the dusty prints of my sandals on the bright crimson
like those fishermen's corks that float
above hidden, submerged nets. Before me I saw the slave-girls
unrolling still more crimson carpets, as if they were pushing
the crimson wheels of fate. A shiver
ran up my spine. That's why I asked you to prepare me
a hot bath. That shiver—glass, glass—you know,
no one wants to die, no matter how tired he is.

My place now is, I am, this weariness of mine; as though I were
    ascending
without effort, almost without legs, the bluest mountain

from which I will be able to survey (and do survey, already) the lower
hills, plains, cities—a little smoke shines gold in the sun—harbors
and the ships of our bitter return in the semicircle
of the deserted shore—white ships, distant, diminished,
like a child's pared nails—like our other daughter's—remember?—
when you cut them in the bathhouse doorway—she didn't like it; she
    cried—so many years ago.

How we've let our hours slip by and vanish, struggling foolishly
to assure ourselves a place in the consciousness of others. Not one
second of our own, in all those long summers, to watch
a bird's shadow above the wheat—a tiny trireme
on a golden sea—we could have been sailing in it
for silent trophies, for more glorious conquests. We did not sail.

At times it seems to me I am a calm corpse that watches
my own self existing; it follows with its vacant eyes
my movements, my gestures—like that time, one winter night,
down below, outside the walls, with an indescribable, cold moonlight
and everything looked marbled, made of moon and whitewash.

I looked around me with the indifference of an immortal, who no longer
fears death, nor cares about his immortality. Yes, like a
handsome corpse strolling through the night's whiteness, looking at
plaster ornaments on houses, garden fences,
shadows of masts on the beach. And then, an arrow
whistled past my ear, lodged in the wall vibrating
like a single string of an unknown instrument, like a nerve
in the body of the void, ringing with inconceivable gladness.

Thus, on occasion, something would bring us up short, even out there—
    you didn't know what was happening—
a reflection in your sword from your eye, the miniature
mirroring of a still cloud on a helmet-top
or Patroclus' habit of putting two fingers
to the tip of his ear, saying nothing, deep in solitary
erotic musing. One day, Achilles took his hand, looked
at his fingers, like a soothsayer, then at his ear. "Autumn is coming," he
    said;

"we must redeploy our forces." And there was a strange connection
between that "redeploy" and Patroclus' beautiful gesture.

And then Patroclus left the tent, approached his friend's horses,
Balius and Xanthus, stood between them, placed his arms
around their slender necks, and there the three of them, faces side by
     side,
stayed motionless watching the sunset. The composition they made
I have seen, I think, on some sculpted pediment, and suddenly I
     understood
how it happens that you sacrifice a human being for a little favorable
     wind.

Little by little everything was stripped, became calm, glassy,
walls, doors, your hair, your hands—
exquisitely transparent glass—not a breath of mortality clouds it—
     behind the glass
you can distinguish nothingness, indivisible—something ultimately
     whole—
that first complete wholeness, unwounded, like nonbeing.

Before I put my hand on the doorknob, before I open it,
before I enter the room, I have already seen the sofa, the chairs,
and the mirror reflecting the opposite wall with a picture
of some ancient sea battle. Before I get into the bath
I look at the myrtle leaves floating on the water and the swelling clouds
of steam rising up to the ceiling, thick round the skylight. I can even
sense the approximate hour of my death.

Forgive me for this view of things, above all for this confession—
it is a way for you, too, to see me; to make us equals—although we were
     already—
altogether defenseless, of course. But, again, at this moment, I ask
     myself once more
what I may be about to reap, to avoid, to conceal
with this confession—what possible new mask
of unbreakable glass over my glassy brittle face—
a great hollow mask, reproducing my features, my expression,
hung high, in front of the palace, on the metope of the gate,
my personal escutcheon only, not that of the dynasty. Sometimes I think

it all happened only so I could be reminded of it one day,
or rather perhaps so I could discover its immortal futility.

Propitious moment—and I welcome it. I look at my hand—
neither for the sword nor for the soft caress—on its own, tied
—tied how?—to invisible strings, like the rhapsode's
hand on a great lyre—if you take hold of it for a moment,
the music will stop in amazement; and the half-finished sound
forgives neither the one nor the other; like a silver ring,
hung in the air by a string, it taps you, mysteriously, on the shoulder.

The others fell—true warriors (and yet, who knows
what bitterness, what fear, they too felt). I didn't envy them their death.
If I glorified their heroism, it was to conceal
my secret relief that I still lived—not at all heroic.

So now here I am, who brought you none of that joy—the renown as
        they say, the glory
that, alas, might even perhaps redeem,
with clanging and counterfeit coin, our silence for ten real years,
thousands of murders, covert and overt, thousands of errors and graves.

Such heroics are far from me—another sort, now,
beckons to me—unheard and unseen. Once at dusk
I saw one last golden leaf on a pure black tree
and it was the naked shoulder of a quiet, handsome athlete who,
        bending down,
lifted all our burdens and set them softly on the ground. Then
a new hunger, a different appetite, made my mouth water
and I felt purl on the edges of my lips,
sweet and soothing, the milk of gratitude. Against my will
I lifted my hand to the spot, to wipe it away
lest it betray me, perhaps even lest people see my new childishness,
my new suckling at the first nipple of creation.

Then they would have realized how strong, how feeble I am—
provocatively in either case. One late afternoon I was walking alone on
        the shore;
a golden stillness; rosy sea; the flash of an oar. On a rock
was spread a large red sailcloth. From the camp above

a song reached me, lonely, sad,
warm and misty, like a garment just removed from a beautiful body—
a warm song, I held it in the hollow of my hands as I walked
in the evening freshness, near the ships. All around
something gave off a scent like roasted corn and seaweed.
A little water, boiling up, may have spilled over onto a burning log.
     Outside the tents
great lanterns had been lit for the evening mess.

Death seemed so easy. I remembered the silent Philemon: one night,
when everyone was drunk, in the tent, babbling endlessly
about exploits, women, horses—Antilochus, taunting, challenged
his calm and his sobriety. And Philemon said: "I'm ready," nothing
     more;
and he stayed that way, leaning over, not drinking, with his elbows on
     the table,
his face in his hands. Behind his fingers
shone a strange smile. "I'm ready." At dawn
Antilochus left the tent, turned toward the east and delivered,
with the grace of an actor and the impiety of youth, his prayer to the
     sun.

I don't know how I remembered his concluding words. "O sun"—he
     said—
"you who open with your finger a golden hole in the black wall
from which two birds emerge, one crimson, the other blue—
the crimson one settles on my knee, the blue one on my shoulder—"
     And indeed,
at that moment, two great birds flew over him—
two crows. Neither he nor Philemon looked back.
On a white lekythos we etched two beautiful birds—one crimson, one
     blue.

Oh yes, of course, our life together will be difficult. But tomorrow, right
     away,
I will move out to the country property. Don't worry. I know:
they may forgive us for everything one day, and yet
their knowing how you view them, how you view yourself,
that no one—neither enemy nor friend—can forgive. Nor
can you hide: in the middle of your forehead is that third eye

which, no matter how concealed and how closed, mocks you with the
    gleam
of solitude and uniqueness—ultimate arrogance and humility.

Years pass. We go away. We grow old—not you. Helen, you know,
after the city fell, would sit for hours in front of the large mirror
that she'd put out and they'd lugged aboard the ship—a strange mirror:
two golden ultra-cunning Erotes, carved on the sides of the frame,
naked, with neither quivers nor arrows, looking suspiciously
at whoever looked into the mirror. Well, Helen

makes up her face now with memory as her model—and perhaps it's
    more beautiful
with recollection, knowledge, desire (and with persistence too)
with secret tints—pure alchemy—ochre, rose, deep blue, silver,
with heavy black shadow around the gray of her eyes,
with deep red on her soft, full lips.

Now she paints her large mouth, as if about to call from the balcony
an inexplicable "no", or to kiss a God. But—what can you expect?—her
    face
is no longer the one for which we set forth, for which we fought,
sowing sea and land with broken oars, wheels, skulls.
A different face now—perhaps more truly hers—but still different.
Beneath the splendid colors of her feminine art,
it's as if she's bitterly concealing or beguiling her death. And she knows
    it.

One day, down on the beach, at the table for the victory celebrations,
when we had buried the dead, and the city, from end to end,
was smoking still in the soft autumn dusk, Helen,
holding her glass to her lips, said: "Listen
to how my bracelets jangle; I am dead"—
and a pure white light streamed from her teeth, which suddenly
all became marble and bone. Her hands and her voice were nailed to the
    air.

All white, pure white—both the masts and the sea; a seagull,
as if struck by an invisible arrow, fell without a sound

right in the middle of the table, next to the wine pitchers. Helen
picked it up, looked at it silently,
moistened her little finger in its blood and traced on the tablecloth
a perfect circle—perhaps nothing, perhaps totality. Later,
plucking, with a gesture of incredible charm, a downy tuft
from the bird's belly, she scattered it, laughing, in our hair. We forgot.
There remained only a flavor of whiteness and that inexplicable circle.

On the voyage home, in the Aegean, one night in a great storm
the helm broke. Then I felt a terrified sense of freedom
right at the heart of this lack of direction. I peered
with unbelievably clear vision through the darkness; saw
a life ring tossing on the waves. I was able, indeed,
in the dim torchlight, to make out on it the word "Lachesis".

And this life ring, that name, and the fact that I saw them,
gave me a curious strength and calm; and I told myself:
"Only let this life ring be saved, and nothing is lost."

The next day, the Aegean grew calm; I saw the life ring floating
amid the wrecked ships and splintered wood. I fished it out.
I have it still in my duffle like a secret life preserver. If you want to,
you can hang it as a momento in one of the rooms
or throw it away—I no longer have need of it. "Lachesis", it says.

Everything was incomprehensible, deceptive—that Trojan Horse before
    the walls,
implacable, with its enormous glass eyes mirroring the sea—
a wooden horse, with azure eyes, fully alive. You'd think
that the same sea saw itself with the horse's eyes,
saw at the same time the horse's belly, pitch dark, hollow,
with the fully armed warriors shut inside. And yet I preserved
that azure vision of the sea, boundless,
compassionate, exhausted. No rancor against fate;
only the sense of a strange ineluctable law that has abrogated
the errors and sins of each individually, and the collective responsibility
    of us all.
Sometimes weariness, too, gives you a presentiment of
    indestructibility—isn't that so?

At a banquet, back there, during a three-day truce in the fighting,
when everyone was drunk (not so much on wine as on death),
they were smashing their glasses on the rocks, and it seemed to me as if I
        saw the broken glasses,
whole again, uncracked, gleam in a splendid line to the horizon's edge,
sparkling in the torchfires; last of all
the half moon shone out—a silver cup, shimmering calmly
full of warm milk.
                        And then Ion, twenty years old,
threw off his chiton and, naked as a god, leaped up on the table,
kicked aside plates and wine jars, poured a pitcher of wine over his curly
        head,
soaked himself, stood there dripping, gleaming. "The unbroken *does*
        exist," he shouted,
"The unbroken *does* exist!" He hurled his glass—it didn't break;
they handed it back to him; he aimed at an anchor, hurled it again;
four, five, ten times—it didn't break (perhaps it was made
of some other stuff—fake—who knows?—or perhaps
that same tipsiness of ours convinced us of the impossible.)
                                                The next day
Ion was killed in battle. I searched for the glass in his tent, in his pack;
I looked everywhere. I didn't find it. But his words—those I remember.

I think you're not listening to me—as though you're in a hurry. But, of
        course we're all in a hurry
for the other person to stop, so we can speak ourselves. And each of us
hears only his own words. What difference do words make? Only action
can be counted and counts—as you always insisted.
                                        Tell me, has the water
you prepared for me cooled? No need for you to come with me;
I can manage by myself—I got used to it back there; and perhaps it's
        better that way.
And besides, to tell you the truth, I would be embarrassed in front of
        you.

So many years have passed—we're out of the habit, we've forgotten. As
        if the body
(not only the spirit) has lost that old assurance it had:
enmeshed and erect in its private delight at existing and being seen. Now

it only watches (suspicious, the body, and old) with an altered
    perception
the world's confident ageless beauty, which it shares no longer.

This perception no one forgives it. And, in fact, it is so independent,
so profound, self-sufficient, and unconstrained. I think it trammels
both us and others—useless.
                         That shiver—not glassy now,
here in my spine—something different. A little while ago
everything was glass—faces, bodies, objects, places, you, me, our
    children—
glassy, exposed, gleaming—of hard, clear glass. I observed them with
    interest,
almost with exultation—as I could, in an aquarium, the movement of
    beautiful, small, strange fish
or even of large, ugly, vicious, bloodthirsty ones—all strange. And so,
    suddenly
as if the glass had softened—no longer held its shape, was no longer
    transparent,
as if it had never had shape or been transparent—it fell in a heap on the
    ground
with all it contained—a turbid mass, like a grimy sack
where they let dirty underclothes pile up to be washed one day,
and don't wash them—they're tired of them; they lie there forgotten
    (they want to forget them), thrown
on the floor, near the door—they trip over it, give it a kick on the way
    out
and, more often, on the way in to the house. And they have indeed
    forgotten them,
and what will they do to remember?—the stuff's rotted completely, shut
    up
in its own smell of ancient sweat, urine, and blood.
                To the bath, to the bath,

the water will cool, it will have cooled. I'm going. You stay here—it's
    not necessary. You insist?—Come.

The man stands up. He begins to walk—clearly toward the bath.
Without speaking the woman follows him. They both go out. The room,
empty now, seems larger. Breakfast is untouched on the table. The

glasses have become somewhat cloudy. The helmet is still there, in front of the mirror. There is a deep stillness both inside and outside the house. An ant recrosses the white tablecloth. Following the ant, you notice near the center of the table an embroidered circle—a ring of red flowers. Suddenly, outside, from the marble staircase, the voice of the foreign woman can be heard, in pure Greek: "Citizens of Argos, citizens of Argos, the great golden fish in the black net, and the sword uplifted, two-tongued, citizens of Argos, citizens. . . . " Heavy drums, trumpets, tumult drown her voice. A man, handsome, bare-headed, wearing a military cloak, with a huge bloody sword in his hand, comes into the empty room. With his left hand he picks up the helmet from the side table. He wears it back to front, the horsetail plume in his face. Like a mask. He goes out. The voice of the mad woman: "Citizens of Argos, late, too late, citizens of Argos . . ." She stops. The drums grow louder. The first woman comes into the room. Pale, tall, very beautiful. She climbs up on a chair. On a nail in the wall she hangs a life ring. "Lachesis" it says. Then she goes to the mirror and fixes her hair.

ATHENS, SIKYON, HERAION, SAMOS, DECEMBER 1966–OCTOBER 1970

· ORESTES ·

Two young men, about twenty years old, pause at the gateway with an expression as if they are trying to remember something, to recognize something. At the same time everything looks unimaginably familiar and affecting to them, only somewhat smaller—much smaller—because of all they have seen abroad, in other lands and at other times— everything much smaller, the walls and the great stones, the lion gate, the palace under the shadow of the mountain. It is still summer. Night is falling. The private cars and large tourist buses have gone. The place relaxes in the silence—the mouths of ancient tombs and monuments breathe deeply. A scrap of newspaper stirs in the burned grass, blown by a vague wind. There comes the sound of the nightwatchman's steps, and the great key that locks the inner door of the tower. Then, as if set free in the night's warm freshness, the crickets begin beating their tiny drums. Somewhere, behind the mountain, lurks an unidentified brightness—perhaps it is the moon. And at exactly the same moment, from the stone steps, can be heard—sharp, harsh, jarring—a woman's lamentation. The two young men cannot be seen. They merge with the lower part of the wall like two great shadows. After a little, one wipes the sweat from his face with his handkerchief, gestures casually in the direction of the sound, and speaks to the other, who always remains affectionately silent and attentive, like Pylades:

Listen—it hasn't stopped yet, she hasn't gotten tired. Intolerable,
on this Greek night—so warm, so calm,
so independent of us and indifferent, allowing us
a respite—to be in its midst, to watch from its midst
and from far off at the same time; to see the night
naked like the most insignificant voices of its crickets,
like the slightest shivers of its black skin.

How did it happen that we, too, remained independent, with the
     delightful
pleasure of indifference, of tolerance, beyond everything,
in the midst of everything, in the midst of ourselves—alone, together,
     under no obligation,
without competition, rivalry, censure, without
any expectations or demands placed on us by others? Thus I need only
to look at the thong of your sandal, which sets apart for me
your big toe, so irreproachable, turns it toward a position of my own,
toward a secret place, my own, near the oleanders,

and the silver leaves of night that fall on your shoulder
and the sound of the fountain flowing imperceptibly under our nails.

Listen to her—her voice spreads over her like a deep-arched vault,
and she herself is suspended in her voice
like the clapper of a bell, and is struck by and strikes the bell,
though there is neither feast nor funeral, only the immaculate solitude of
    the rocks
and, below, the humble quiet of the countryside—underlining
this unjustifiable passion—which move around her
as innocent children's kites circle countless stars
with the light papery rustle of their long tails.

Let's move a little away from here, so the woman's voice won't reach
    us;
let's stand further down; no, not at the ancestral tombs;
no libations tonight. I don't want
to cut my hair—this hair
where your hand has so often wandered. What a beautiful night—
our own in a sense, receding, torn from us, and we can hear it
like a dark river flowing down to the sea,
gleaming now and then under branches, to the sparkling of the stars,
amid this powerful, pitiless summer,
with imperceptible pauses, momentary, with haphazard jumps (maybe
    someone
is throwing stones into the river)—this small leap
and the vinegrowers' greenhouse panes shining near ground level.
    Strange,

they prepared a complete life for me and for this I prepared myself. And
    now,
before this gate, I feel completely unprepared—
the two marble lions—did you see them?—they've been tamed,
those lions, that started out in our childhood years so resolute,
wild, almost, manes bristling, poised for a daring leap,
they've settled down now, reconciled, at the two upper corners of the
    outer gate,
with lifeless pelts, vacant eyes—they frighten no one—with the
    expression
of whipped dogs, not even especially unhappy,

faithful, blind dogs, without rancour,
tongues licking, from time to time, night's soft warm sole.

Unprepared, yes indeed—I can't do it; I lack that essential
relationship to the place, the time, the situation,
the facts. It's not cowardice. I'm unprepared
before the threshold of the deed, a total stranger
before the destiny that others have decreed for me. How is it
that others establish our fate, little by little, prescribe it for us
and we accept it? How is it that with the smallest threads
of a few of our moments they weave for us
our whole time, harsh and dark, thrown
like a veil from our head to our feet, covering
our faces and hands completely, where they've secreted
an unknown knife—quite unknown—and it lights up,
with its harsh glint, a landscape, not our own—
that I know; it is not our own. And how does it happen

that our own fate accepts it, stands back
and watches, like a stranger, ourselves and our strange fate,
dumb, austere, resigned, aloof,
not even with the dignity of magnanimity or stoicism,
without even disappearing, without dying,
and that we remain, prey, it may be, to a different fate,
but to one only—not in two minds and divided. Look at it, still there,
as though drowsy—one eye closed, the other dilated,
letting us see it watching us and discerning
our endless hesitation, with neither approval nor disapproval.

Two opposing forces seem to pull equally on our legs
and one force moves far further away than the other,
stretching the stride of our legs to the point of dismemberment; and the
     head
is a knot that still rules this weary body,
although, I know, legs are made to move
one by one of their own accord, both in one rhythm, in one direction,
in the fields below, near the clusters of grapes, as far as the reddening
     horizon beyond,
moving our whole bodies—or perhaps

because of this great and terrible stride of ours we were fashioned
over the unknown abyss, over graves and our grave? I don't know.

And yet, beneath the many layers of shock and fear, I divine
endless silence spreading out—justice,
a self-existent balance that contains us
in the order of seeds and stars. Did you notice?—at noon
as we were coming here, a cloud-shadow passed across the plain
covering wheatfields, vines, olive trees,
horses, birds, leaves—a transparent sketch
of a distant landscape of the infinite, here upon the ground;
and the peasant who was trudging along at the far end of the field
seemed to be holding, thrust under his left armpit,
the whole shadow of the cloud, like a huge cloak—
majestic, yet simple as his sheep.

Thus the earth becomes familiar with the infinite, taking on something
of blue and of vagueness; and the infinite, in its turn,
takes on something from earth, chestnut and warm, something of leaves,
and of sheepfolds and roots, something of the eyes
of that patient cow (remember?)
and the strong legs of the farmer disappearing in the distance.

Meanwhile this woman shows no sign of being quiet. Listen to her.
How can she herself not hear that voice of hers? How can she stay
shut suffocatingly in one instant of past time,
past feelings? How can she, and with what,
renew this passion for retribution and the voice of passion
when all the echoes belie her, mock her even—the echoes
from the porticos, columns, stairways, furniture,
from the jars in the garden, the caves of Zara, the water channel,
from the stables below for the horses, the guards' watchtowers on the
    hills,
from the pleats on the statues of women in the outer courtyard
and the noble phalluses of the stone runners and discus throwers?

The vases in the house still, as it were, set against her lamentations
the merciful gesture of a few tender-hearted roses
arranged charmingly by Mother's own hand,
there on the carved sideboard, in front of the great, ancestral mirror,

next to a light, reflection against reflection, watery—I remember it
from my childhood years—it remains for me unshadowed—
watery light, impalpable, neutral—an unknown quantity—
timeless, innocent—something smooth and wonderful
like the soft hair at the nape of girls' necks or on the lips of youths,
like the smell of a newly bathed body on the sheets,
the warm freshness in the breath of a summer night, filled with stars.

She understands nothing, not even the echoes
that mock her harsh voice. I am afraid; I'm powerless
to respond to her challenge—so exorbitant and at the same time so
        comic—
to these pompous words of hers, old-fashioned, as if unearthed
in a linen chest "from the good old days" (as the old folks say),
like great flags, unironed, the seams of which have absorbed
naphthalene, denial, silence—so very old
that no one doubts their age, and they persist
in flapping with archaic gestures above the unsuspecting passers-by—
the busy ones, the tired ones—above the asphalt-covered streets,
modest, for all their breadth and length, with elegant shop windows
all ties, crystal, bathing suits, hats, gloves, brushes,
which correspond quite beautifully to our needs of the moment
and so also to the age-old needs of life that rule us.

And she persists in preparing hydromel and food for the dead
who no longer thirst or drink, no longer have mouths
or dream of restoration or revenge. All this invokes
their infallible nature (—what way infallible?) perhaps to escape
the responsibility of her own choice and decision—
when the teeth of the dead, bare, scattered on the ground,
are white seeds in an endless black valley
sprouting all by themselves, infallible, invisible, pure white trees
that glow in the moonlight, till the end of time.

Ah, how can her mouth bear those words,
drawn forth, yes, from old linen chests (like the ones
decorated with big nail-studs), dragged out
from among Mother's old hats, in an outmoded style,
which Mother no longer wears—she despises them. Did you see her

this afternoon in the garden?—how beautiful she still is—she hasn't
    aged at all,
perhaps because she watches time and manages it
every moment—I mean she's renewed by the recognition
of the youth she's losing—perhaps in this way she gets it back.

And Mother's voice, how real, ordinary, precise—
she can make the biggest words seem natural,
or the smallest, in their deepest significance, like:
"A butterfly came in through the window,"
or: "The world is unbearably wonderful,"
or: "They should use more blueing on the linen napkins,"
or: "One note of this nocturnal fragrance escapes me," and she laughs,
perhaps to anticipate someone else who might laugh—

This depth of understanding and tender indulgence
for everyone and everything—almost contempt—always amazed and
    alarmed her
with that conscious, lofty dignity of hers,
mingling her tiny, artful, complex laugh
with the little hiss of the match and the match flame, as she lit
the hanging lamp in the dining room, and there she was, lit up from
    below,
with the light focused more strongly on her shapely chin
and on her thin, flaring nostrils, that for a moment
paused to breath in and narrow,
as if she would stay near us, stop, be motionless,
lest she dissolve like a column of blue smoke in the night wind,
lest the trees seize her with their long branches, lest she wear
a star's thimble for some endless piece of handiwork—

Thus Mother always found her most precise movement and stillness
precisely at the moment of her absence—we were always afraid
she would vanish before our very eyes, be taken up, rather—whenever
    she bent
to tie her sandal, which left uncovered her marvellous,
painted, curved toenails, or whenever she arranged
her hair in front of the big mirror
with a movement of her hands so graceful, youthful, and light,

she might have been rearranging three or four stars on the world's
    forehead,
or setting two daisies to be kissed beside the fountain
or watching with the effrontery of affection two dogs
making love right in the middle of the dusty road
at noon, in burning summer. Mother was so simple and persuasive
and at the same time strong, commanding, and unfathomable.

Perhaps that was what my sister never forgave her—her eternal youth—
that old woman of a child, cautious by contrast, given to denial
of beauty and delight—ascetic, odious in her moderation,
solitary and detached. Even her clothes,
stubbornly old-womanish, baggy, tattered, old,
and the cord at her waist limp, worn out,
like a bloodless vein around her belly (and she tightened it even so)
like the cord of a fallen curtain that no longer opens or closes
thus revealing obliquely a landscape of perpetually crabbed harshness
with jagged rocks and huge trees, naked, branches stretching up
into hackneyed, pompous clouds; and there, in the distance,
the barely perceptible presence of a lost sheep,
a living white spot, a speck of softness—it can't be seen—
and that same sister of mine an upright rock
encased in its hardness—intolerable. Listen to her,
almost quibbling—she keeps a stern eye on Mother, is continually
    provoked
whenever Mother puts a flower in her hair or her bosom,
whenever she walks down the corridor with her confident, lilting steps,
when she tilts her head, in melancholy relaxation, a little to one side,
letting fall a small drop of sound, charged with meaning, from her long
    earring onto her shoulder,
that she alone hears—her own sweet prerogative. And she, the Other, is
    furious.

She sustains her anger with the pitch of that voice of hers—
(if she ever lost it, what would become of her?) —I think she fears the
    accomplishment
of her revenge, lest nothing be left of her at all. *She* never
heard the grass rustle secretly in the night from the passing
of a lithe, unseen man outside the window, at dinner time;
she never saw the ladder, propped without reason

against a high, bare wall one holiday; she paid no attention
to that "without reason"; she didn't notice
the tassel of a corn-ear grazing the sole of a tiny cloud,
or the shape of a jug against the starry sky, or a sickle
abandoned, all by itself, beside the well, one noontime,
or the loom's shadow in a locked room, when they fumigate the
    vineyards
and the laborers' voices can be heard below in the fields,
while a sparrow, all alone in all the world,
pecking in the courtyard at insects, seeds, a few crumbs,
tries to spell out its freedom. She saw nothing, ever.

Completely blind, imprisoned in her blindness. But how can it be
that she lives a life entirely based on opposition to another,
entirely out of hatred for another, and not out of love
of her own life, without any place of her own? And what do they want?
What do they want from me? "Vengeance, vengeance," they cry.
Let them take care of it by themselves, then, since vengeance nourishes
    them.

I don't want to hear her any more. I can't stand it. No one
has the right to control my eyes, my mouth, my hands,
these feet of mine that tread upon the earth. Give me your hand. Let's
    go.

Long nights, summery, perfect, our own,
assorted stars, sweaty armpits, shattered glasses—
an insect hums politely in the ear of tranquility,
lizards warm at the feet of young male statues,
slugs on the garden benches or even in the locked forge,
strolling on the huge anvil, leaving behind
on the black iron white trails of sperm and spittle.

Let's leave this land of Mycenae behind us once again—how the earth
    here smells
of bronze-rust and black blood. Attica's lighter. Isn't it? I sense
that now, this appointed hour, is the hour
of my final abdication. I don't want
to be their theme, their servant, their instrument, not even their ruler.

I too have a life of my own and I must live it. Not vengeance—
what could it bring back from the dead, one death more,
and that a violent one?—what could it add to life? Years have gone by.
I don't feel hatred any more; perhaps I've forgotten? grown weary? I
    don't know.
Indeed, I feel a certain sympathy for the murderess—she took the
    measure of great chasms,
great understanding has widened her eyes in the darkness
and she sees—she sees the inexhaustible, the unattainable, and the
    unalterable. She sees me.

I too want to see Father's murder in death's palliative generality,
to forget it in that totality of death
which awaits us too. This night has taught me
the innocence of all usurpers. And we are all
usurpers of something—some of the people, some of the throne,
others of love or even of death; my sister
usurps my own life, and I yours.

Oh my dear, how particularly you share in all
these strange, foolish undertakings. And yet, my hand
is yours; you too must take it, usurp it—your own,
and because of this also my own; take it, clasp it; you expect it to be
free from retributions, reprisals, recollections,
free—I too want that,
so that it belongs wholly to me, and only thus
can I give it wholly to you. Forgive me
this secretive solitude and division—you know it well—
that splits me in two. What a beautiful night—

a damp smell of oregano, thyme, capers—
or perhaps geraniums?—I confuse fragrances; sometimes,
blood smells of sea salt, and sperm of the forest—
a willful displacement perhaps—that's what I seek tonight,
like that soldier who told us, one night in Athens, how when
the beach was loud with groans and the clang of arms,
he hid in the withered bushes, above the shore and
watched in the moonlight the swaying shadow of his manhood on his
    thigh
like a doubtful erection, striving to exist, testing

his willpower over his own body, for a displacement away
from the plain of death, in hope of a dubious independence.

Let's go further down; I can't bear to hear her; her cries
batter my nerves and my dreams, just as those oars
battered the floating slaughtered corpses
momentarily lit up by the ships' flares, the shooting stars of August,
and they were all agleam, young and erotic, unbelievably immortal,
in a watery death that cooled their backs, their ankles, their legs.

How quietly the seasons change. Night falls, limitless.
A wicker chair remains alone, forgotten under the trees,
amid the light dampness and mist given off by the earth.
There is no sorrow; scarcely any expectation; nothing.
A motionless motion spreads out to yesterday and to tomorrow.
The tortoise is a rock in the grass; after a little it stirs—
unforeseen calm, hidden complicity, happiness.

A tiny spot of vacancy remains in your smile—perhaps
because of what I'm telling you or what I may tell you, things I don't yet
    know myself,
things I have not yet found in the rhythm of speech that travels
ahead of my thoughts—far ahead—that reveals to me
my own rhythm and my self. Like that time in the arena,
when the runners arrived, bathed in sweat, and I noticed one
who had tied a bit of string around his ankle,
for no reason at all, quite at random. Just that, and nothing else.

Sacrifices, then, and heroics—what difference do they make? Years and
    years. Maybe we really came
for these small revelations of the great wonder
that no longer contains small and great, nor murder and sin.

All one passion—enchantment and amazement (as Mother would
    sometimes say),
when the leaves of night—broad, fleshy, cool—
brush our foreheads, and the falling fruit
is a message, fixed and incommunicable,
like the circle, the triangle, or the rhombus. I muse over
a saw rusting in an abandoned woodshop,

and the house numbers changing position out there on the horizon—
3, 7, 9—the innumerable number. Listen; she's stopped.

A vast, inachievable quiet—I think thousands of pure black horses
must be climbing darkly up to the mountaintop, while on the far side
a golden river runs downhill toward the plain
with its lifeless springs, uninhabited camps and stables
where the straw steams with an ancient heat of stray beasts,
and the dogs, with their tails hanging, wander
like dark scars in the silver depth of night.

She's stopped at last—peace—deliverance. It's beautiful.
Look—the shadows of hurrying insects over the wall
leaving behind a dewdrop or a tiny bell
that rings a little later. Beyond, a brightness—
a prolonged suspicion, purple—the moon,
small, solitary conflagration behind the trees, the chimneys, and the
    weathervanes,
burning the great thorn trees and yesterday's newspapers,
leaving behind this approval—glorification, almost—
of not waiting, not hoping, of manifest vanity,
moving out to intrepid isolation, to the end of the road
with the ghostly, violet passage of a cat.

When the moon appears, the houses sink down to the plain below,
the corn-ears crackle with frost or from the law of growth,
whitewashed trees gleam on their boles like agonized columns
in a silent war, while the signs of little shops
hang like fulfilled oracles over the locked doors.

Countrymen will go to sleep with their huge hands on their bellies
and the birds with their tiny feet curved lightly around branches in their
    sleep
as if they made no effort to hang on, as if effort were nothing,
as if nothing had happened, as if nothing were about to happen—
light, light, as if the sky had penetrated their wings,
as if someone were walking the long narrow corridors, lamp in hand,
and all the windows were open and outdoors could be heard
beasts calmly ruminating in the midst of eternity.

I love this fresh quietude. Somewhere, close, in an upper gallery,
a young woman will be combing her long hair
while her spread-out underclothing rests beside her in the moonlight.
Everything fluid, smooth, happy. Great water jars in the bath rooms—
I imagine them pouring water on the necks and breasts of young girls—
small bars of sweet-scented soap slither on the tiles,
bubbles rise through the noise of water and laughter,
one woman has slipped and fallen,
the moon has slipped through the skylight,
everything's slippery with soap—you can't get hold of things
or keep a hold on yourself—this slipperiness
is the returning rhythm of life; the women laugh
shaking white, light-as-air mounds of soapsuds
above their little forests of pubic hair. Is this what happiness is?

This night of waiting has left me an opening to the outside
and to within. I can't describe it exactly. Perhaps it is
huge masks destroyed, metal buckles,
and the sandals of the dead, warped from the damp,
moving all by themselves, as though walking without feet—but they
     don't walk;
and that great net in the bath—who wove it?—
the knot, the knot—unloosable—black—it was not Mother who wove
     it.

An immense shadow spreads out over the arches;
a stone works loose and falls into the ravine—and yet no one passed
     by—
then nothing; and then a branch that snaps
from the light pressure of the sky. Small frogs
jump, soft and silent, in the damp grass. Peace.

Ash-gray mice fall into the wells and drown,
dense constellations slowly turn; down inside there
they toss the trash from banquets—pitchers, cups, mirrors, and chairs,
animal bones, lyres, and clever exchanges. The wells never fill up.

Something like fingers of light and freshness pass in succession over our
     chests,
drawing circle-traces around the nipples,

and we too are winnowed by the air, circle upon circle, around a center
unknown, ambiguous, and yet fixed—endless circles
around a mute cry, around a knife thrust; and the knife
is driven into our hearts, I think, forming the center of our hearts
like the stake in the middle of the threshing floor up there, on the hill,

and around the horses, ears of corn, oil lamps, mule drivers
and reapers beside the hayricks, with the moon's head on their
    shoulders,
hearing the neighing of horses till the very end of their sleep,
hearing the bulls piss among willows and brambles,
the thousand feet of the millipede on the jar,
the slithering of the quiet snake in the olive grove,
and the cracking of heated stones as they cool and contract.

One erotic word stays forever locked in our mouths, inexpressible,
like a pebble in our sandals or even a nail; you get tired
of stopping, removing it, loosening your straps,
being delayed—the secret rhythm of your walking has possessed you
more than the annoyance of the pebble, more
than the stubborn reminder of your weariness,
your procrastination; and there is still
a small thorny exultation and recollection
in the fact you've brought that pebble back from a beloved shore,
from a pleasant walk with good conversation, with watery images,
when the tobacco merchants' talk could be heard in the seaside taverna
with the song of the seashells and the song of the sea,
far off, far off, lost, near, alien, our own.

That wretched woman is still quiet. In the midst of her silence I seem to
    hear the justice of her claim—
she is so vulnerable in her fury, so wronged,
with her bitter hair fallen about her shoulders like grass on a tomb,
walled up in her narrow righteousness. Perhaps she's fallen asleep,
perhaps she is even dreaming of an innocent place with good animals,
whitewashed houses, the smell of warm bread, and roses.

And now I remember—I don't know why—that cow
we saw, toward evening, in a field in Attica—remember?
She stood, just unyoked from the plough, and looked around,

with two thin streams of vapor from her nostrils steaming over
the purple, violet, and golden sunset, mute, scarred
on sides, back, beaten about the forehead,
familiar perhaps with resignation and obedience,
implacability and hatred in her acquiescence.

Between her two horns she held
the heaviest piece of the sky like a crown. In a little
she lowered her head and drank water from the stream,
and licked with her bloody tongue that other
cool tongue of her waterborne image, as if she were licking
broadly, calmly, maternally, inevitably,
from the outside, her own inner wound, as if she were licking
the silent, vast round wound of the world—perhaps also to quench her
    thirst—
perhaps only our own blood will do to quench our thirst—who knows?

Later she raised her head from the water, not touching anything,
herself untouched and calm, like a saint,
and only between her feet, both rooted in the river:
there remained a small changing pool of blood from her lips,
a red pool, in the shape of a map,
which little by little widened and dispersed; it disappeared
as if her blood were flowing far away, freed, without pain,
into an invisible vein of the world; and she was calm
precisely for this reason; as if she had learned
that our own blood is not lost, that nothing is lost,
nothing, nothing is lost in this vast nothing,
disconsolate and pitiless, incomparable,
so sweet, so consoling, so nothing.

This nothing is our familial infinite. Useless, then,
this gasping for breath, or anxiety, or faith. Just such a cow
I drag with me, in my shadow—not tied:
she follows me of her own accord—she is my shadow on the road
when there's a moon; she is my shadow
on a closed door; and you're always aware of this:
the shadow is pliant, bodiless; the shadows of her horns
may just be two pointed wings and maybe you can fly
and perhaps you can get past the locked door some other way.

And now I remember (this, too, may have no significance) the cow's
eyes—dark, blind, huge, convex
like two hillocks of darkness or black glass; their surface
faintly reflected a church tower, and the jackdaws
perching upon the cross; and then someone called out
and the birds disappeared from the cow's eyes. I think the cow
was a symbol in some ancient religion. Not for me
such ideas and such abstractions. An ordinary cow
for the villagers' milk and for the plough, with all the wisdom
of her labor, her endurance, her usefulness. And yet,

at the last moment, just before the animals returned to the village—
    remember?—
she let out a heartrending bellow, toward the horizon,
so loud that from branches around the swallows and sparrows
    scattered,
horses too, goats and farmers,
leaving her alone in a naked circle,
out of which rose, much higher, in the distance,
the spiral of constellations, until the cow ascended; no, no,
I think my eye picked her out from among the herd
climbing the overgrown path, quiet, docile,
toward the village, at the hour when lamps were lit in the courtyards,
    behind the trees.

See where dawn is breaking. There—and the first cock crows in the
    yard.
The gardener's woken up; he'll plant a sapling or two in the garden. The
    familiar noises
of working tools—saws, pickaxes—
and the courtyard fountain; someone washing; the smell of the earth;
water boiling in coffeepots; peaceful columns of smoke above the roofs;
a warm odor of sage. So we've survived even this night.

Let us now lift up this funeral urn with my purported ashes—
the recognition scene will begin in a moment.
They will each of them find in me that person they expected,
they'll find the just man, in line with their legislation,
and only you and I, only the two of us, will know that in this urn
I am holding my own real ashes.

And while the others are triumphing through my deed, the two of us
will weep over the gleaming, bloody sword, worthy of glory,
will weep for these ashes, this corpse, whose place
has been taken by another, completely covering his flayed features
with a golden, respectable, venerable mask,
perhaps even useful, with its crudely worked design,
as a precept, an example, opium for the people, terror for tyrants, an
    exercise
that slowly, heavily, pursues history with repeated deaths and triumphs,
not with terrible knowledge (impossible for the multitude)
but with hard action and easy faith,
inflexible, necessary, unfortunate faith,
disproved a thousand times and held fast a thousand more
tooth and nail by the soul of man—ignorant faith
that does great deeds secretly, antlike, in the dark.

And I, the faithless one, choose this faith (the others do not choose me),
yet in full personal knowledge. I choose
the knowledge and the action of death that enhances life. Let's go
    now—
not for my father, not for my sister (and yet, they too, perhaps
both he and she, had to give up at some point) not
for vengeance, not out of hatred—absolutely not out of hatred—
not even as punishment (who'd punish, and punish whom?)
but perhaps for the fulfillment of appointed time, for time to remain
    free,
perhaps for some sort of useless victory over our first and ultimate fear,
perhaps for some sort of "yes", that shines, ambiguous and
    irreproachable, beyond you and me,
to give this place, if possible, a breathing space. See how beautifully the
    dawn is breaking.

Mornings in the Argolid are a little humid. The urn
is almost frosted, with some condensation
as if, as they say, rosy-fingered dawn had moistened it with her tears,
holding it between her knees. Let's go. The appointed hour
has already come. Why are you smiling? Do you agree?
Was it this that you knew already yet never said?
This is the right ending—isn't it?—after the most righteous of fights?

Let me, one last time, kiss your smile,
while I still have lips. Let's go now. I accept my fate. Let's go.

*They walk toward the gate. The guards stand aside as if they were
expecting them. The old porter opens the great door, keeping his head
bent submissively as if to greet them. In a moment there comes the
sound of a man's clotted groan, and then a woman's startled, harrowing
cry, followed by a great stillness, broken only, in the plain below, by the
occasional report of a hunter's gun, and the countless twitterings of
unseen sparrows, finches, skylarks, tomtits, blackbirds. Swallows circle
persistently over the north wing of the palace. The guards calmly take
off their helmets and wipe the inner cloth band with their sleeves. Then,
right under the lion gate, a large cow stops and stares at the morning sky
with her huge, black, unwavering eyes.*

BUCHAREST, ATHENS, SAMOS, MYCENAE, JUNE 1962–JULY 1966

· THE DEAD HOUSE ·

EXTRAORDINARY AND AUTHENTIC ACCOUNT

OF A VERY ANCIENT GREEK FAMILY

*Of the entire family only two sisters were left, one of whom had gone
mad. She imagined that their house had been moved to somewhere in
ancient Thebes, or, rather, Argos—she mixed up mythology, history,
and her own private life, past and present, but not the future. Never
that. Later she recovered. And it was she who spoke with me that
evening when I brought them a message from abroad, from their
uncle—their father's brother. The other sister didn't appear at all. Just
from time to time a muffled shuffling of slippers was audible from the
next room, while the elder one went on talking:*

Now we two, the youngest sisters, traipse around alone in this
     enormous house—
youngest, so the phrase goes—we too grew old years ago,
we were the youngest in the family, and besides, we're the only ones left.
    We don't know
how to manage this house, or ourselves:
to sell it strikes us as improper—we've spent a whole lifetime here—
and the place of our dead is here too, you can't sell *them,*
and anyway who'd buy the dead? On the other hand, lugging them off
from one house to another, from one neighborhood to the next—
so exhausting and dangerous: they've settled in comfortably here,
one in the shadow of the curtain, another under the table,
another behind the wardrobe or the glass doors of the bookcase,
yet another inside the lamp-glass—modest and undemanding as ever,
and one, unobtrusively smiling, behind the two thin crossed shadows
cast on the wall by my "young" sister's knitting needles.

We've shut up the heavy furniture down on the ground floor,
along with the thick carpets and the velvet or silken curtains,
tablecloths, embroidered napkins, crystal, dinner services,
great silver trays that formerly mirrored
the whole broad countenance of hospitality,
blankets, silk quilts and bed linen,
woolen clothes, handbags, overcoats,
ours and those of the dead all jumbled together,
gloves, lace, and ostrich feathers from Mother's hat,
the piano, the guitars, the flutes, the drums,
with wooden horses and dolls from our childhood years,
Father's dress uniforms and our big brother's first long pants,

the ivory locket with the younger one's blond ringlets, a knife inlaid
    with gold,
riding habits, haversacks, cloaks, all jumbled together,
with no mothballs, no lavender potpourri in tulle sachets.

We've even nailed the rooms up. We've only kept
these two rooms facing west on the upper floor,
with the corridor and the staircase, of course, in case
we sometimes need to go out at night and stroll in the garden
or do some emergency shopping in the neighborhood.

Don't get the idea, even so, that we've found peace. We've certainly rid
    ourselves
of superfluous activities, ridiculous chores, vain efforts to carry out
impossible orders, unrealizable arrangements. Yet
the house, so closed, so naked, has developed
a frightening, most delicate echo to every
movement of mouse, roach, or bat.

Every shadow in the depths of the mirror, every grinding
of the tiny teeth of woodworm or moth
is prolonged without limit, reaches the delicate fibrous vessels of silence,
    enters the veins
of the most implausible delusion. You can hear distinctly
the clack of the tiniest spider's loom, in the cellar, among the jars,
or the sawing of rust in the handles of knives and forks
and a sudden loud thud in the downstairs entrance hall
when a section of rotted baize breaks loose and falls
like some ancient, much-loved building's demolition.

And when, sometimes, at dawn, the trashman's going through the
    suburbs,
his distant bell echoes back from all the glass or metal objects,
bronze bedsteads, the frames of ancestral portraits,
the tiny bells on the pierrot costume our young brother once wore
on a beautiful carnival night—on our way back home we were scared,
dogs snarled at us, my dress got caught in the fence,
I ran to catch up with the others: the moon thrust down its face
so close upon mine—I couldn't move any further
and the others were calling me from behind the trees

and somewhere quite different I heard the glass beads of the
     masqueraders
and the glass fringes of the stars, far distant, above the invisible Cretan
     sea,
and when at last I reached them they all stared at me, bewildered,
because my face was shining, all layered with gold-dust
like that they used to gild the old dining room chandeliers
or the drawing room mirrors with their elegant, fine-carved consoles—

These too we've locked away in the downstairs rooms. We could, it's
     true,
have kept one or two of these things for our personal use,
a rocking chair, say, for relaxation, or a mirror
to comb our hair in sometimes. But who'd look after them? This way at
     least
we can hear them wearing out, but not see them. Everything has
     deserted us.

And these two rooms we've kept,
the coldest, the barest, the highest, are perhaps to enable us
to look at things from above
and from a certain distance, so we have the sense
of overseeing and controlling our destiny: above all
when dusk is falling, and all things bend down to the warm earth,
the chill here is sharp as a sword
to cut short the urge for a new agreement or the hope
for an unrealized meeting: there's a kind of healthiness
in this pure, supercilious cold.
And these two rooms are suspended in the boundless night
like two snuffed lamps on a wholly deserted beach:
only the lightning briefly reveals, then eclipses them,
pierces and nails their translucency in the void, and they are void too.

But if someone should chance to be walking on that hill over there, with
     the thornbushes,
late, when the sun's going down, when everything's pale, lusterless,
     violet,
when all things seem lost and all things attainable, then
that lonely figure strolling on the hill
looks gentle and compassionate, like someone indeed who could

still find a little compassion for us. The hill too looks
peaceful then, at the same level as our window, so much so
that if the walker turned this way to look at the cypresses,
you'd think one further step would take him over our doorsill,
that he'd enter the room like an old acquaintance, would even, I think,
ask for a brush to dust off his shoes. But he
very soon vanishes behind the hill
and once more all that remains across from our window
is the curve of the hill, as silent as remorse,
and the bitter afternoon, reconciled, sinking down amid its shadows.

Not, on the other hand, that we're wholly resigned to it—but what can
        you do? all things
have forsaken us, and we them—that way something close to a just
        balance
has been restored, with no mutual rancor,
no remorse, no sorrow even—how else should it be?

So here we remain, just as when you cut flowers in the garden
at dusk, lots of flowers for the dining room vases and the bedrooms of
        the dead,
and yellow stains from the pollen are left on your hands
and the dust from the road that drifts through the lattice and powders
        the stalks
and a few very tiny bugs, some winged, some not,
and one or two tepid dewdrops
plus the inevitable cobwebs, gossamer-fine,
that always adhere to the flowers: and as afternoon fades, rose-pink on
        the windowpanes,
you have the sense of the keen knife losing its edge
from the blood and milk of the flowers—a complex, strange sensation
of terror and slaughter, a blind, fine, fragrant, and boundless beauty,
a stark naked absence. So it is. All things have forsaken us.

That last day, the slave-girls screamed and ran—
a shrill scream that remained nailed in the shadowy corridor
like a huge fishbone in the throat of an unknown guest
or like a rusty sword in the slain man's long coffin,
a scream—no more, no less—and they took off running
hands pressed to expressionless faces: only when they reached

the top of the marble stairway, behind the colonnade,
they looked black, tiny, hunched,
infinitely wary and opportunistic,
deceitful, vindictive, with deliberate and calculated eagerness—
they stopped for a moment, wholly strangers to their earlier screaming,
uncovered their faces,
studied the steps with care so as not to slip
although their feet had learned every riser by heart
and they knew the whole flight, top to bottom, with all its pauses,
like a poem on the back of a page in a calendar
or like one of those songs soldiers sing after a battle
learned from the few troops returning at times from the front—

a few soldiers, still handsome and somehow sad,
with big feet and big hands, with lice in their undershirts,
with underground galleries and fallen stars in their eyes,
with curling blue-black lashes, like a fortress's shadow in the fountain,
with something hard and intolerant about their mouths,
something intensely virile, and at the same time indifferent, as though
they'd kissed too many corpses on crossed hands or forehead,
as though they'd left their wounded comrades, running sleet-pelted to
      the ravine,
and, most of all, as though they'd stolen the sick man's water bottle that
      he used for a pillow. Yet

the soldiers would sing in the kitchen at night (we were little then,
we'd eavesdrop behind closed doors—they didn't let us
into the kitchens with their strange unfamiliar gear,
their mysterious smells, peppers, garlic, celery, tomatoes,
and other intricate odors that didn't betray their source,
with the sibylline voices of fire, smoke, boiling water,
the crisscross clatter of quick knives,
the menacing towers of unwashed plates,
the huge bare and bloodied bones of mythical beasts.

There the slave-girls queened it in their suggestive aprons
amid the alchemy of vegetables, meat, fruit, fishbones,
clandestine witches with their enormous wooden ladles,
delivering oracles over steam from the cauldrons,
fashioning from smoke a slender slaughtered woman in a white tunic

or three-masted ships with heavy rigging, oaths, and sailors
or the long beard of a blind man, transparent, with a lyre on his knees—
perhaps that was why Mother wouldn't let us go in there:
and sometimes we'd find a handful of salt behind a door
or the head of a cock, its comb like a miniature sunset, on a broken tile.

We'd say nothing to the grown-ups, because when the kitchen swing-
    doors opened a crack
the spirit of smoke would sidle out and stand for hours in the passage,
tall, threatening, with a glass helmet and a horsetail hanging from it.
    This spirit
was solitary, odorous, brutish, incorporeal,
totally boneless and yet all-powerful. So we'd eavesdrop
behind the doors till well after midnight, till a sleep
red with sparks finally calmed us.) Well, the soldiers used to sing,

and sometimes crack jokes with the maids,
and tug off their boots and rub their coarse toes with their hands
and later wipe the wine from their fleshy lips
or scratch at their hairy chests and legs,
make random grabs at the women's breasts, and then
start singing again. We could hear them even in our sleep. They sang

with their faces hidden behind their greasy hair
imperceptibly keeping time with their bare feet on the tiles
or with their fingers on the nearest jug or glass
or on the wood of the table (used for dicing meat),
quietly, very quietly (so the masters inside wouldn't hear):
and then their Adam's apples would go up and down
like a knot on a thick rope tugged from either end,
like a knot on a rope coming up from a deep well,
like a knot in the guts. At that the women

hearing them would weep hysterically,
tear off their clothes, stand there stark naked and beg them
and then take them on their laps, like sick children they insisted on
    coddling,
longing to put them whole inside their bellies—
maybe to fill their own emptiness,

their own wombs—to shut them in
deep, deep, to throttle them
for their own protection, to be the only ones
to keep them—and then to give them birth

at a more auspicious moment, in a whiter house,
an airier, sunnier house, with fewer shadows
of columns, jars, murders, swords, moments of glory, coffins,
with fewer invisible holes in the walls—holes made
by nails for hanging steel mirrors or evening dresses,
nails for uniforms, trumpets, drums, helmets, shields,
or the strings of mute toys belonging to dead children
or portraits, wedding garlands, pots and pans: covered over, of course,
all these holes, filled in, masked with fresh plaster and whitewash,
yet ever opening further, deeper, in memory.

So that's how they wanted to give them birth, in more spacious
        surroundings,
lighter, more solidly based, somewhere not undermined
by crypts, catacombs, tombs,
in a house with doors that don't lock, and from behind them
come whispers, sobs, and the intense sound
made by a woman's hair tumbling down to her knees, or the sound
of a shoe falling, far from the bed: finally,

in a place of elusive solitude, sincerity and security,
in a spring landscape, amid the new-grown barley,
beside a sorrel horse and a nice little ash-gray donkey,
next to a dog, a cow, two sheep,
in the lonely shadow of a plough. But these soldiers

heard nothing, saw nothing, felt nothing,
manly and unconcerned, intoxicated with death,
sunk deep in their private song—a song
not in the least heroic, but not what you'd call sad either, much less
        halting—
a song they'd undoubtedly learned from the women in their village,
and now, coming back from the front,
were teaching the girls. Well then, this staircase

was as familiar to the maids as the song they'd relearned,
with all its breaks and intervals and measures,
with all its stones, stressed and unstressed,
slashed in two midway by the landing: thousands of times
they'd been up and down it on other occasions, festive days
when they brought the roasting pans back from the baker's oven
or the big pitchers of wine up from the cellars
or the great round loaves and the joints and the fruit
or armfuls of roses, carnations, daisies,
or modest olive branches and laurels bright with morning dew—

on other days, at weddings or baptisms, feast days, birthdays,
days of triumph and glory, when the dusty messenger
would collapse, gasping, on this very staircase
and kiss the marble and weep
and announce his news in a manly, slightly gravelled voice,
unexpected amid the ripple of his final sobs;

and the house-slaves and one or two old men passing by
would crowd together in the colonnade to hear him,
and the maids in doorways, aprons raised to their eyes,
and our mother, their mistress, out there in the forecourt
and Nanny beside her like a lightning-blasted oak
along with the tutor, yellow as candlewax behind that thin beard of his,
like a long fleshless hand clutching the strings of a harp
and the younger girls stock-still at the windows
hidden behind their dreams and their suspicions,
listening and not comprehending,
observing the beautiful bend of the messenger's knee,
his youthful chestnut beard and his black hair,
curly, matted with sweat and dust,
and a sprig of broom caught on his tunic—So
forests walk and tables rear up on their hind legs like horses
and triremes cruise over the trees at sunset
and their rowers bend and rise, bend and rise, bend and rise
in the very rhythm of sex: and the oars
are naked women suspended by their hair
who thrash and shudder, gleaming, in the sea
till the foam of the Milky Way is scrawled behind the triremes. So
   then—

And the messenger was announcing the brilliant victory
at the cost of two thousand dead—not even counting the wounded—
was announcing too, at last, the arrival of the master
with loads of booty and banners and carriages and slaves
and a wound—he said—in the middle of his forehead
like a new and wonderful eye from which death kept watch,
and now the master could see right through to the inner guts
of landscapes, objects, people, as though
they were all made of transparent glass; he could read easily
the pulsing of our blood, our moods, our destiny,
the veins of gold running at the core of the stone
and the branches of coal spread out in the underground darkness
and the silver nerves of water ramifying through rock
and the tiny shivers of guilt under skin and clothing.

Everyone listened—we too—as though petrified,
all anxious, heads bowed, tearless,
as though already turned to glass,
with everyone watching them and them watching themselves—
their skeletons, naked, in glass, and of glass, brittle,
no refuge for anyone. And yet

amid this total absence of protection
amid this deadly weakness
amid this shadowless transparency

they felt suddenly pacified, dissolved
amid the boundlessness of transparency, being boundless themselves,
as though sinless amid the general sinfulness, all
like brothers in the general desert of reciprocal hatred
as though armed by mankind's dearth of arms
finely and nobly clad in worldwide nakedness.

"Let the master come," said the mistress, our mother.
"Let him come, and welcome. He too is glass.
Glass. Glass. There it is—we too know this eye of his—
we have it too, look there, in the middle of our foreheads.
We too have come to know death well. We know it. We see it.
He was the first to teach us. We were the first to see true again.

"So welcome to the glass master with his glass sword
back home to his glass consort, his glass children,
glass subjects, dragging behind him masses
of glass corpses, glass booty, glass slaves,
glass trophies. So let the bells peal out,
from peak to peak let the watchmen light signal fires
for our glass victory—yes, our very own victory,
the victory of us all. Because we too fought
through our endurance, and even more
through our impatient and myriad-eyed expectation. And those who
     died
are victors too, in the front rank, *and they can see.*

"So let the bells ring out to the furthest horizon!
And you slave-girls there, why are you standing around? Go set out
the glass food, the glass wine, the glass fruit:
Our glass master is coming. *He is coming.*"

So spoke the mistress, and on her temples showed
the hammer-beat of her blood, you could see her sweat
before it formed, before it coursed down her pallid cheeks.

The old nurse, who for one moment held her
as though she was going to faint, stood by her now with her well-
     practiced silence,
covered her with her wise shadow under the great domes
of her dilated eyes. Then she shook out
her black apron as though chasing away
a black bird. And the messenger fled.

An owl skimmed low in the forecourt
though it was still early afternoon—
dusk hadn't fallen, the owl's shadow was indelibly imprinted
directly above the gate. It's still there. The slave-girls ran inside.
The mistress forgot to dress her children. She went into the bathhouse,
filled the bath with hot water, didn't wash. A little later
she locked herself in her room and made up in the mirror,
red, red, deep purple, like a mask, a corpse, a statue,
like a murderess or her victim. And the distant sun was setting
yellow and fiery like a crowned adulterer,

like the gilded usurper of another's power,
savage from cowardice, and frightful in his fright
while the bells rang crazily throughout the country.

So the slave-girls knew this stairway well,
all those years in this house, and yet
they uncovered their faces and studied it,
they even turned back for a little in case someone might have seen them,
then put their hands over their faces again and fled,
small, black, hunched and disgusting,
like black dots, like flies in the swamp-fever season
under the stone rain of the colonnade, leaving
the big broom upside down behind the kitchen door
like a nightmare, hair standing on end, unable to scream. They all left
    us.

We brought in outside charwomen to wash down the stairs,
to mop clean and scrub the marble. That marble sweated
blood again after a little. They went too. They left us.
We too abandoned everything—sweeping, mopping, cleaning off
    cobwebs.
And the stones still kept at it, spewing up more and more blood.

A red stream ringed our house,
we became cut off from the outside world;
later the world forgot about us,
feared us no longer; we too were afraid no more.
Passers-by, it's true, still gave us a wide berth
but they no longer crossed themselves,
no longer spat in their bosoms to exorcize the ghosts.
The road nearest our house
became overgrown with weeds, nettles, thorns,
even a few blue wildflowers—it no longer looked like a road.

At night, if some woman working late was still
doing her washing down by the river, and the regular thump
of her beater could be heard on the soft damp fabrics, no one
would say that a knife was being thrust into flesh,
or that they were shutting a secret trap door,

or that they were dumping a corpse in the ditch from the north
        window—all they'd say
was that a beater was being used on the washing;
they could even tell from the sound
if the fabric was woolen or cotton, silk or linen,
and they'd know when a woman was bleaching her daughter's
        trousseau,
they'd even picture the wedding day,
the bridegroom's pallor, the way the bride would blush,
the entwining of the two bodies, made somehow insubstantial
by the tulle bed curtains, astir in the night breeze. Such details
and such accuracy too (a proof of balance, perhaps?)
together with this sense of the essential,
as though what happened, and its consequences, were necessary—
the sense of something inevitable, unaccountable, as well as
a vein of music vibrating in the air
and you hear it over and over, and you don't know

just where it's coming from—a little above the trees?
below the empty benches in the garden?
that bathhouse? over the red river?
or Father's locked-up armory with the trophies of all those futile wars,
or the empty sandals of the elder brother, the sailor—he's been away at
        sea for years,
and who knows if he'll ever come back—
or the younger brother's sketchbooks (he's stopped writing us from the
        sanatorium),
or poor Mother's clothes closet
with those long white pleated dresses and the wide forged metal
        buckles—

(often, at night, from the window, I saw the dresses
strolling around by themselves under the trees,
blown lightly like moonlight shadows, and behind
their white mist, behind their pale undulation,
you could make out the dry fountain with its bronze dolphin
curved in a final gleam of flight—that glassy transparency
that left no marks of remorse or recollection
since memory too is useless in a lasting absence or presence). In any case

that vein of music was audible everywhere, and you don't even know
why you're happy, what happiness is; you simply perceive
things that before you'd never noticed or seen
yet devoid, now, of their weight. We had no knowledge
of messenger, murder, or the terrified slave-girls who fled,
and I was one of the two girls who stood at the two windows
and who also looked at the two maidens as though from downstairs or
    from the road,
just about from the messenger's viewpoint, or that of the youngest slave-
    girl,
I who always stood at the window (I often envied those slave-girls
their splendid garrulity, their cunning, their cheerfulness, and their
    freedom,
that deep freedom of slavery that preserves you
from initiatives and decisions—yes, I envied them).

Ah, I saw nothing, remember nothing; only that rare sensation,
so delicately felt, a concession from death, of seeing death
to its transparent depths. And the music went on
as sometimes at dawn when we wake early for no reason
and the air outside is incredibly dense with the morning song
of countless invisible birds—so dense and steamy
there's no room in the world for anything else—bitterness, hope,
    remorse, memory—
and time is indifferent and alien
like some stranger going quietly by down the street over there
without a thought for our house, not a single glance at it,
carrying under his arm a stack of opaque, unwashed panes—
you don't know why he needs them, where he's going with them,
what they mean and which windows they're designed for,
and indeed you don't even wonder, and you don't see him disappear,
unobtrusive and silent, round the last bend in the road.

Who preserved all this for us, then, with such precision, in so many
    dimensions,
all scrubbed, bright, clean, and set in order,
stripped of every wound and every death?
And the red river round the house is nothing,
just ordinary clear water from the warm rain two days ago,
reflecting the red sunset till late evening, till the time

when that boundless, glassy translucency spreads abroad
and you see to the heart of the boundless, the imperishable, the invisible
being boundless, imperishable, and invisible yourself, surrounded
by the muted whispers of furniture and stars. And Mother sits
on a carved chair, stitching her eternal embroidery
under the triple-flamed lamp, each flame aquiver
in the draught that's created between the two windows, while Father
has been away, out hunting, since early morning
and in his ears the melancholy spiral of the huntsmen's horn
and the impatient, friendly barking of the hounds.

Our youngest sister, escaping her nanny's vigilant eye,
dreams in the cool of the garden, riding the stone lion,
and everything is so quiet—
no one was at fault and nothing happened,
only the creak of a door on the lower level
and the wrought iron garden gate—perhaps the milkman bringing
a bowl of yoghurt for Mother's diet—she's afraid of getting fat,
and it's good news for the children when she goes back to watching her
    weight,
takes care of herself a little, sometimes looks in the mirror,
arranges her lovely luxuriant hair in a chignon. The yoghurt
takes on a cool, bluish, marbled brightness
under the starlight, the trees' shadows. You can hear
the quiet voice of the youngest servant-girl
as she pays for the week's milk and lingers there
counting, recounting her change. And the garden,
up at its furthest point, in its darkest corner, sometimes
glitters and gleams, when, during the night, the big
heliotropes shift their warm shoulders
and an azure mist shimmers under the statues' nostrils
as though they were secretly breathing the moist fragrance of the roses.

Our youngest brother is always painting away
in the workroom where the looms are, such delicate watercolors
with a style reminiscent of Knossos—he's never shown us his
    paintings—
or else in the pottery studio, decorating jugs large and small
with black or tile-red lines that affect austerity,
depicting youthful warriors, or dancers, entirely hidden

behind enormous shields—so that if you don't look closely
you think it's just a row of circles, a black linked chain. Our elder
    brother's
resigned his commission in the royal navy; now,
ever solemn, he reads all day in the room next door. Amid the quietness
    of time
you can hear the page turn as though a secret door were opening
on a white, translucent landscape. And indeed

at that moment a door *does open*. Father is coming.
They're laying the table, calling us.
We all troop down the inside staircase.
We sit at the table and eat, while from outside in the courtyard
come the sharp yelps of the hounds and the voice of the kennelman.

Life, after all, is so simple. And so beautiful.
Mother bows her head over her plate and cries.
Father places his hand on her shoulder.
"It's from happiness," she says, by way of excuse.
And we look out through the open windows
at the boundless translucent night with its sliver of moon
like a finger forgotten between the azure
pages of a serene closed book.

Tonight there's a touch of chill in the air. Autumn's coming, you see.
In a day or two we'll shut the windows again. We may
have nothing else, but there's plenty of wood for the fireplace,
and not just from the woods: we can use our old furniture,
solid doors, rafters, sofas, coffins, gun-butts, pipes,
even Grandfather's wooden carriage that he left us years ago.

If you're going, please tell our uncle not to worry about us. We're doing
    fine.
And death is as soft as a mattress we've got used to,
stuffed with flock, cotton, down or straw—the mattress,
    accommodating,
has taken the shape of our body—a death entirely our own—
death at least neither deceives nor evades us, it's sure,
and we're sure of it—the austere, the exquisite certainty.

But if you're not leaving Argos, it would give us great pleasure
to see you again in our home. Just for you, I'll even unnail
a door to let you inspect Father's armory,
to let you inspect that shield that still bears, on its black metal,
the imprinted reflections of countless warriors' deaths,
and show you the bloody fingerprints, the fountain of blood,
and the underground passage through which, dressed up as women,
the twelve bearded war chiefs escaped with their pale leader,
who, though dead, led them unerringly to the exit.
At the other end the entrance remained open,
dumb, deep, and dark like an unknown error.

And the evening star—perhaps you noticed it?—the evening star as soft
as an eraser—it keeps rubbing the same spot
as though to efface some error of ours—what error?—
and a faint sound can be heard as the eraser goes back and forth
over the error—and the error can't be rubbed out;
minute shreds of paper fall glittering on the trees;
it's a pleasant distraction, and it doesn't matter
that the error can't be rubbed out; the star's movement is enough,
gentle, persistent, perennial
as a first and last meaning—rhythm: heavenly power
and practical too, like that of the loom or of verse—
to and fro, to and fro, the star among the cypresses,
a golden shuttle among the long mournful threads,
now revealing, now hiding our error—no, not ours,
the world's error, a fundamental error—why should we take the blame
        for it?
an error of birth or of death—were you paying attention?

Autumn evenings are beautiful—reconciliatory—
erasing with a serene, universal guilt the guilt of each one of us,
consolidating a secret friendship among us,
a friendship of rhythm—yes, yes, that's just it, a rhythmic friendship,
        rhythmic—that's it—to and fro,
to and fro, birth-death, love-dream, action-silence: it's a way out, I tell
        you,
to the far side, the dark dark point, the straight path to heaven—

a breeze blows from there, sweat dries—a respite, my God, relaxation at
     long last,
and from all around you can hear the roof-terrace conversations
clear in the night, and the cool sound of the bucket raising water from
     the garden well,
and the voice from under the trees that says "I'll be back", and the
     breathlessness
of the child untying his shoe by himself for the first time
and the sound of the flute from the student's open window—an amateur
     player—
yet a music notwithstanding that soars up to become one with all
the splendid, pointless, concerted music of the stars.

And yes, I assure you, though dead, he did lead them unerringly to the
     exit—
even though we know that the exit, more often than not, is just
another death: necessary, cunning, inevitable.

So please tell Uncle not to worry about us
out there in that marvellously disciplined Sparta of his.
We're doing pretty well ourselves, back here in Argos.
Only—he has to know this—it's the end of the road. This he has to
     know.

*"Yes, yes", I muttered automatically, and stood up. I hadn't understood
a thing. A feeling of magical terror had overcome me, as though I had
suddenly found myself face to face with all the decadence and
enchantment of some archaic civilization. Night had now fallen. She
accompanied me to the stairs and lit the way down for me with an old
oil lamp. What had she been getting at? What about that corpse who
conducted them to the exit? Could it be—? No, not Christ, surely not.
And the house—not Agamemnon's. And that younger brother with the
bent for painting? Who was he? But—there was no second brother.
Then—? What was the point of this house? And why was I trying to
make sense of a madwoman's words? By now I was outside. I began
walking briskly, but when I heard my own footsteps I stopped.
Something astringent and unsatisfied remained in my mouth, dissolved
in my saliva by all this black uncertainty, as though I had bitten into a
cypress cone. And yet, at the same time, I felt something solid, rich,
pure, which gave me a peculiar sense of euphoria, and made me think,*

with mathematical precision, how easily I would surmount tomorrow's difficulties in my work, something that had struck me hitherto as insuperable. A harvest moon had risen among the cypresses. Behind my back I could feel the dark mass of that house like some majestic ancient tomb. And, if nothing else, I had at least learned what I must avoid, what we all must avoid.

*P*ast midnight. Spring. A big room, cluttered with antique furniture. A large hanging oil lamp, gilded, casts a shadowy light on the room's round central table, spread with a faded purple velvet cloth, on which stands an engraved brass flower vase empty of flowers, not in the middle but somewhat off to one side, next to a glass of water. Brother and sister are sitting more or less opposite one another, on low armchairs, with the table between them. They do not speak; they might be suffering from insomnia or killing time before a departure. Neither inside nor outside the house can a sound be heard—not even the murmuring of the night, though one window remains wide open. The servants, or those of them that are still alive, bowed with age, shadowy and mysterious figures, are undoubtedly asleep. On a chair rests a charred log, somewhat resembling a woman's torso minus arms and legs. The sense of pointlessly banished sleep hangs heavy in the atmosphere, like a punishment, together with a certain vague impression as though some kind of obligation had ended. Apparently their two sisters are on the estate, out at the big vineyards. The rest are shut away in their vaulted tombs. Brother and sister remain silent now after the innumerable exchanges during the course of their long-drawn-out return journey, amid the tensions of the danger they fled and those other unknown dangers that lay in wait for them. They look as though they have freed themselves from words, sensations, memories—as though repenting their earlier exaltation and, above all, their unavoidable excess, during that period, of gesture, expression, tone of voice, things that betray the person without either reserve or forethought, who seems to be making, in absolute sincerity, some enormous promise that he will never be able to fulfill, keep up, or repeat. Perhaps that was why her brother's faithful comrade was forced to flee as well—more emotional, though suffering a lesser ordeal—foreseeing the change of tone in their relationship, their attempt to preserve their original intensity of feeling by redoubling their cordiality. He couldn't endure this isolated sense of guilt, though all three of them recognized their deeper common complicity. What they felt, in the last resort, was shame. They must have wished that they'd controlled themselves, or had separated earlier, or had never met at all. Yet the daughter still makes one last effort—on the common ground, at least, of their solitude—to talk, indeed to ask questions, in an area where, she is certain, questions are unnecessary, and answers do not exist. Perhaps she wants, one more time, to demonstrate some sort of naïveté, some sort of innocence and guilelessness—to be judged without

that sense of premeditation, somehow to camouflage the disproportion
between before, now, and afterwards with an agonizing and compulsive
sincerity:

Three days already we've been home now. The journey's over,
the adventure's ended. Well? Did this happen? Did that? Did the other
    thing?
You're not smiling, not at all. Nor I. Of course it isn't
the things that are missing, that we didn't find—and which, in any case,
we never expected to find. Perhaps it's ourselves
who are missing. We've returned (we say),
and we scarcely know where it is we've returned from, or to. We're
    shifting ground
between two unknown points. Don't hang your head.
We'll escape, you and I both. One won't dominate the other. So sit up
on your chair! Our friend's going too. We've scarcely met
before we're parting again. Oh yes, of course, one day
our destinies will be fulfilled. We've broken free
in the midst of a new slavery—it's not giving up on us, it's lying in wait
at the outer postern, beside the dried hay, the burrs and nettles
and the abandoned keys.
                    Things
seem, sometimes, at once different and the same. The piano
in the columned hall—how small it looked to me that first day! But now
it grows big in the night, its joints creak, it's silent, it becomes
a whole world covered with a marvellous tarpaulin,
tough, blackened—it doesn't fit the things it covers,
just like what they use to protect sacks of grain, down in the harbor,
the moment it starts to rain. The covered
sacks swell, swell, take away
something from us, making us feel
totally vulnerable; making us comprehend
general vulnerability—since even the tarpaulin
is full of holes, water drips through it, the grain gets sodden, rots,
becomes neither bread nor cakes.
                    So the piano
useless, heavy, imposing in its muteness,
reminding us vengefully of the fact that it keeps silent,
with its deep covered tones, is a black coffin

full of bones, buttons, twisted shoes
and a heap of unmatched earrings.
                                    The dead
always and everywhere outnumber the living. They don't speak—
that's what thickens the silence. But they can hear,
hear sounds before they're made, hear our footsteps
before we get out of bed to go to the tap
for a glass of water. And the water has
an icy tepidity, as though they had held it
in the palms of their hands, in the wall, in the dark. This water doesn't
      refresh—
and besides, you're not after refreshment; you're really afraid
lest somehow the intense cold will reveal more deeply
the difference from our own slack warmth, with its touch of comfort.

They fled into their rowdy glory, into bloodshed
clad in their great cloaks, wearing their great helmets,
up onto flowery hills, their swords in marble,
a glove on the steps, in front of the peristyle, there,
unmoved by the breeze—there are certain things
that day by day acquire an inexplicable weight,
remain immovable, you can't pick them up or hide them away in a
      trunk.

Perhaps, it's possible, our hands have grown weak. A strange, hollow
      echo
reverberates from mask to golden mask. The plates in the kitchen,
for all their breakages, are far more fitting,
much bigger and whiter, especially the dishes
for those fabulous fish they used to bring whole to the table
when we entertained much-travelled guests. Most of the servants, too,
have died in their fortunate anonymity. Those that are left
hurry vaguely, dawdle vaguely, bow and scrape vaguely
before invisible huge-bodied shadows,
before something that isn't us, isn't even
our own past.
                  Their movements
remain almost motionless, decisive in their inconstancy,
while from the pockets of their striped vests emerges

one corner of some undelivered calling card, or the petal—
sere, brown, crumbling—of a dried-out carnation, who knows how old.

When a maid climbs the stairs, so carefully, so noiselessly,
the tear in the curtain lining can be heard distinctly, and then
you no longer know whether she'll enter the room with a tray
or a slaughtered chicken or the big wooden ladder
to clean cobwebs off the chandelier. And they've forgotten
to knock at the door before coming in, there's that much more risk
every moment of the unseen being seen, of each "I remember"
in its quiet intermission signifying "I am not".

"I am not," we say "we are not"—we don't really believe it. Amid this
    nonbeing
we confirm as probable our own existence in the dumb crush of those
    who are absent,
who miss us, whom we miss; for suddenly we see
that our coatsleeves are out at elbow. Above the table,
back there in the second gallery, there appear hung up
by the feet, on a yellow string, two brightly colored
dead birds—it's possible that they are
two of the three parrots belonging to our mother
who never taught them (remember?) to say a thing
except for the word "light" over and over, "light," all day long, the year
    round,
and when they woke sometimes during the night, "light," "light,"
    "light,"
even with the lamps out, even with no moon—
especially when there was no moon.
                           That used to bother me
like Mother's private stubbornness, which didn't tally at all
with her great mourning eyes, her great beauty,
or our own childish credulity in those days.
                                   Later on
I was no longer able to sleep. I eavesdropped inside my self,
found a more powerful silence, the quicker rhythm
of an unaccountable, inconceivable growth (and perhaps we begin to
    decline
the very minute we're born), while at the same time

I heard outside, on the ramparts, the guards playing dice—
a bonelike clatter, as though they were playing with *our* fate.

How remote things have become (or we ourselves, perhaps?). Facts,
    intervals
intrude between one's hand and sense of touch, between
the eye and what the eye sees—a rope still tied to a tree,
the horse, dog, sheep that's got loose and taken off,
a nail in the wall, hills, islands, tobacco warehouses, a pitcher,
the angle of a temple's metope, the light on a headland. At night,
time and again, in bed, I try
to touch the wall with my foot; and the wall
recedes endlessly, and my foot recedes too,
and makes contact far further off; for instance, I touch
the stones on some other bench, or the knee of the still air
that has never been stiller; and this
is by no means unpleasant, since along with the sense
of remoteness, or even dissolution, there is left to you
something of the freedom of the infinite, the chimerical,
something of the stillness of peace, in the surface of which
the knife and the wound it gave are no longer rooted,
nor the bird-snare, the chair, the rock, nor even
one weightless dried flower from those we used to preserve
between the leaves of a book we never finished reading.

At the precise moment of this dissolution we perceive, as night falls,
that secret joy of mutual reverence
between us (which us?) and (whom?). Calm knowledge
of integral ignorance—a silent gratitude,
a general sickness, an accepted end.
                                And yet
why, once again, this fury with our self
that won't accept the inexplicable? Why this fury of ours,
this recurrent rage in us?
                        Maybe the trees understand things better:
they don't question the fact of their leaves or flowers,
the why of their fruitfulness. That Sunday I climbed the hill
I was thinking about the bell rope—always ready to hand
for pulling, to signify births, deaths, feast days,
weddings, assemblies, requiems, wars,

with a movement always in the same direction,
a movement that's almost immovable.
                                    How late and how well we learn
the law of loss (durable, jural loss)
and the other, of return, somewhat deeper (that is, of non-loss). The
    houses
have no walls, they stand on air, pure air;
they aren't even glass (as Father sometimes declared
during his illness). Without going into the houses you can see people
shifting weightless objects from one room to another,
a chest, a bouquet, an outsize picture frame,
a folded woolen blanket or the boots of the nightwatchman,
a brush, the broom, a sealed bottle—all weightless,
all transparent, inside and out, wrapping and contents;
you see bubbles in a glass, you see a fine
hair under the tongue of an embarrassed woman; you see
corpses and newlyweds sprawled on the same big iron bedstead,
oblivious of each other. A little warm air
remains caught in the empty overcoat hung on the rack by the door;
the old lady is knitting a marvellous sailor's jersey; her needles flicker
in vaguely hostile movements
above her lap.
                    In the other room,
three men are arguing, gesturing, pacing to and fro,
committed to that uncertainty which, once, we stubbornly
sought to define in deeds and words. And for all that we learned
much about what's inachievable, we persist still, persist—our persistence
    never changes.

The stone lions of the gateway are mist; if you blow on them
they shift and vanish; and the gate doesn't fall
because there is no gate for you to go in and out by,
only wet laundry spread out on the line,
stirring with an awareness of defeated indifference.

Tell me, then, why all this business? What was it, what is it? Murders,
    expeditions,
reprisals, sunken ships, ruined regimes,
and above the ruins a towering marble column
(Did you notice that photograph in Father's room?), and on the column

a standing figure in marble, blind, with a lyre.
Underlining, you feel, with his blind erectness
the absence of all meaning.

And as for us—
here we are, back in Argos, on that red earth
where we first set foot, only to leave it, finding now
neither our own footprints nor the print
of Mother's damp sandals on the upper landing when she'd come,
they say, from the bath house. Here we are, then,
victors, seemingly (vanquished) having brought to conclusion
a "grand design" that we never set ourselves. And, look,
the image of the goddess that we brought back—look at it, there on the
    chair—
a plain log, naked, roughhewn. From my earliest days,
long before Aulis, I always used to feel
that they had blindfolded me with a foreign kerchief,
that they had disguised me—I didn't know as what—very likely an angel
or a deer or a butterfly—I didn't know; only
I felt that right under my shoulders they'd glued (not hung)
a basket, maybe, full of white paper flowers
or some theater program, and I needed
to walk backward so they could see it,
or a pair of marvellous papier-mâché wings
that every so often came unstuck because of their weight, removing
bits of my skin as well—they glued them back
right over the sore places—and of course I could neither fly
nor lie down. And if a spider settled on my foot
I couldn't bend down to get rid of it. Only upright, only with my hand,
like the blind, could I now recognize air, objects, walls.

I know—it's the same for you as for me, my dear; even worse, perhaps.
    In your case
they'd glued two daggers to the palms of your hands. They didn't do it
so you could fly, as they did me, but so you could run. Since that time
we've been invalids, supervised by third parties. Into our rooms
they'd march, at any old hour, autocratic and unknown men;
they'd remove their big hats (not from respect, but for their own
    reasons)
and install themselves on the sofa, laying their hats on their knees—

perhaps to hide something inside them—the wiry hair, maybe, on the
     backs of their hands
or the warm steam from their hair. They sat there awaiting our certain
     death, waiting to take
our glory, which *they*—despite all our expense—had ordained.

And we, to escape their gaze, would concentrate ours
down on our hands, which grew weaker from moment to moment, and
     very soon
we'd hide them under our armpits, arms crossed, shutting our eyes,
pretending to be sicker than we were to calm them
(and, of course, to hide); we squeezed our eyelids
tight, tight, yet with a relaxed appearance—our eyes, my God,
that were already closed. Nothing remained for us
but to look inward, ever more inward; to see
beneath the unanswered questions, beneath the fear and the heartache
that tender, hopeful submissiveness,
that boundless, serene indigency of ours. The three maidservants
had gone out a while before to shop, and were late returning;
the smell of food from the kitchen climbed the stairs,
made stronger and nastier by the impatience of the hungry;
the pendulum clock in the dining room had never stopped.

That summer I really took sick. I especially remember
how after my illness I came out all over in pimples. And I knew that
     inside me
the unknown had grown like a tree. I got very ugly. The sympathy
our two brothers had shown me during my illness
changed to repugnance. They shrank from meeting my eye
as though I were blaming them for something they didn't want to admit,
as though I'd betrayed some secret of theirs. And so
in the end I was left alone, essentially alone,
to get used to my new face. They left me in peace
in whatever room I was in. I was able
to try on Mother's jewelry, in front of the mirror—
long earrings like comets' tails, bracelets fashioned
as gold serpents, coil by coil to the elbow, that necklace
with the masks set next to each other,
one tragic, the next comic, joined by rings
in the upper parts of their ears—Mother wore it

on rare occasions only; you'd think she went in awe or fear of it. I
    loved
their cold and alien texture, the wise secretiveness
under that crafted surface of artifice. In the mirror
darkness dissolved my features as night came on,
dissolved the ornaments' template. All that remained
was something like a spark from ancient hilltop fires
or a vague glow that probably emanated from her.

I remember then it was close to carnival time. Mother
planned me a deer costume. She'd already made
a lovely mask, the mask of a little doe,
maybe to hide those pimples. When I wore it
I felt drowned in a black abyss, yet one from which
I could see more clearly. It smelt
of oil paint, pasteboard, fish-glue, and besides
it had an odor of preserved and essential void. For the first few moments
I was surprised by a rough sensation on my cheek—as though I didn't
    fit. But very soon,
and with no great effort, it was perfectly adjusted. I felt
protection, remote but real, and a kind of freedom.

This fine mask virtually deprived me of control
over all my movements. I was no longer myself,
I was the Other—yet beneath, or within the Other,
I was wholly, only myself, I could make
leaps that before I'd never even have tried. I rejoiced in
an agility, a delight, a rigorous adroitness. My own words,
traversing the passage of that alien mouth, took on
an alien boldness, alien resonance. Speaking the language
of deer (since deer do not speak) I unexpectedly discovered and uttered
thunderstruck truths, sounds more profound than I knew or imagined.
    And I had
a special sense of the word *source*, and also, perhaps, for me,
a hidden coquettishness that before I'd have thought altogether
    unseemly in me.

This mask, yesterday afternoon, I rediscovered
in one of Mother's drawers, packed with cotton wool
in fine silk paper, tied with blue ribbons. Here and there

the paint had flaked off, the hair fallen out. I wanted,
just for a moment, to put it on again. I didn't dare to. You see
since then other deer had appeared, other deeds, wars, myths,
and the fitting of skin to skin would have been a difficult business.

In those days, while abroad, I got some relief from the knowledge
that here they believed me long dead; from my having remained
a small unchanged girl, as at the hour of my death, while within
I grew, strangely, freely, to an all but timeless age.
Perhaps the lucky report of my death helped me endure
my life, and our certain death. That mythic
moment of time was my freedom and my enslavement both, the measure
for my every action, deed, word. I should always
have carefully mimicked the self of that one moment,
standing there, with a withered coronal on my hair,
staring in the old wardrobe mirror, while inside
the wardrobe the clothes changed, and outside the wardrobe
trotted the maidservants carrying birthday trays
or cardboard boxes that undoubtedly contained
every sort of wind-up toy, which even the grown-ups
examine with great admiration.
                                        Outside in the garden
the young birds were singing differently from last year, despite
their immutable vocal equipment. Only I
shouldn't have cared about that, should have stayed where I was
eternally reproducing my image, which dwindles as it recedes
for my eyes and the eyes of others,
or that has been altered at the hands of those who on top of it
were admiring the statue of their own unfulfilled ambition,
completely ignoring me in the midst of my silence.
                                        And then
I longed to kick up a horrible fuss—to throw down
that statue of me in the marketplace (and I wonder who looks at it?)
on some Sunday afternoon when they're all out for their promenade—
carefree men and women with stupid babies in prams
and an ice cream cone in one hand and the other arm
tucked round their partner's waist, or less often, clutching a book or a
        flower,
feeding the swans on the lake—so carefree, my God,
completely forgetting the way they've abandoned behind them

sick relations in stuffy rooms, with flies
stuck to the lemonade glass. Yes,

a horrible fuss that makes them suddenly turn their heads
to see, to recall that *there* stood the statue of a live girl whom they killed
    young,
a fine statue now in fragments and in its place
there now stands an airy facsimile. Nothing. Nothing.

Men continue to go on like this
oblivious to those who fled, to those who are fleeing, to themselves,
who are fleeing too: they circulate naturally
amid their own death.
               Fork or spoon
finds their mouths unerringly, without pause or hesitation,
while close to them, right at their side, the dead
watch the mechanical movements of their lips without eating
    themselves. And the apple
that rolled under the table and afterward
under the sofa and vanished—through a hole in the floor, very likely,
or the wall—was kicked by the dead boy,
and maybe the children found it, on the road, in the sunshine,
and shared it, taking bites from it each in turn,
leaving different sets of teeth marks, and it was the same one
we found the day before yesterday in the garden, among the dry pine
    needles.

So, what are we waiting for amid this desolation? What are we waiting
    for still?
Because (no use in concealing it): we still wait
behind the door, behind our clothes, behind our death,
behind our eyes, amid the wavering darkness,
in these ancient rooms with their long, decrepit curtains
drawn shut emphatically, to indicate that we're not,
supposedly, waiting.

            Sometimes,
when I open the windows, I have the impression the trees are leaping
    into the room
like sunburnt men, strong and clumsy in their strength,

embarrassed by my pallor (from lack of sunlight,
from being shut up inside myself). And I'm confused. I feel
very experienced, very penetrating, as though just a moment before
I'd worked through my hardest exercises on the harp. The walls
are still hung with obscure bits of music on animal skins; and then
I force myself to smile, to offer some pretext,
make some elementary excuse. I go to the kitchen,
fetch a tray with glasses and the big cut-crystal pitcher,
and leave it on the table. The pitcher is empty. I go out again
and hear, from outside, the men conversing alone
with a splendid, unsuspecting simplicity, never noticing
the empty pitcher, one cracked glass. And suddenly it's dark.

Outside, the people walk with lanterns, deliberately, not to see,
just because of the great shadows that climb up walls and stairs
and spring from the fanlights on to curtains and sofas,
creating arches where in fact nothing exists
or only a chair forgotten in the dew-damp garden
or a half-used spool of thread on the floor
and the one-eyed dolls on the beds of those who have died.

Oh, yes: there's no one who's not waiting—especially in the morning,
at the time when you wake up and delay putting on your slippers,
delay because you're eavesdropping on every sound, inside and out,
every creak, footstep, crackle, cough, since you'd so much like
to preserve a stance of indifference, to restrain
that animation of hands, eyes, lips, which marks
an inexhaustible secret impatience. How profound mornings are,
with all their profundity enclosed by the light, the time of ablution, the
    time
when you drink your coffee, looking at the window, through the
    window,
and the window's unwashed, and the light above it level,
and you don't hear the maid when she asks you a question. Your ear
is held elsewhere, by an unheard phrase
like the water in your glass: "Today for sure."
                                        In the air
hangs the insidious scent—abstract, you might say—
of old leather, one of Mother's bags,
or the bag of the mailman.

Two steps in from the threshold
there stands, indeed, a handsome messenger, not a speck of dust on him,
though he's come from a great way off. His hair
carefully combed, still damp. On his lips
the reflection of the mirror.
                         "You are immortal," he says
with youthful respect. "You are immortal." And goes.

You see the carpet—he left no footprints. So,
he must have flown in and out, though you'll recall
there was no sign of wings on his shoulders or ankles. Then you get up,
put the same record on the gramophone, sit down again,
adjust your body, more or less, to the rhythm—since music
always eases waiting, in some sense fills the gap
between two imperceptible points, combines
in an ephemeral unity those things and *that*, kills time
by leaving perceptible the linked sequence in a translucency that permits
     you
to look once more into a calm abyss, immutable colors
of rocks, subaqueous forests and the lost key of the casket.

You didn't tell me, in fact—is Pylades gone for good?
We'll miss him a lot. You especially. His sword belt—did you notice?—
was always buckled up crooked, and *he* never saw it; that showed
that he never took thought for himself, or that others
at some time had done it for him. And this indifference of his
displayed an orphan's toughness that made you inclined
to look after him.
                      His mother, I think, must have taken
a peculiar pleasure in straightening his sword belt, every so often,
with a feigned display of anger, and in observing
above her hands, so close to his body, that clumsy smile of his
at not knowing where to stand, what posture to adopt
in his fleshly pleasures and sorrows. It wouldn't surprise me
if maybe his mother sometimes privately prayed
that Pylades would fall sick one day, so she could warm his feet
with a hot water bottle, screwed tight. But he's
so healthy, so unsuspectingly handsome, that I tell you
his mother could never have managed to get the water in the bottle;

she'd have spilled it on her hands, she'd have scalded her hands, and
    she, of course,
wouldn't have wanted her son to see her hurt hands. Luckily, he didn't
    fall sick.
Anyway, I believe she'd have hidden her hands in her pockets
when she was in his presence, since hands are always betrayers, and sad.

Everything, then, just for this desolation? For this minimal
allotted span of ours? What significance, then, to fortune and
    misfortune?
On Mother's bedside table I found—faded now and yellowed—
our childhood photographs. How miserable, how unready
our faces, our hands, as though already marked by fate!
In one of them you're sucking a finger as though you want
to nurse yourself on your own, by yourself, and yet are also ashamed
of wanting to be nursed; that's also why you display it
with a rough and precocious impudence in your childish eyes.

How *alone* we are, my God, what strangers, for all our common fate!
    The time
I spend talking about myself, though I well know
that you're still further from any goal, completely cut off
from all continuity, in a place where words vanish, and silence
does not accord well with anything, cannot even relax on its own.

None can endure that—perhaps it's why I'm still waiting
for discussions, comparisons, expectations and recollections,
for some predetermined attempt at change or, yes, masquerade
as then in front of the Altar—so alone, so defenseless and scared,
weeping with mean little sobs that sounded louder
to me than to anyone else.
                        And suddenly
I noticed a burr on the fringe of Mother's dress and understood in a
    flash
the final inevitability of my death. "Get it over," I said,
stressing each syllable clearly. "It doesn't matter
since it is for *my* country; since it's to raise a wind,
for *our* ships, I'm not important." And I saw in their eyes
amazement and sorrow (so at the very least
I tried to exploit my death—if it should happen). These words

I've seen carved in marble a thousand times. They make me blush. I've
    wished
that I'd died then in fact, so as never to hear them again. And yet
at the heart of my shame was a kind of secret delight,
perhaps like the actor's success.
                                  But now
the drama is over; we have no more spectators, no more listeners. Change
is impossible now, and the masquerade
empty of all significance—it doesn't even free us ourselves—
in relation to whom? looking in which mirror?

That's why I've never put on the deer mask again, which Mother kept
for her own emotional needs, since she certainly was aware
that I had no further need of it. She'd already
figured the whole thing out, long before, never dodged or backed off.
And you, my dear, I'm quite certain, despite her hounding of you,
she loved more than any of us—because you were a man. In your
    persona
perhaps she exacted the penalty for her own bondage. Mother loved
    greatly,
and that was a thing in herself which that arrogant,
beautiful, autocratic free spirit couldn't forgive; she could never
forgive her own non-self-sufficiency.
                               It occurs to me now
that most of her jewelery she wore with no thought whatsoever
of adornment, but more to avert or divert the attention of others,
or rather to conceal some parts of that body
which was so sensitive to cold, to heat, to light or shadow,
to the fleeting wind of an insect, to the touch of damp. You remember
how easily she would shiver? Her skin flushed and changed color
through a whole spectrum, from ochre to pure scarlet, and all the time
she kept her gaze fixed unwaveringly on some point
like the tightrope walkers who, despite their motley costumes,
always have gloomy eyes. Of course, it's their eyes they use
to hold steady in space, it's by means of their eyes
that they balance their limbs, maintain that disciplined stillness
in the midst of their fine-balanced motion.

                                Oh, yes,
Mother loved you a lot, as much as we envied you. Evenings

in the dining room, on the big sofa, after dinner,
she'd often stroke your hair (always with unmoving eyes). Then I
    convinced myself
that her fingers would stay stuck to your neck or that
your locks were alive and her fingers holding them down, while you
were already asleep, or pretending to be asleep.

One New Year's Day, just before the great expedition,
she'd made you a present of a fine blue velvet uniform,
with gold belt and a gold dirk. You, without a word spoken,
had become cross; you didn't want Mother to dress you, you dressed on
    your own.
You stood in front of the mirror, so handsome, so handsome,
as though you'd grown up in an instant—a rather angry angel. I noticed
    then
that there were two of you: one you, one (not the same) in the mirror.
    Mother
unexpectedly knelt before you—the simplicity overdone—
to smooth out a fold of the velvet on your legs, while we,
your three sisters in the doorway, at once turned our backs
and hurried down the staircase—I don't know
if it was out of jealousy, or if we'd already guessed
that something, at last, was going to happen.
                                    Your toy wooden horse—
I found it yesterday, not in the storeroom with our old furniture, no,
I found it stowed under Mother's bed; and strange but true,
my mind turned to the Trojan one.
                        So, my brother,
you shouldn't have any complaints. From time to time
what happened to me seems as though it never took place. Don't you
    think so too? Last night
I heard once more, behind the walls, that word—
light, light, light, light, mechanically uttered, again and again,
encouraging and ironic at once—perhaps it was
Mother's third parrot—tell me honestly, might it not have survived
through some housemaid's secret attention? I heard it so clearly.

I got up. I stood still to hear better. I couldn't tell
what side it was coming from—now there, now here, in the house or out
    of doors;

I looked out of the window: nothing. Down there in the countryside
the whole world was asleep, just one or two lighted windows. No moon.
Then, again, *light*. A pause. *Light*. Another pause. I thought:
that answered something within me, deeper than memory. My eyes
searched the darkness without my volition for a tree, a chimney,
an insect, an odd-shaped star, or the garden railing,
for a small fire from hill to hill, for something
I could say "Thank you" for.
And I saw,
right under Father's room, his two white horses,
throats stretched to gaze upward, just as though they'd seen
Father standing erect by the doorway (I couldn't
see that far, though I'd bent to the waist)
standing there in his uniform, the light from his helmet reflected
on their nostrils, their eyes, their manes—
the white of the horses gleamed pure
like two angels on earth, wings folded to their flanks,
a twin glow only, weighed by the parrot's cry
of *light, light,* stronger now, and more diffuse.

I may even have been asleep—I don't know. In the morning I really saw
Father's horses, scrawny, aged, deadbeat,
coming through the gateway, laden with big baskets,
returning, perhaps, from the estate. I looked them in the eye. They
    didn't know me.
They were blind. The carter greeted me. Once again I heard
that cry, *light, light,* but softer now, more compassionate, more
    sorrowful.

Don't you hear it sometimes too, my dear? Don't say no.
Try again. I'm like you. I know the thing when I hear it,
it's what, despite all that business, we long to hear,
it's what can't be heard, what we don't hear.
Look: daybreak.
That's surely the light? (Don't let it make a sound.) And look how
    calmly
the water shines in the glass. Just so there shines
on your features a sweet acquiescence—what a beautiful light!

Perhaps the two of us, having found that there's no comfort in the
    world,
perhaps, for that very reason, the two of us (though each in isolation)
may once more succeed in giving, and maybe getting, comfort.

*She stands up. In the morning light she looks very pale and exhausted.
She goes up close behind her brother's chair, bends down, and kisses his
hair. He makes an attempt at a smile, amid his alienation, which can be
sensed, cold and harsh, not merely in his hair and shoulders, but right
down to his toenails and the hollows in the soles of his feet. At that
moment can be heard, outside in the courtyard, the sound of horses'
hooves and wagon wheels. An extremely elderly maidservant comes in,
skin drawn tight over cheekbones, chin, and nose, as though she were a
mummy. "My lady," she says, "the wagon's down there waiting." She
goes out again. The woman says nothing. She wraps up the goddess's
image in a small white tablecloth, and settles it in the crook of her left
arm, like a child. She draws her ash-gray mantle across her face. She has
brought no other baggage with her, nor does she take any. She goes out.
Her brother follows her without speaking. He pauses, and stands
motionless on the landing. She goes down the marble stairway,
mechanically, as though carrying out some previous decision, as though
her memory were a blank. She deposits her wrapped burden in the
wagon, then stands as though she had forgotten something. She goes
back into the house, and stays there a little while. When she reappears at
the door she is clutching three shabby, empty birdcages, and, under one
arm, a parcel wrapped in paper—perhaps the deer mask. She stops on
the landing and, without drawing back her mantle, rests her cheek
against her brother's lips. None of the servants is to be seen; it's as
though they were all away at some Sunday morning service, or hiding
behind the shutters. The wagoner is still clutching his cap in his hands.
She gets into the wagon rather awkwardly with the birdcages. The
wagon moves off. It appears that the ceremonial ritual will take place at
Brauron on the arrival of the image in the hands of its consecrated
priestess. And, in fact, it is Sunday. The light shines more brightly than
it should. A chorus of birdsong can be heard. A little dust glows golden
in the distance. And the horses of the dwindling wagon, too, gleam
white.*

SAMOS, ATHENS, SAMOS, NOVEMBER 1971–AUGUST 1972

On the lower slopes of a high mountain, an old half-ruined mansion.
An autumnal evening. In one of the bedrooms the oldest unmarried
daughter, a woman of about seventy, is talking with her old nurse. The
Nurse has to be over a hundred years old, maybe even two hundred. She
looks like a mummified eternity: absolutely silent, patient, enigmatic, as
though kneaded from earth in which the clay has cracked, here and
there, through sheer length of time. You cannot tell whether her silence
is due to exhaustion, wisdom, ignorance, forbearance, comprehension,
general condemnation, general acceptance, affection, affirmation,
denial, hostility, stupidity, or some private dream of her own. The rest
of the house is apparently uninhabited. A bat flicks against the
windowpane. At intervals the call of an owl can be heard from the
mountain, between the eternal virgin's sentences:

Nanny, don't put out the light yet. Sit with me a little.
When the light goes out, I no longer have anywhere to stay,
I lose that defined space which is almost mine. It's then I'm aware
of the giant mountain's sovereignty over our fate—this mountain

set sheer in front of the window, blocking the window,
stuck fast to the house—it gives the house no breathing space,
especially on the side of the women's quarters. A mass of rock
keeps the window obstructed. Since childhood I've feared it. Afternoons
its shadow fell early, the entire house was submerged;

only the aqueduct, cut through the heart of the mountain,
kept some sort of independence, a voice of its own,
like a vast intestine, soft, that pierced the stone
and worked solo with the water, with purpose and the will
to get somewhere, do something, disregarding
the mountain and the shadow of the mountain.
                                        During my childhood,
at night, in bed, when they snuffed out the lamps
and the smoke turned blue in the darkness, before sleep claimed me
I'd hear the colossal sole of the mountain lifting
to tread right into the room, and then
I'd think of the aqueduct to find myself some courage,
it was my only protection;
and a small reflection on the silver candlestick
was like a thin hand that had survived the shadow of the mountain,

a hand that kept me too on the surface,
and so I was somehow able to sleep, knowing
that above me was an opening or a tiny grapple
I could grasp in the morning, to get out of bed.

On the other side of the house
was the wide open countryside (I say "was" as though
our house no longer exists, as though we don't exist);
but there too darkness fell suddenly in the late afternoon
and the panorama was vague, the prospect insidious—
only, sometimes, a cloud, delicate, violet-tinged,
would journey alone through the dull sky, above the darkened plain,
like a small, uprooted garden
or like a diaphanous trireme, hung high in the heavens
by some mirage of a distant, invisible sea
lit from within, projecting
the rosy shadows of ships on the twilight air.

That scared me too, perhaps even more intensely
than the mountain, as though they meant to take something from us
or bring something to us, and we were unprepared—
that's why I'd tell you then to light the lamps,
to cut short this waiting and uncertainty,
to preserve intact the resolution of night
with all its ratified and accepted weight,
as well as the eternal presentiment that after midnight
twelve maskers would decapitate
the two stone lions at the gateway—as in fact happened.

If sometimes I stayed up late, out in the forecourt,
it wasn't to welcome my friend the night (why my friend?),
to borrow her black clothing, have her familiarize me
with that permanent mourning garb, that never left me
from my tenth year on, like my own skin—no, rather
it was so I could see the last reflections of the sunset
on the windows of the houses down in the plain,
like fire signals set by vigilant secret watchmen
from hill to hill, from one quarter to another,
for something else at last; till the stars would light up and the lamps
behind the windows, and all the late evening's fluidity

would form a definite arm, a tattooed arm—the arm
of a prisoner who is a prisoner and nothing else.

I don't know, tonight I feel the urge to talk—now
that it makes no difference whether I talk or not. This afternoon
was so remote and indifferent that it left you a kind of freedom.
You remember those afternoons? Their supposedly noble pallor
contained a gray enmity. I'd listen to the shadows
falling from the sloping rooftops, drop by drop,
silent, invisible rain—especially the gutters,
like exhausted larynxes, stuffed with silence,
and the shadow within them grew round, was sliced
into dark non-negotiable coins that dropped from the gutter's mouth
down to the earth, became part of the earth. What can I say,
now that time has run out for me, and confession in no way
benefits me or anyone else
and I'm not in the mood to reckon up credits and debts—

Such things have never preoccupied me, much less now—
but perhaps I have thought about them—I don't know, I don't
        remember—
and perhaps even now I still seek to reap the benefits of something
and even perhaps to help someone—whom? I don't want to ask myself,
I no longer want to understand myself. Enough. We wear ourselves out
        on our own
far more than we're worn out by events and time.

Nanny, how did the two of us survive like this—you the more ancient,
and I the more weary, you only remembering
while I reflect and forget—the two of us
each at an absolute point of private futility—
no, not you, perhaps; I always see your hands tremble
when they strike a match every evening—could it be
from the emotion of seeing that they still work
or perhaps out of fear for what vanishes from the light
or what's revealed in the light? How have we lived?
And this mountain—how have we stood it? A black and stony palm
presses heavily on our breast from earliest daybreak
when a scatter of numbed stars, like drops
of white wax on a polished board, dissolve themselves

like the hushing to silence of our own sleep, avoiding
any word about the four wax tapers melted
at the four corners of an outsize coffin.

Winter nights when it was raining
streams poured violently down the mountainside; I used to think
that they'd sweep away the house, the columns, the tombs,
and even the mountain itself—the water was always
some sort of consolation, a concept of motion, the idea
that amid the general destruction what had destroyed us
would itself be destroyed.
                            Then, in summer
the entire mountain burned like a furnace,
steamed from its stony nostrils like some exotic monster,
its hot breath wafting straight at our house; it kept up the heat
well past midnight, till two or three. And the cicadas,
those stupid, frivolous creatures, beat all day (and all night)
on their tiny drums the password
for a dawn alert, without reason or danger
or at least no visible danger—we got used even to them, we almost no
        longer heard
these loquacious dwarf soldiers of the blazing noontides
in summers as boundless and bright as if they were dead,
when the least drop of dew went to ground in the covered cisterns
or the cloisters of the dead where their clothes dissolved
and the golden pitchers we'd set by them rusted from the moisture.

Then the one reminder that you were alive
was the sweat on your forehead soaking the pillow
and especially the sweat at your throat
with its humiliating annoyance and the realization
of the pettiness of this annoyance, which stretched out
in a boundless, permeating displeasure to the roots of the world
and above it floated nothing but flies,
enormous black flies, buzzing and shameless.

Perhaps that's why our own people migrated abroad,
went down to the coast, fitted out ships,
made expeditions, fought sea battles, so it's said,
toiled and sweated this way and that, perhaps only

to wash off the sweat of the mountain in the sea,
to wash themselves, drown in the water, escape
from this sheer rock—I don't know how
to define the why and how of it, everything's interwoven:
those hot, astringent odors of fern and lentisk,
of stone, mold, whitewash in burning noontides,
sweat, the cicadas, the mountain, the ships,
all those slain on dry land, all those who drowned
when the sea tossed them up one night on a flotsamed shore
with a yellow moon skewered on a javelin,
and the drowned had not one wound on their bodies,
so how did they die? I'd never seen anyone drowned.
And the silver specter of a slaughtered maiden
floating ethereally over the drowned men
with a long-stemmed lily in her hands—immaculate, untouched
by sweat or by our own obscure, our rodent pangs.

It may be that men are not bothered by those
vulgar rivulets of sweat
that high-handedly use you as their bed
as though you were stone or earth or parched grass. I don't know.
At midday they'd seek refuge in the public baths,
horsing around and maybe laughing naked, one chasing
another, one soaking another with water
hurled from big pitchers—how can anyone
run or laugh when he's naked?
That's something I've never understood. When they emerged
from the baths (I encountered them sometimes) they were more
    handsome,
politer, as though vaguely guilty—their faces,
dew-fresh and flushed then, underlined
a strange maidenly modesty, and only then did I feel
that men too can be lonely, that they can die.

They, of course, forgot this, or never gave it a thought. Afternoons
the shouts of the crowd could be heard from the arena. Then I got
    angry,
even, on occasion, thought about bribing
the elderly changing-room attendants to remind them—
at the precise moment when they'd be drunk with their victory,

at the precise moment when they'd be left to their splendid exhaustion,
at the precise moment when they'd be proudly naked and unprotected—
to remind them that they too would age,
to remind them, above all, that they too would die. I never dared to do
    it.

I had seen the gods' statues naked, and I knew
how vulnerable they all were—the statues
gleaming and shivering at high noon
with the huge shadows of their bodies like knives
driven into their own bodies, or, at nightfall,
blanching mistily in the darkness, unapproachable, insubstantial,
even though of stone and beauty. Both men and statues die,
sooner, perhaps, than us, and perhaps even more profoundly
because they do not acknowledge it.
                         From time to time
I would notice my father aging—still handsome,
but less nimble, less vigorous—a different handsomeness—
and see under his skin the face of death
drawing breath through his fine nostrils, as if through the gills
of a long invisible fish that was swimming in his blood
and sucking it; or on another occasion I saw,
already molded to his face,
gold, tragic, immobile and splendid,
the glittering mask of death.

Death cruises within us or we ourselves cruise
from our very cradle in his secret waters. Yet I kept
this proud reflection to myself,
I concentrated it, I pressed it closely to me
to absolve them and maybe also to protect them
like infants who smile in innocence before their fate
or like unnatural, savage beasts that tremble
before our implacable experience.
                       My mother, in contrast,
had lost her looks after her last confinement;
her forehead full of freckles, her breasts
gone shapeless—she knew it and concealed it,
she was annoyed, out of sorts,
almost dislikable. The thing we conceal is

what reveals us the most—isn't that right, Nanny?—
and maybe it's this that makes us guilty and ugly—a breaking off,
a transformation and distortion of life
because of our own futile intransigence and harshness,
because of our own pride—a veil for our cowardice—
unseemly in the light; while the furniture
ages without resistance, always keeps its place in the house,
has an expression of sweet humility—
and the arm of the armchair, when sometimes by chance a streak of
    sunlight
happens to light on it through the eastern window,
resembles a genuine arm, exhausted,
gratefully akimbo on the hip of the world,
somehow approving, I think, somehow saying: "I existed;
I still exist; my thanks; that's enough for me."

So I imagine that your hands too, when day is ending,
are set on your waist, as though they were reposing
in a closed, perfect circle, like a crown of glory
circling the forehead of someone unknown and invisible—
or perhaps even the head of the sun?
I saw you standing this way once, like a column in the forecourt,
black in your black dress against the sunset,
with your hands on your waist, around the setting sun,
while through the openings made by your two arms
the last rays lanced my eyes. I didn't understand then.
Honestly, Nanny, didn't your eyes hurt from the sun? What did you see
    out there?
The countryside or the distance? Life or memory?
Or all of them together? So abandoned, so yielding. How can you
    know?

Meanwhile my mother would stand motionless, for hours at a time,
in just the same posture, but unyielding, her gaze
fixed on the broad metal mirror; she used a burnt
bay-twig to make up her eyes—I could tell
from the scent as I entered her room.
That bothered me, because bay was always meant
for the brows of athletes and poets. She also used an array
of exotic herbs, picked in secret under the waning moon,

herbs that raise rashes on the skin, color the face a fierce red
like a theatrical mask. One evening
she saw in the mirror that I was watching her,
perhaps had already sensed my gaze on her back,
and shivered all over; she made a movement
as though leaping a flight of steps at a single bound
that, sooner or later, she'd most certainly have to descend,
or as though she'd seen my eyes in a deep black well,
looking like two white circles that gradually spread out
and one circle entered the other until they mingled
and filled the whole circle of water in the dead depths.
The water must have whitened then, wide and neutral as truth,
and my mother must have seen in the white water her dark face
beyond all denial, and then she said
in a terrible voice as though from out of a well:
"So you too have seen how much older I've become?"
And suddenly once again she became simple, beautiful, loved,
as she'd been long years before, before her own murder
and before the tiny untraceable murders of time.

After that she no longer made up. She let herself go. We women
age faster, learn faster. What can we ever do
with this knowledge? To whom can we bequeath it? What use is it?
My mother softened a lot (and she was hard—remember?)
and I tell you my brother's vengeance was no longer needed
at a time when her weariness and dejection were absolute,
when her anger had already passed, her remorse and repentance too,
and all the passion that might have vindicated her earlier crimes. She
    almost didn't defend herself
and perhaps she saw it as a fine excuse for a tragic death,
if not a heroic one, because from start to finish
she uttered one cry only, so exact in its sound, as though premeditated,
as though imitating the pain of all life, and fixed her eyes,
with self-control and a vague expression of tenderness, on her ring,
which had grown very loose on her middle finger. Mother couldn't have
    stood
dying the way we die, in bed,
tangled up in her white wispy hair,
as though trapped by a white spider's legs.

Perhaps this mountain is also to blame. My mother was hard. One
    afternoon
a shepherd passed in front of the house with his geese (he'd clipped
the tips of their wings so they couldn't fly). My mother
leaned down out of the window and haggled over the geese,
something she'd never made a habit of—she said something
about Saturday dinner—I couldn't hear clearly, but just from the sound
    of her voice
I knew the shepherd was nineteen years old, swarthy and handsome;
I opened the window, and then
I saw the geese all at once rising skyward
and I was in time to catch sight of my mother's eyes, dilated, frightened,
amid the shadow cast directly on her face
by the geese, a dense darkness, as they ascended—so dark
that for an instant they hid the sun. And the shepherd
wanted my mother to pay for his flock
because—he said—she'd frightened them. But she instead
ordered the guards to give the shepherd a whipping: never in my life
had I seen her so enraged. And they really did whip him. I myself
looked after his wounds, and for safety's sake went with him
two streets further down, him and his geese. They raised
a cloud of dust and hid him, almost entirely, that midafternoon
in a bluish cloud—because, I forgot to say,
his geese very soon returned—or perhaps
they never took off at all? I just don't recall. Perhaps you remember?
The incident was much talked about at the time—words and more
    words—
the geese, it was said, were omens. The import varied. Some said one
    thing, some another,
and all these rumors blurred, transforming my memories.

Who lived through all these things? How did they happen? How end?
Is it we who lived through them? How many ages ago?
And the struggle: a nothing. And the pain:
a tiny dark spot, a silly fly struggling
pointlessly in a brilliant summer, and all around
formal, inexorable, serene and unaffected,
the superlative immobility of death.

How many changes of king since then? How many revolutions?
We had, too, it's said, brief periods of an incredible mob rule.
And one moment of genuine democracy. I don't know.
I think they dug up, with honors, someone they'd executed
and set him, a skeleton, on the throne—they'd fixed
his bones together with wire, and draped him
in a purple mantle, sprinkled the hall with rose water,
made speeches from the balconies that no one understood. Someone else
they buried with unimaginable honors—a whole thicket of flags at half
    mast,
not a square or park without his statue. A little later
a kind of madness overpowered them all—I don't recall this clearly—
they waved their arms, they ran, screamed, smashed up his images:
it was odd to see men battling with statues.
Others carried off bits of marble by night,
turned them into stools, or made fireplaces out of them. They also found
a soldier who'd hidden under his pillow
the marble hand of the deposed one, fingers clenched
as though hiding something, as though it still retained some shred of his
    old power,
or of a different sort—the timeless power of death. What can you
    believe
among so many accounts? Another counterrevolt broke out,
drums beat all night long, at dawn it was trumpets,
the flags on the public buildings changed their colors,
you didn't know who was coming in, who on their way out,
the guards at the barrack gates were changed, but still
young as ever—the same ill-fitting uniforms—brutish and stupid,
yet likable in their irresponsible youthfulness,
and when they were suddenly lit up at night by the headlights
of big covered automobiles, you could see
in their delicate pallor that they were quite innocent,
that the one thing they wanted was to sleep, in their clothes and boots if
    need be—
and when men feel sleepy they're so nice, so lovable,
isn't that right, Nanny? The dead and the sleeping
we can love quite freely, they're adversaries no longer,
they've already given up. So we too, without
humiliation, can surrender ourselves to them. You're sleepy, Nanny.

Once they mobilized the old men too. They looked so silly (remember?)
in their outsize uniforms. Their miserable eyes
peered out from under their helmets like cockroaches
or small gray frightened mice. That same night
they surrendered their arms en masse to the enemy
and he clapped them on the back like a good friend. They grinned
and accepted honorable discharges. From that time on
they've never showed up in the marketplace. They retired
to country homes with gardens and devoted themselves to breeding
dogs or cats, chickens, rabbits or canaries;
one took care of a wounded eagle;
another nice little old fellow, three hawks. What did they want with
    them?

I no longer remember anything, about myself or others.
It's as though it all had happened somewhere else, outside time. As
    though it hadn't happened. It didn't happen.
Nothing any longer is another's or mine. Brooding on these things so
    much,
I've forgotten everything, or dissolved it, or assimilated it—I don't
    know.
Between myself and such things came foresight and foretaste
as an advance bridgehead—a barrier bridge—
since you could cross it beforehand, you didn't go over,
but you could cross it no longer, so you never knew for certain
if the bridge was firmly secured on the other side,
and the idea of the bridge remained always
a disguise masking bond or distance,
an untested proof. Who can cross
over that? To go where? From earth to heaven or the reverse?
Even words are lacking. We left everything half-way done,
we left everything to chance. And it all happened
without us. We stayed behind
repentant or unrepentant—what does it matter?
humiliated or arrogant, it makes no difference.

Certain large, incomprehensible words
entered our daily vocabulary. I never
looked them straight in the eye, never tried to pronounce them—

as though foreign invaders had come and I had had time
to hide in a secret retreat
between ceiling and roof beams,
with barely enough food and water. And I didn't know
what had become of my people—perhaps they too hid somewhere
or were killed in their bedrooms or on the ramparts? I imagined
the lord chamberlain strangled with the curtain cord
and two thick silk tassels hanging over his belly
awkwardly and unbearably; or the supreme commander
being dragged in his bloodied uniform through the dust of the road
while the cicadas chorussed madly, and a fly
stuck tenaciously to his ear
like some strange green-gold earring—I saw it;
and who, I wondered, would water the young saplings in the square
or the flowers in the garden? Summer season crimes
amid a fearful brilliance that seemed to me
more fearful still as I pondered it in my dark hiding place—
a brilliance that would have shown everything up as
pitiless, insignificant, nonexistent.

Such things weren't so common at the beginning, or later—they came at
        some point in between;
my sole concern was watching my movements to prevent
my being noticed, apportioning my supplies
each day into shorter rations for a longer time span. And time,
within this caution and precaution, was extended beyond measure,
passed through time, abrogated time. A vague awareness
became identified silently with sensation, deepened endlessly, lost itself;
recollections dissolved, and there remained
nothing but memory, vacant and unencumbered,
itself forgotten through too many recognitions,
just as a beat is no longer heard after constant repetitions—
pulse, breathing, the tick of a clock—
a silent uniformity, rich and indifferent
amid a unified, exhausted fortune or misfortune.

A tiny crawling creature with countless feet inched slowly across the
        wall
in a primeval, isolated landscape of creation
with neither purpose nor necessity—not even for me to see it,

and that I saw it was already an indication
that I exist—a preposterous pride
and, elsewhere, distant pain; the veins of the wood
bore the weight of an unknown touch, a heavier load
than all these mindless events. One day I stuck my finger
into a knothole in a board. It got wedged there. I didn't try
to pull free—I'd become one with the wood, the tree, the forest;
on my knees small leaves and stalks had already sprouted
and an inner calm possessed me—until I took fright
lest I vanish in that faceless unity,
above all lest I lose my voice (as happens in nightmares
or, so they say, like those women whom the gods, as a mark of their
        favor,
turned into trees, or marbled as splendid statues
on the lip of the precipice, to save them from the fall,
and the cry they never uttered remains eternally scored
from their toenails up through the roots of their hair,
a drawn-out, disembodied "Help!"—may we be spared such favors!).

Then I wrenched out my finger by force, and it was bloodied,
and I felt sorry for my finger, quite apart from the pain—
like a final, broken engagement, the wooden
ring of the forest torn away from my hand—
it still hurts me, did you notice that, Nanny?
But you don't know what this pain is, even though all
your fingers are raw from washing, sweeping, kneading dough for
        bread.

Another thing you never learned: the joy of disobeying life and time,
that naked joy of willing deprivation,
that supreme chill of denial, when
what we denied and what we might have given
are presented to us whole and unified
in an inconceivable, neutral space
void and replete, unexplored, beyond verification,
yet there, and translucent to infinity.

But once more the mountain's shadow was present in this translucency
like an inverted cone, decayed, hollow at the core,
and I was inside it, while over me

stood, always, the rocky cone of the mountain, and I couldn't
hack that out too in order to struggle upward
or to get out once more so as to climb from the outside
and let the sky lean down upon my cheek.

And if you keep talking of dates—nothing: I'd forgotten
even the numbers of the house and telephone,
places that even if I'd remembered would have changed with time,
the sequence of numbers, the street plan, the form, the physiognomy of
	the landscape, the phone book,
and at times I'd ask myself how I must have seemed, outside the house,
to those who might have seen me inside it—I
who never emerged from my house, who saw no one, who never looked
outside the house. And I stared at myself
in a cup of water in order to see my face,
especially my mouth because I had the impression
that my lips had been eaten away, and all that was left
were my two naked jawbones. I couldn't make out a thing.
And that tiny puddle of water in the cup
was a black hole over my face.

But I tell you, even if I'd come out by the main entrance
under the two decapitated lions, I might still have been recognized
by the ancient dog from my movement of self-withdrawal
or the smell of my torn dress—
because material always retains the scent of the house
and reflections from the positions of all deaths (they say
that dogs have a most delicate sense of smell). Then I'd have given it the
	last of my water
and I'd have been ready, with a final smile on my lips,
like the gold and proper obol between the corpse's teeth for the ferry
	fare.

Perhaps even you might have recognized me—don't you think?—
from my broken shadow on the paving of the courtyard,
from the curvature of my back, which bore
all those years, and proudly, the mass of the mountain, or even
from the tiny wrinkles of sympathy for my own ordeal
surrounding my eyes, like some very delicate army,
just a few trusty guards around

the ruined tower—yes, you'd have recognized me,
by the style of my breeding, by the gaze
that never drops down, that isn't fixed
on faces and objects, but paces
directly forward, alone, five yards above the helmets
of the drawn-up firing squad. You would have recognized me,
dear Nanny, poor fellow sufferer, you who never
in your whole life understood anything, yet sense it all
through your worn, dead fingers, even through your nails.

Tell me, do you remember the old guitarist? His fingers,
translucent, bright, long (just like mine),
touched the strings and vanished with the sounds,
touched everything yet remained themselves intangible,
offensive, horripilating, as though stripping, effortlessly,
a supercilious woman, only to leave her thus,
naked, kneeling, her hair
spilled in a black tide on the ground. In total contrast
were the fingers of the masons while they were building
the right wing of the house or, later,
Father's or Mother's tomb—there was real power
in those fingers: whatever they grasped became theirs,
they themselves were built of stone, or rather whatever
they were building was built over them, increasing their bulk—
each one of them an entire fortified city,
castles and all, free (yes, indeed) and impregnable. When they quit for
     the day
and washed off, sunburnt, uncomplicated, fierce,
at the garden fountain, I'd listen to their black hair
raining drops on the marble, as though somewhere, at the close
of a summer day, they were sprinkling the hot-baked roads
on the vast site of a trade fair,
with thousands of horses, cattle, pitchers, fiddles, baskets,
little paper flags, barrel organs, grapes, lemonade bottles, gypsies.

Now the fingers of the young groom—remember him?—
were rough and adroit. One summer
he thrust out his hand, palm up, and I stepped on it to mount,
just as with his predecessor, who had retired—a broad
and solid band of heat like red-hot iron

pierced through my sandal, burnt my sole. All day
I galloped below on the plain. I got home late, pursued
by that contagious, animal heat and the eyes of the groom,
large, gentle, respectful, and precisely as strong
as they were respectful—a hostile strength (I saw that),
flush with self-confidence, and perhaps showing some contempt
for my own proud frivolity. I galloped:
a branch whipped across my face. A little further on
I kicked off my sandals.
                         That summer
was heavy—the most unbearable of my life—
fearful heat waves, the plain a blinding glare, strewn
with shards of broken glass; rage and dull sultriness,
swamp-fever, nightmares, insomnia.
All night the horses' hoofbeats could be heard on the rocks;
around midnight the guards would start chasing the cats, would kill
     them
with sticks or javelins, or just kick them to death.
All day long there were flies, at night came the mosquitoes,
a thick black veil to blot out the cherry red sunset,
and the locusts in the vineyards—they even bothered the groom.
Everyone dreamed of war as a solution—soon war broke out in fact
and the country was stripped of its men. The garden fountain
seemed all at once like a glass tower, uninhabited,
shining with a fresh, inexplicable, and pointless freedom.

That summer jewelery scorched
at the throat, on hands—you wouldn't know, you've never worn such
     things.
Why, Nanny? Didn't you like them? Or perhaps you never had any?
You never told me. I could have given you some. Only your wedding
     ring,
of blackened iron—why do you still keep it?
Could it be that iron is cooler, a circular rivulet
around your desiccated finger? I dumped all that stuff in a casket—
this bracelet of my great-grandmother's is the only thing I kept;
I got used to it finally, it's no burden to me. I'm rid of the rest.

Not one single ring stayed on my finger—
was it perhaps the fear of slavery? Was it fear

of seeing my own solitude more clearly, set against
another, parallel, closed solitude? Of course I preserved
virginity of soul and body, a shrivelled virginity,
dry and astringent, whining like an old worm-eaten door
on its rusted hinges, in the upper keep, on windy nights—
a nasty assurance of unneeded security
when neither friend nor foe is left to assail it,
and the guards died long ago at the look-out posts,
arms, uniforms, helmets and all; some of them are even
standing still erect, elbows on the cyclopean walls, with two holes for
    eyes
through which the wind whistles in winter, out of which in spring
sprout nettles or the occasional camomile.

One spring evening at dusk I met, on the upper ramparts,
a dead warrior chieftain, all wasted away,
with two poppies for eyes.
                  Don't get up, Nanny.
Sit on the stool more squarely; all guardedness is now superfluous
and class distinctions a joke. I'm quite sure
that you too met them like this. Each time the swallows return
like black arcs, blind, javelined into light and air
by invisible dead soldiers, doesn't your mind follow?

You, surely, must have had the benefit of a different experience.
You've lived, toiled, been involved with objects, implements,
you'd no time to think—you've escaped knowledge.
You used to plant trees, taste their fruit, yet never knew
what a tree *is, how* a tree is,
bare on a winter morning, with its branches
spread against the grayness like the dry raw veins of the world,
desolate, unprotected, and vivid. That you never saw.

You had your life, you bore children. They were killed,
in the mines or quarries or wars—so I've heard.
Yet what is your pain compared to my own deprivation,
my own circumspect precautions against pain and sin,
my own orderliness and inflexibility? compared to the oppression
that thwarted both joy and pain? You don't know.

Yet death you do know. You too have seen my corpses.
Maybe you even saw death spread out whole, like a sheet on your bed.

No, I don't want confessions from you. I'm not asking for that. You too
    gave up whitewashing
the courtyard and the tree trunks. You heard the creaking behind the
    plaster,
the creaking of wood and stone. Only, I beg you,
hold on a little longer, hold on, don't go,
hold on tight to the rails of your cot,
hold on to the silverware, the handles of the buffet, cupboard, drawers,
hold on to the cellar padlock—don't leave before me,
since no matter how differently we shared things' shadows and sounds,
the way sunlight and window shone back from the glass panes in the
    bookcase
or the books that you used to dust and I used to read
or the maquis from the shadow of the mountain falling upon
the corners of the rooms, and even the day's broadest and smoothest
    surfaces—
yet the two of us lived amidst the same
objects—yes the same—with the same names.

Once I found a feather from your duster
in a book of mine, and for an instant I imagined
that it came from some mysterious bird that flew high at night
and threw me a downy feather as a message; though quickly I realized
that it was from your duster—I recognized the colors—
and wished I'd never found it.
Yet may not this too be a fine domestic bird,
reliable in your hands? It makes no demands, is songless
(silence is always more expressive), is all-giving—
yet it too ages and moults. You, I know,
preferred the canaries (they're gone too)—I saw the love
in your concern for their water, their birdseed,
when you washed out their tiny cup, when you
carded out bits of wool for them in their mating season;
that day when one of their eggs rolled out and smashed on the tiles
I saw in your eyes that it was like the collapse of a white dome
in some ancient Helladic cult. You too had your deaths,

and all deaths, however different, resemble one another,
and there we assuredly have met. That's why I say to you,
don't leave before me. Who will look after me?
Who will slip in my dentures for me, so people won't see me
in my last hour with an empty mouth, like some useless hole
gaping in greedy betrayal in the bright golden daylight?
(Yes, that's what they'll think: *greedy*.) I don't want that. Who'll dress
    me
in that formal white gown of mine, designed for modest nuptials,
which I in my solitude kept immaculate for death? Don't go—
please, Nanny, do me this one last favor.

The terrible summers are gone. Any day now
autumn will leave us too. Winter is coming. Don't be afraid.
Winter's the best season of the year—really the best—
a general contraction, a return to the center of our self,
concentration, thickening, reduction,
ending in the total disappearance of the seed in the cold's domain,
a calm death, met with self-knowledge—
the frozen roots of the trees indifferently entwined
with the hair of the dead. The beautiful pitchers—
cool, decorative, all in ice-cold order—
to you seem pointless, since you're not thirsty;
precisely because of that you see them, independent of you
even though fashioned by you, in their own shape,
far out beyond our needs. We too are independent.

What about food and fire, then? I don't want to know.
Pour out the oil and the flour. Kindle no more fires.
Don't light the lamps. Let the cold
lay siege to us, let it at last win free mastery over the house,
let it sit cross-legged on the chairs. I see the cold already
sitting there as master at my table,
tucking a white starched napkin around his neck
and voraciously gobbling our food, even our very hunger.
And the cat we'd thought lost is lying dead
under the sofa—look at her lifeless tail,
like a black, frozen fishhook dragging
the whole house toward death. Don't be frightened, Nanny.

Make our coffins ready now, our last housekeeping act—
from tomorrow we may be sleeping in our caskets
as though in my finest carriage—we must be prepared.
Perhaps someone can be found to inform the authorities—
there's even a chance that passers-by will notice
because of the smell. They'll realize who I am
from my wide bracelet with its nine sapphires
and from the royal cut of my chin—not, of course,
from the curve of my forehead—such things they don't understand.
And if nothing else, right above me
will be standing the high mountain, significant and proud,
worthy memorial of my immortal line. I need nothing else.

Nanny, where are you going? Are you too deserting me? How
    unyielding you've become.
Remembered your humble origin, have you? Are you going with them?
Your eyes are so round and scary. What do they see
that I can't see? Do you still bear a grudge against me
because I once beat you with your broom? You know
what a miserable creature I was. Wait, Nanny. Wait. Wait.

*The Nurse exits through the door, as unbending as archaic Fate, or like
some terrifying sleepwalker made from clay, as though her joints no
longer allowed her to stoop. Her footsteps, as she descends the stairs,
make firm thudding echoes in the empty house, among the casks down
in the cellar, even outside in the courtyard. Presently they can be heard
on the road. The sound goes on all night, as though some vast and
undefeated army were on the march through the ages. The Other
Woman calls out "Wait!" once more—a cry that seems to evoke some
immeasurable anguish—then runs, trips over her coffin, which is set to
the left of the door, falls, and lies motionless. The lamp gutters out by
itself, and from the mountain the call of the owl can be heard more
distinctly.*

*A week later, a certain traveller, returning to this ruined city, with all its
huge Pelasgian stones, bare foundations, shattered columns, gymnasia,
baths, theaters, tombs—as it might be Epidaurus, Delphi, or Mycenae—
where the midday wind whistles among the marble blocks and tall
dried-out thorn bushes, does indeed realize what has happened from the
smell. A few other people who have just stepped down from a new*

tourist bus also gather round. They bundle her up in a threadbare purple rug and dump her in a makeshift grave, holding their noses. Thousands of flies have gathered. Her gold bracelet with the nine sapphires they put in the Museum. Suddenly clouds gather, and lightning begins to appear above the mountain peak. A moment later comes a torrential downpour. They all pile hurriedly into their bus and leave, welcoming with relief the powerful smell of sodden earth, rocks, and trees, as though the world were being washed clean of some archaic pollution.

MYCENAE, MAY 1960

· CHRYSOTHEMIS ·

A quiet afternoon toward the end of summer. Sunshine. Scattered clouds. A hint of the first breath of autumn. A young woman journalist, commissioned by one of the big newspaper chains, makes her way up the ancient, legendary hill, passes through the now unguarded entrance gate, ascends the stone steps, and strikes the knocker on the half-ruined palace's main door. She feels the heat of the metal on her palm. The aged Lady comes down and opens the door herself, conducts her visitor into a large drawing room redolent of dust, withered roses, musty silk and velvet. The young woman addresses her with great respect, explaining the purpose of her visit—an interview, she says. She goes on to say something about the Lady's "pure, silent, solitary freedom". The Lady—obviously moved, a childlike blush on her pale and wrinkled features—keeps twisting, with the thumb and middle finger of her right hand, an unusual ring she wears on her left ring finger. She listens with well-bred attention, in which, nevertheless, there is visible a certain degree of abstractedness, embarrassment, and an impalpable sense of foreknowledge. Silence. The dusty crystals of the chandelier glint from time to time. From outside, in the garden, comes the faint sound of the old gardener's voice—perhaps talking to a bird, a dog, or a flower— followed immediately by a sudden frenzied outburst from the cicadas. Then the aged Lady, as though encouraged and protected by this confused din, begins to speak, in measured tones that do not, however, conceal some hint of remote and inexplicable happiness. A bird perches on the windowsill. She lets it be. It goes off again.

How did they come to remember me? No one ever remembers me. No
    one
ever paid any attention to me. I'm not complaining. Everything was just
    fine for me,
and maybe better that way.
                    You know, with the passage of time,
all things, however bitter or terrifying, come to seem indispensable—
useful, attractive even. And this rough hill above me
was company, almost protection. I put on its shadow.

So, in my obscurity, I liked looking and listening. I could
dream freely. It was marvellous, really—as though I lived
outside of history, in my own intact and absolute realm,
protected, and yet present.

Whole hours on end I'd watch
water left in a glass with the rotten stalks
of forgotten flowers—something velvety, viscous remained
in the glass, permeated the room, the entire house—

And that weariness and postponement, so thick with good breeding—
not being able to take the flowers, toss them through the window
into the garden, to wash out the glass (why, I wonder?). The rotten
    garland
would have stayed there secretly in the glass, in the house, around our
    foreheads—
something deep and fearful, yet not without its charm.

What was all our meddling for, then? Very early I learned
that there's nothing anyone can avert. Each evening
the warm breath of the house walls pours out into the street,
a huge horse's shadow steams in the moonlight. If this is not
an answer to something, I don't think an answer exists.

Huge biers passed through this gate—as huge as ships;
corpses in ceremonial gear, with tall helmets, covered with flags and
    flowers,
and others naked, clad only in their pallor and their perplexity,
and one slaughtered girl, wearing a marvellous pure white robe; the
    breeze
lifted the robe high up, set it on a spring cloud,
and it stayed there, fluttering in solitude, from time to time
casting its sky blue reflections on courtyard and stairway. Perhaps there
    were also
reflections from the kites her girlfriends were flying in a nearby
meadow, since every so often they changed color—I saw them
on the thighs and breast of a statue out in the garden. But really
there was nothing except the white robe's sky blue movements.

All gone. Nothing's left. They squandered everything on their name,
not on themselves (are we the same, perhaps?). They never repented.
Besides, they were always too late to repent. They didn't need to.

On our way back from the cemetery, we all kept our eyes on the ground.
There was a long pause, so long one might have supposed

we were giving some thought, at last, to where she might be.
                                                        And suddenly
came the sound of countless loud hoofbeats down in the plain, on the
     roads—
the troopers were charging back out from the poplars, blocking the
     fords; there were some
flags at half-mast, and other still flying high amid the shooting.

You couldn't tell who was coming, who going, what was happening.
     Some ran for it,
some hid, some scribbled notes on their knees, some killed themselves,
some ended their lives in front of the bare brickyard wall,
some fiddled with the two waistcoat buttons they'd left unfastened.

Abandoned cows wandered warily through the market,
staring at clocks, mirrors, shop windows
as though they were there to shop for new furs. An antique set of scales
lay overturned in the big warehouse. They stood it up any old how
and started weighing stuff again—sacks, barrels, packing cases,
baskets, tin cans, demijohns. Some weighed their own small children.
One person brought a bird to weigh. The bird flew out of the door.
The man exclaimed: "It weighs nothing, I weigh nothing. We're
     weightless.
We're losing our way, we're lost, we've lost our weight, we're flying"—
and spread his arms wide, as though really about to become airborne.
His laughter rang out past midnight, down by the river.

Afterward, nothing. No more cheers or curses. The only form of
     freedom left
was silence. In the deserted gardens
nettles grew rank, and asphodel, and some unusual thorn bushes
with unfamiliar golden flowers like stars of desolation. The wells ran
     dry—
if you threw a stone down it struck stone, and the sound continued
down to a fathomless depth, right through to the other side; and if you
     peered in,
a single eye, dark, without lashes, was staring straight at you,
making your whole face hollow, like a bottomless hole.

Later the great cold set in. Packs of wolves descended upon
city and villages. We all locked ourselves indoors. It snowed, too.
An indescribable whiteness had blanketed roofs, trees, memory,
like devotion, like absolution—like that robe I told you of—
and behind it we saw all that blackness: undivided, anodyne, tranquil.

Mornings found the roads cluttered with starving sheep, dogs, donkeys,
and a few sad scrawny horses. The bees had left their hives.
Prices rose for corn, barley, and wheat. Yet, one morning,
when I opened the shutters, I saw, set round the garden wall,
a whole mass of children's paper windmills. Maybe the man
who wanted to weigh the bird was there too. From the road
a boy could be heard hawking rolls—his voice, and the smell of hot
bread and sesame restored form to the trees, the doors,
faces and hands. The diaphanous morning moon
withdrew with guilty, rose-pink footsteps,
beside a servants' iron stepladder, twisted and rusty.

Then I called my big sister. "Look, look!" I told her. I counted
the windmills: "Two, three, seven, sixteen, nineteen—" She
turned that way, but saw nothing; spun round and eyed me,
took off at once, in a rage. I felt sorry, as though I'd done something
        wrong.
I peered down once more from the window. Nothing. Really. The
        windmills had gone.

In those far-off days, I remember, once, down in the garden,
the music of the cicadas, very much as tonight, dropped from the pines
amid the noisy light, interrupted at times
by the breath of a breeze. And then, for a moment,
the eucalyptus leaves touched silence. The shadows on the ground
turned golden blue, dark, elongated. Soon
they swallowed up everything. Yet that brief silence hung
like a cobalt spot in the bright-lit air. I remember
the wicker garden chairs, warm from the sun, set firm
—precise, reliable, positive—on their four feet. Only that.

And that spot, as though reflected from a distant windowpane,
moved from the woven chairs to the table, and settled there
beside the silver teaspoons. Glasses left under the trees from breakfast

became blue now, with green patches. One day some water
was spilled on my sister's dress—the dress had a pattern of flowers
printed on it. "Give it to me," I told her, "I'll wash it."
"It's nothing," she said, "water doesn't stain." "Give it to me, give it to
    me,"
I repeated. Everyone stared. I fell silent. The flower print grew,
filled the whole dress, her arms, her legs, her face—
my sister had turned sky blue, only the tip of one sandal
stayed white. No one sees the obvious. All those other things—
other things, like, well, what? moves, jobs, gestures,
amid (as they say) the immutable and the immovable. They don't see at
    all.
Better so, maybe? Worse? Who knows? They just don't see.

I've retired to this corner. It's quiet. No clamor reaches here
from births, marriages, deaths. I'm tired. The same things over and
    over—
some people rising, some descending—all alike, first, second, or third
(even the best, you know, when they get power). A wall
with rusted pitons rising high in the night. Never
have I managed to grasp a piton and climb. Of course, I didn't try.
I lost myself watching a star dissolve in water like a drop from a lemon
in tea—somehow it turned the darkness light. Everyone panicked—they,
    perhaps, more than any.

Yet this wearisome repetition, finally, seems transformed
into something good, almost wholesome—it gives you the vague
    impression
of being at once fleeting and inexhaustible, a tranquil endurance,
something unknown yet familiar—it relieves you—a notion of fearful
    eternity—
but eternity, notwithstanding.
                                    A quiet smile hangs within us,
as we hang a picture in an empty room, an old sea battle
in dark green tones, at night, with gold and red stippling; to one
side, on the sand, in the foreground, a lame old sailor. He's lit
a small fire and propped up his pot on two stones—
he stands alone, past active service, as though outside the world,
securing the world on two smoke-blackened stones.
You can sense a smell of fish soup in this picture,

a smell of humbleness and dumb freedom—the only kind.
Saliva fills your mouth. You realize you're hungry again. That pleases
    you.

For the rest, we learned neither what nor who was at fault. The lot was
    cast long before.
I never liked lotteries, games of chance; never gambled. Once
Mother drew a ticket in my name, and I won
a huge Chinese vase—it's still there, in that room
where we store the junk. "Strange," said my mother,
"that this child should turn out lucky. Strange," she repeated.

"Strange, strange." And I smiled. The year went by,
everyone else forgot. But I remembered. "I'm lucky, I'm lucky,"
I repeated, over and over, as I climbed the stairs at night,
or as I lay with the light out, watching the pink sliver of new moon
glued to the windowpane—"I'm lucky, I'm lucky." And then
a thin girlish laugh, like water from a narrow-necked pitcher, poured
down from some high sunny window on a shadowy summer garden.

Oh yes, I always stayed lucky. Strange. Not even I myself
wished to believe it. I'm still surprised, even now—
which explains my shrinking gratitude when someone—
tutor, musician or gardener—happened to wish me
"Good night" or "Good evening". I'd look around carefully,
to see if it was someone else they were greeting. Then a huge grin would
    spread
all round my face, spill past my ears—most unbecoming. I know it—
I tried, really hard, to control it, but simply couldn't.
Only by knitting his brows can anyone control
a smile (and perhaps they're right, those who say:
Frowning men are the mildest, sweetest, most humble,
yet strong too, very strong—yes, perhaps they're right); *I* couldn't do it.

Late afternoons, winter or summer, out in the garden, or here by the
    window,
under the influence of the evening star, I'd raise my left hand,
trace round my lips, slowly, with care, abstracted,
as though to help in the shaping of some unknown word, or to send
a long delayed kiss God knows where.

Back in those days,
many times, as I strolled alone in the garden, the moon would chance
to steal up noiselessly behind me and, quick as a flash,
clap both hands over my eyes, asking "Who am I?"
"I don't know," I'd reply, "I don't know," just to be asked again.

But she'd never ask again, just let go. Then I'd turn round,
and there were the two of us, face to face, her dewy cheek
above my cheek; and the whole of that smile of hers—I'd just snatch it
    and run.
She'd chase me all round the fountain.
                           One night
Mother caught me right in the act. "Who's that you're talking to?"
"I was chasing the cat to stop it from eating the goldfish." "Silly child,"
said my mother, "don't you ever mean to grow up?" At that instant
the cat really came by, rubbing against my legs. An enormous goldfish
gleamed out clear from the fountain. The cat scooped it up
and vanished into the rose bushes. I shouted—I chased it—
I was scared it might eat one of the moon's arms—and my mother
    believed me.

That's how it always happens. We no longer know the right way
to behave, or speak, or to whom, or what we should say. We're
    left on our own
with invisible obstacles, to invisible wars, sans victory, sans defeat,
with a mass of invisible enemies, or, rather, enmities. Yet
we have numerous allies as well—they, too, are invisible—like the moon
in the old garden, the goldfish, even the cat.

Another night (in high summer, the dining room sweltering hot,
curtains drawn back, windows wide open) Mother
looked angry, and so did Father and my big sister;
they were talking loudly—their mouths grew big, full of darkness—and
    at times
their tongues gleamed in the lamplight as though they were trying
to swallow a mouthful of light. They couldn't do it, though. They
    choked.
They all choked each other. I watched them. I couldn't make out their
    words.

At that moment a bat flew in through the window,
bringing with it a few stars, a piece of the velvet night,
two mulberry leaves (yes, mulberry), and the faintest bleating
of a little lamb by the river, at the hour when the shepherds' star
shivers in water, so crazy for solitude, so deeply moved,
when sparrows sigh in their sleep, turning over
on their other side, and sheep promise their god
to be better still. At once the grown-ups stopped talking.

Maybe they even eavesdropped on that bleating. Maybe they feared
what was distant, lovely, unknown. Still, they heard it. Then Mother
snatched up a napkin from the table, went after the bat—
she almost swatted the lamps out.
                                        I really adored
my mother on this rampage—though she was still
arrogant, aggressive, imperious. With that white napkin flying
from one hand, she was like a single-winged bird, and she couldn't fly.
     In her huge eyes
glinted a secret passion to run out into the night, right into the night.

Then I too grabbed a napkin and thrust it, like a second wing, into her
     other hand.
She smiled in complicity, but then exclaimed, at once,
furiously, "Have you gone crazy?" The bat had vanished,
vanished, along with the river—I was in time to see
the bright leap of the river over the sill. The talk
began again, louder than ever. I didn't care. I kept quiet. I was just sorry
     for them.
I had my secret allies too—as I told you—including,
now, a second wing in my mother's eyes.

That "Aren't you ever going to grow up?" hadn't bothered me for some
     while now—
I felt it all right, but as a sort of privilege—my special vision, my secret
     joy. Mornings
I'd go out alone with the innocent garden dew, sit down
and study the birds for hours.
                                  Very often a sparrow
would fly down to earth and hop around perkily, giving an accurate
     imitation

of a girl on her first date—I didn't tell the girls this
in case they got angry with all birds—though I desperately wanted
to reveal this discovery of mine—revelation you might call it, why
     not?—
that's what I believed then (and maybe still do)—such insignificant
     things
sometimes brighten our faces, and the world too, don't you agree?

Maybe the birds know that; it could be that's why they too
don't intend to grow up—they're on their guard, perhaps; perhaps
     they're scared;
they change color, hide among leaves. ("Obscurity," said
my old tutor, "is profundity's mask.") But their song, no,
they can't hold back, can't conceal it to the end; and then
every missile, every slingshot's aimed at their voice. They betray
     themselves.

During my childhood they never gave *me* a doll on my feast day.
I collected my big sister's broken dolls, glued them back together—
their arms, legs, hair, eyes. I made them new clothes,
combed them—they became beautiful, more beautiful than before. My
     sister was jealous, she took
them back from me. I felt sorry. I wasn't cross. More than anything
I was sorry for my sister. Nothing satisfied her.
                              One day
the prettiest doll lost an eye—a big, bright blue eye.

Did you ever happen to see a one-eyed doll? A hole; a chasm—
and out of it there watches us something vague, remote, yet our own.
With that very hole the doll watched me, confided in me:
it was her true eye. We became friends.
                              Years later,
after Father's great journey, I found that eye
in a black velvet box. I said nothing to my sister,
just set it in one of my rings as a ring stone. No one worked out what it
     was,
they all admired so unusual a precious stone.

Could that be why I told you—oh yes, it was all so lovely—what
     meaning

grief and joy may contain in their indivisible nothingness? what meaning
may inhabit that fortunate and indifferent landscape—no, not
     indifferent—
a boundless benign death—and perhaps when I say "benign"
I'm transferring to it my own momentary feeling toward
this evening's resplendent twilight—my God, what colors!—
or assuming my pose (my comfortable, genuine pose),
just as though it were our secret mirror, that showed us,
     incontrovertibly,
our entire face, clear, undiminished, beautiful,
almost immortal—why *almost*, though?—truly immortal.

In one big uninhabited room there'd been hanging for years
an old gilt-framed mirror. No one ever went
into that room. They just dumped there in confusion
everything worn out and useless, lamps, armchairs, candlesticks, side
     tables,
ancestral and other portraits of retired generals, poets, thinkers,
oddly shaped crystal vases, tripods, bronze braziers,
big plaster or metal masks, and small ones of black velvet,
stuffed heads of deer and wild beasts, stuffed
birds of all colors, golden and blue, with curved beaks—I never knew
     their names—
coat hangers, armor, consoles, heavy curtains
(most often purple or dark green). That was my refuge.

It smelt of moth-eaten clothing, of dust and damp. Well, the mirror,
hanging high on the wall, would collect all the light—it was
the eye of that blind labyrinthine room.
                              That eye
reigned peacefully, in kingless kingship, over uselessness and
     desolation—
made them, indeed, immortal: sacred memory amid deep forgetfulness.
     One afternoon,
late, I climbed up on a linen chest, looked in the mirror, saw nothing,
nothing, only light, a dim light, as though I myself
were compounded wholly of light. And in truth I was. I understood then
(remembered, rather) that I'd always been light. A spider
moved into the light of the mirror and over my face. I didn't flinch at all.

I wasn't the spider. A strange, most delicate body, slipping
on that glassy surface, with countless angular legs—I saw them
    magnified
with their slow-moving joints, in slow motion, slow time, almost
    motionless. Little by little
I made out my solid face, pink and dark blue, in shadow;
my eyes sea green, full of wonder, and always around me
that hazy light—I was haloed amid my heedlessness, my isolation,
my invisibility. I couldn't endure this secret
happiness, being all light, with a delicate mask of reality,
rose and dark blue. I jumped down from the linen chest,
caught up an ancient key left lying on a marble washstand,
clasped it and kissed it. And then, at the outer gate, the hunter's
horn resounded, strangely melancholy and wearied—irrevocable.

It got dark late. The mirror continued to shine on the wall.
The spider had gone. I could still perceive light shining
from inside me. All alone, at one with it, in love,
clutching the cellar key in both hands.
                            That's why
I told you how I assume the pose (my most genuine pose),
the pose of my death. That is, of death.
                            So now you know
just how privileged I was. Yes. That made me ashamed, I felt guilty,
I'm even more ashamed now that I admit it. But what privileges?

I came to know splendid futility—so serene, almost, in a way, cheerful;
I relaxed in it or on it, as on a summer haystack, watching
the evening sky, the woods, the blue hills, deeply inhaling
warm moisture, thyme, straw, the distant river,
the sweet scent of harvested wheat—not at all with the notion
of bread, water, usefulness—with the notion merely
of a general harvest, a solace, while from hill to hill,
from vine to vine, the farmers' and herdsmen's dogs bayed a dazzling
white full moon, queen of heaven, a queen with arms folded, childless.

There was a taste, I don't know, of deep blue diluted,
a taste of existent nonexistence, underlined at moments

by the movement of some bird in its sleep, a resonant stillness—
and I was wholly the silence, and part of the silence. I bit on a myrtle
     twig
to stop myself crying out. Because I felt it: my mouth opened
in vast amazement, for a great shout, and my teeth
parted, opened wide to leave free passage
for that shout. I held it back. It dissolved inside me.
This was the silence. And I was light as air—I could fly.

I remember, at Mother's funeral, a velvet-black butterfly,
with orange spots, fluttered lightly past, hovered over the bier—
ah, that secret buoyancy, it lifted the whole weight of us,
things lightened, we lightened. Then only,
even the coffin could fly—and it was heavy, laden down
with flowers and pearls; though sixty horses drew it, it still
moved slowly in the fierce sunlight. Horses and men both sweated.
     Suddenly I saw
that all decorations are heavy, even flowers. The butterfly—
black, as I said, with orange spots—shouldered the coffin and vanished.

The light had bleached everything. Only one white cloud hung quiet
on the hill, looking elsewhere—I saw that too. (Strange how you see
with such sharpness, indeed with delight, at such times.) As we returned
     home
we were met by the smell of celery, carrots, and boiled potatoes.
We ate in an angry mood, with slow, stubborn movements.

After dinner, our brother left—dogged, they declared,
by the Furies. Nothing of the sort. He took off quietly,
only a little more circumspect and somewhat hunched over. At once
the rooms expanded immensely. Not one corner for us to hide in.
     Outside,
that indescribable sunlight blazed on. The cicadas were chirring:
they got inside the house, one perched motionless
on the lace inner curtain, like a plump fluffy musical note, somehow
     discordant—
"Here, here, here," it kept calling, "here." Which "here"? I wanted
to ask. I controlled myself. Not a sound escaped me.

That day the maids talked louder, banged the doors,
stamped their feet on the floor, on the stairs (they who till then had been
    so silent),
clattered the knives and forks in the kitchen, broke a few glasses.

A beautiful yellow dress, worn by Mother the day before,
was left crumpled on a chair—a focal point
for all the light and silence. And when I went into the bathroom
her toothbrush grew and grew, till it filled the whole mirror. As I passed
    the door
it scratched my knee. I was scared it might snatch me out of my dress
and keep me shut up in the bathroom, eyes fixed on our brother's net
in the corner, the net he used to hunt butterflies as a child.
                                        Then
I went up to the mirror and tried, for the first time, to paint my lips
with that secret and sacral red stuff of Mother's. Upon my lips
a fine rueful sunset spread, a grieving scarlet brightness.

Only then could I weep—happy that tears would come.
And the toothbrush grew small again, smaller than ever. And I wept
for my mother, for her lover, for her husband,
for the little slain girl, for my other sister, the way
her eyes had gone blank in an instant—it's as though she didn't know
why she should go on living. I wept even more
at the quiet flight of my brother. As he crossed the estate boundary
he cut a small shoot of willow, tucked it through his belt, then
slowly sniffed at his fingers.
                        In that pose, as he went,
he seemed to be holding his chin to keep himself still
with his elbow propped on an invisible table. And in fact
he *did* hold still, I think. He'd move around while sitting—perhaps
because there are times, as they say, when each fresh displacement
nails us down to the selfsame spot—there's nowhere else.

I wept that day for my whole life, for the proud horses,
for all hunted dogs, for the birds, for the ants,
for the old peasant's donkey feeding quietly out in the country,
in a bone-dry yellowed field—I could see it from my window.

"Little donkey," I silently called, "little donkey—" and when I said it
I meant the whole world.
                            Then I found myself crying still harder,
maybe to make my unweeping sister hear me. The maids collected
the big warm rugs outside—I felt their red warmth, huge
and health-giving, spread through my body. My eyes dried. The world
was hot, downy, all purple—and the dead, too.

At night, in the small hours, you could hear on the road,
right below my windows, a warfarer's footsteps—
perhaps no one ever walked in that fashion under the moon
and perhaps no one had ever heard, as I heard, such footfalls.
He was the first man who ever came into the world.
He was the last to leave it. And no one had ever
come, or gone.
            As I told you,
the world was hot, downy, all purple—without one break or flaw.
Only the moon bedewed the nap of a blanket, left out on the balcony.

At first light I stole out into the garden, sat on the furthest bench
with a book in my hand, not reading it. A small strange insect
fell on the page. I pushed it out of my way. Then it turned
upside down, waving a mass of delicate legs in the air—
a whole world of infinite movement. At that instant
my sister called to me from the doorway.
                                    In the voice addressing us
there is always (you'll have noticed this)
an upside-down insect that suddenly
flips right side up, and is gone.
                        Behind it remains a certain
perplexity for us: which was its true posture? and our own?
This one, or the other, amid the leaves of sleep, dropping from on high,
    or flying?

Later a great wind blew, sweeping away
thorns, newsprint, paper lanterns, bay leaves, bridges;
doors slammed open, stood ajar. Yesterday's royal steward,
the knife still in his belly, went up the inner stairs.
Ribbons of blood striped the tiles in the corridor.

Outside, in front of the balcony, the mob was shouting, with strange
    black banners.
That huge equestrian statue suddenly fell down. Then
people scattered in terror and the place was left empty.

The next day (truly a new day) I faced the vacant square
all whitewashed with silence. Except that five eggs had been left
on the base of the ancient lamppost. A woman emerged cautiously
from the stable. She took the eggs. At once
they turned red. Said another woman, on the lookout at the window
    opposite:
"Have your hens started laying red eggs, then?" And the first one
    replied:
"They just caught the sun," and stuffed them into her apron pockets.

A handsome soldier came up the road, passed close beside them.
The two women laughed twin giggles. From the hills
the day streamed down like milk—in fact smelling of milk.
One woman went into the stable. The other shut her window. The
    soldier
had vanished into the whiteness. Those five red eggs floated in air,
bobbing slightly, as light as though they were hollow.

This I remember well. But as for the rest, what the grown-ups did,
I never understood, not a thing. They raised their hands up,
high, high, as if to support some heavy beam
that was going to fall anyway. To be sure, they regarded
this posture of theirs as majestic. They opened their mouths,
grab, gabble or wail, a hole full of darkness,
and gleaming inside it, an antique iron ladder, unsupported.

They all went away. Now I sit here and watch and forget and remember.
Everything was just fine. I need nothing—enough is as good as a feast.
I place my hands on my knees, I touch the void, I'm controlled
by the void. Now I stand erect on a splendid, tottering balcony,
held up by the rails—almost airborne. In these rails,
smooth and metallic, I grasp the seasonal changes, cold, heat,
moisture, the stars—symbolic changes. A sparrow sometimes
sits there and watches me. We're acquainted. We've nothing to say to
    each other.

CHRYSOTHEMIS · 163

I remember one afternoon—Mother had just gone out on a visit—
I went into her room, put on her shoes, still warm from her feet—
strange, that warmth—I grew taller at once, as if acknowledging
an unexplained crime. All week I didn't dare
look Mother in the eye. I hid in the garden shrubbery,
waiting for punishment or a reward, I don't know which.

Oh yes, I too was waiting. I was always the first to run
when a knock came at the door—even though it wasn't for me. The
    mailman
stood out clear in the flatlands below with his leather bag, as if
he had a square chunk of light slung above his thigh.
                                                    I waited
for a letter to come for me too. Among all those
official reports and documents and petitions, a pink envelope
with my name written on it. "Chrysothemis, Chrysothemis!"
I'd hear everyone shout in surprise. "A letter, Chrysothemis—for you!"
    Then I'd take
the letter offhandedly, shut myself into that room
as one closets oneself with God—only the two of us,
the whole world left outside, because the whole world
was God and myself, and our identical image in the antique mirror.

The other girls spent all day under the big pine trees,
a little wild from their longings and their beauty,
prancing vivaciously, laughing, hair flying wild
and flecked with those dried-out, double pine needles,
wearing crazy eardrops of cherries (the spots of light that flickered
on the old room's walls and mirrors might have been from
the roundness of their knees), while I, forgotten, alone,
proud with a heavenly pride, read over and over
the letter I'd written myself. (Isn't that what always happens?)

How hard it is to find words—don't you think? Our genuine speech
is addressed to ourselves alone, or, at the very least, we are
the only ones to hear it correctly. Everything else
is minor or major excuses, haggling, masquerade.

When darkness fell, I'd go down the inside stairs as though down a well,
with that invisible light from the mirror all round my head,

164 • CHRYSOTHEMIS

spilling down to my feet too—that's how I saw to walk—
the flowerpots beside the staircase glowed too. In the dining room
they'd already lighted the lamps. That was lucky. My own light didn't
    show at all.
All that talking, the glint of knives, and hunger—where can you hide
    from it?

Night spread thick-leaved over the house, all aglitter
with dewdrops and stars. A horse vanished into the distance
that was blue slashed with silver. The mirrors closed. In bed
I dreamed of sleeping herdsmen. Their cheeks
rested on their flutes. When they woke
they'd have a red furrow there like the scar from a wound
got in far-off and secret combat. The herdsmen, being alone,
always looked handsome to me; those who are solitary
dream, and we dreamed them too, high up on the hills, in the bushes,
unseen, free from watching eyes—alone, we and they together.

Only love, they say, and beauty somehow withstand time—
though what either means I don't know—something like
a light touch on the neck.
                     At midday, in summer,
I'd gaze out from the window at the low hill nearby. Upon it
the hunters, come down from the forest, devoured huge watermelons;
their teeth gleamed as they bit into the red flesh—
gleamed so bright that I stubbornly squeezed my skirt
between my knees. Afterward the black seeds lay waiting to dry
on the earth, under broiling sunlight,
like scraps of a beautiful night—scattered ashes
from hidden conflagrations, tiny black tokens
of a peaceful, tender repentance before the offense.

At times an unexplained smile floats in the air. One late afternoon, in
    the garden,
bent over my needlework, reckoning the pointlessness of events,
even this stitching of mine (yet not ceasing to stitch),
suddenly my hands and eyes flooded with light: two enormous feet,
youthful, unshod, with well-trimmed nails, had passed
there right in front of me. Our young gardener

was sweeping the fallen leaves away. I never raised my eyes—
the image of those bare feet, that broom, sufficed me.

Each day leaves us something for the night. Sleep's difficult sometimes
if you lack something good to set against the darkness that awaits you.
    Now
only the statues are there still at my disposal—intact too, naked,
    unlaurelled,
or those distant trumpeters up on the walls, standing tall, inscribed
on the evening sky's gold and purple—that's more than a little.

Hence my thanksgiving, my prayer before sleep,
and good sleep, and fine waking, and a good death,
may it come easily. I've no complaint. We're acquainted,
we've long been friends. I owe death the most:
the conscious awareness of life—I mean the lack of all conscious
    awareness. We learn it late, late—
the brush of a peaceful wing—and the wing imbued with height
(or so at least we say)—excuses, changes, sad tricks.

Would you like me to put on the lights? It seems to have grown rather
    dark.
We've kept our old-fashioned oil lamps here in the house—
we're used to them, you see, and attached to them, even though
I rejoice in new things—they allow me to see,
amid all the changes, what we call the immutable element. I
have great fun with improvements in hats, clothes, umbrellas, cars,
cellos, cooking, jails, airships—oh my God,
the fine, the inexorable change that's no change—and no one makes a
    decision.

Oil lamps, candlesticks, lanterns have been replaced by
electric light—convenience, inconvenience. At night
I gaze at the far-off town with its big polychrome billboards;
sometimes I snuff the lamp, let my room be illuminated
by the distant glow from outside—now blue or yellow or violet,
now orange or rose—a strange room, with strange light,
and I'm a stranger too, familiar with what's remote, inaccessible, with
    that most profound

understanding of the serene, universal alien realm, like a mystical
    friendship
with everyone, everything—since nothing now touches us
and, naturally, cannot offend us—a divine illusion.

And my room, a violet-gold ship, riding through the night,
and I all alone on board, not distressed in the slightest—
no helm, no oar—knowing the uselessness (and indeed the danger)
of helm and oar and compass.
                                        I remember
that landmark night—the eve of the murder: my brother
stood for a moment outside, on the turn of the marble steps,
silently watching the sky, his head elegantly tilted:
"Maybe," he said, "the stars are nothing but our oars—yet even them
we can't control, so how could *he*?" I took his meaning at once.
My big sister didn't. She gave him the sword from under her apron.

Well, so we didn't put electricity in the house. We kept the lamps,
they were more to our liking, the smoked-up glass, the smell of oil,
a comforting warmth, big shadows on ceiling and wall. Sometimes
we hang one of Mother's old hairpins on the glass
so it won't crack. Then the hairpin looks, to me,
like a tiny horseman complete with steel cuirass
astride his glass horse, on a stormy night.
                                        Everything of my mother's
gave me this impression of armor—why *armor*, really?
She too left us, an ax in the side like her second wing.

Later the big mice came, rust, moths, and termites—
in time they grew bold, openly gnawed the woodwork, the walls,
the fabrics, the door bolts—you couldn't keep anything.
So we abandoned the place to them, to us it made no difference,
not even their nonstop crunching. It was precisely then
we discovered the untamed element in total surrender.
                                        Giant rats
squatted in the big storage jars, drank the oil, climbed to the ceiling,
ate the wicks out of the lanterns, voraciously nibbled
our shoes right under our beds.

                              And there were moments
when you thought people were traipsing about below, down in the
        basement,
while we, high above, kept still, above the ridiculous bustle,
above the fear of decay, as though indestructible, perfect.

One night, a rat climbed up on my bed, maybe planning
to gnaw at my hand. I met its eye, almost with fellow feeling.
It flinched from my gaze, turned, fled. In the end
even the rats left us alone—not because they'd no more to eat
but because we weren't frightened of them. Though once, I recall, my
        sister
stood for a long time at her mirror, well after midnight,
carefully combing her hair. Then she gathered it all up
and put on a helmet of Father's. She slept like that, wearing the helmet.

I pretended I was asleep. She still said to me: "You know,
I'm afraid they'll devour my hair—and all bald women look like
those madhouse patients with shaven heads. No, no, I couldn't stand
        that—,"
and at once she resembled Father. After a little while
she took the helmet off again, laid it down on a chair, fell asleep.
The candle flame flickered green on the helmet's surface.

In time everything retreated, like the mice, the flatterers, the servants,
the waves of the sea above all. Nothing left but a whiff of salt,
the smell of an era, with us, without us—what does it matter?—
that salt in the bread, in the water, in the air—
what we call freedom, though not knowing what we're searching for,
        what it is.

This was just what my big sister couldn't stand. One afternoon
she squeezed into the chimney, got covered with soot—arms, face,
        legs—
then stood in front of the mirror and looked at herself. "Aiee," she
        lamented,
"burnt out and burnt to cinders; mourning black triple-blackened," and
        shed black tears,
really black from the soot. I had no idea what to do;
I took a piece of red silk and cut it in strips. Then, at once,

she fell silent, stared out of the window, almost calm,
tying a scarlet rag around her forehead.

"The sun's a red monarch," she said. "My God, what a red!
Well, we all get by, find peace." And suddenly the evening
blazed up red, with deep blue and green streaks. I crossed to the
    window. In the garden,
under a chair, I could see some outsize sandals,
really huge, and bright purple—none of ours. On the hills
the evening bells had begun to ring. A maidservant ran down
from the eucalyptus trees, hiding something in her bosom. And night
    fell.

So the years passed (how passed? I never noticed them) and I
always marginal to events. Can I say that I *am*, having lived
while not living, so many countless lives, and my own life? Except that
    once,
when my big sister was being punished for her stubbornness,
I took food and water to her in secret.
                                        I was delighted
to be able to take care of someone, that someone had need of me. I
    enjoyed
the whole business of preparation, the secrecy, the danger. I didn't make
    it.

They caught me outside the door. They punished me as well.
It was a private joy to be punished for someone and for something—
that I, my own punisher always, should at last be found worthy
of punishment for an action—I was so proud of this.
From then on I saw things, and myself, in a clear relation to others. I
    remember
being shut in a room and counting the buttons on my dress,
and there were five of them—I'd not known—a beautiful 5—I saw it
writ large on the wall—and there, precisely, were my five fingers
    counting.

As for Mother, poor thing, she was never punished, she only
inflicted punishment (I think that only the punished
have time and means to reflect; only the punished

really grow up—best not to show it—preserving right to the end
all the stages of their growth).

My hapless mother
paid for everything at one stroke. I never saw her cry
or beg for anything. Only in that last moment her darkening eyes,
failing, were huge, confused, beautiful, as though they'd suddenly
     grasped
all the meaning of life, the futility of all power whatsoever,
perhaps the whole meaning of beauty—unattainable always, yet lived.

"The perception of beauty"—I remember our tutor saying—"is always
     bound up
with the idea of futility." And only beauty, I think, can hold out
against all that's futile, inexplicable, minus all hope
of vindication or resurrection. Ah, that noble unselfishness! My sister
couldn't stand the inexplicable. Maybe that's why she went crazy.
     Except
that during her last years she plunged into knitting—vests, socks,
gloves, scarves—not because she was cold, she never wore any of them,
just filled an entire chest, that she sat on in the evenings,
hunched up, arms folded. Oh, maybe she *was* cold. But she didn't wear
     them.

Once, during her illness, when her stock of yarn had run out,
she unstitched an old, worn-out, linen coverlet,
thread by thread, snipped it knot by knot, and fashioned with her needle
a marvellous prize of patience, a little napkin—she gave it to me—
(despite her failing reason, she'd remembered it was my birthday).

I never received a more priceless gift. I still keep it by me. And truly,
each beautiful thing has an endless prehistory, countless invisible knots,
and a tiny needle of patience with fingers endlessly pricked. Perhaps
the other vision of beauty is holiness, who knows? I've learned nothing.

All gone. Nothing left but this boundless calm. I wonder:
did I really exist? all those faces, all strange, all mine, all loved—
my very own face. And this marvellous sense, on occasion,
that nothing's been lost, nothing's been lost. Are you listening?

They're shutting the shops down there in the market. I love
the rattle of keys and padlocks, of steel shutters. "Finis, finis,
finis," the keys seem to call, from door to door,
from hill to hill, year to year, these brazen messengers—
a finish to trade and exchange, don't you think?
                                    In the background
the hills are turning blue. A rosy cloud still rests
above the gardens. Someone carefully climbs
a wooden ladder, comes out on the flat roof, looks about him. Up there
the moon's out already, beside a glass
forgotten last night on the parapet.
                              Always the moon
reminds us of this glass—sometimes full of milk,
sometimes full of water, ice-cold or tepid, or at other times
filled with a strange yellow liquid, in which have been dissolved
two or three strong white sleeping tablets—one sends
a trail of tiny bubbles up from the bottom,
a fine plume of invisible, silent triumph—a murmur, my God—
of sweet sleep's approaching, dreamless, the final sleep.

The years have passed indeed. I've grown much lighter—heavier, too. I
    rejoice
at this lightness, this heaviness. A huge smile
raises me by the armpits, I'm not touching ground—I'm ashamed
that someone might see me roaming the garden like a bird. I'm
    ashamed
of this childish lightness of mine. I settle here at the window
with rain and sunshine. I still haven't had my fill of looking.

Spring mornings I rise very early, at a time when the whole
world around us is shining calm, with the sweet sorrow
that's as pointless and blameless as life itself. The faintest hum
from a bee's wing casts an enormous shadow over the whole length
of this translucency. Other times, I'll sit and listen to the cicadas,
those mad dwarf drummers, all around the embrasures,
at the blinding height of noon—their voices
leave no gaps at all: they plug up the very cracks in the walls. Down
    there
the plain with its wheat-ears gleams in a golden breathlessness.

So, I've not had my fill. I still can daydream watching
a cloud in the west, a strange cloud, as though made from tiny pocket
     mirrors—
it reflects its light in my eyes, won't let me be serious, although
I can sense, behind all that brightness, the coming of night, although
there's a diffuse taste in the air of ashes and ground cinnamon.

In autumn I like to watch the faded trams rounding the bend
beside the maternity clinic; long sullen afternoons, naked trees,
and the voices of children down in the playground, so wistful
and at the same time so unsuspecting.
                            Through the western window
there's a view of the cemetery and its statues behind the olive grove—
marble youths, marble birds, marble angels with vast wings,
while above them flare and fade the rainbow fires of the west.

Until evening comes, and the statues peacefully whiten—a distant
     whiteness,
soothing, consoling; and night draws on, transforms it
into a nacreous blue, striped with rose. Out there too
is the figurine of the slaughtered maiden, small as a tooth
that gave you much pain, was extracted, and hurts you no more. At
     midnight
I hear a tablecloth flapping against a garden table.

A ship sails into the mirror. A rope ladder
hangs from the dining room chandelier. You can feel
the moisture falling on the park benches, the lichen
spreading gradually over the statues. And then peace returns again.

I have nothing left to wait for. My end is here. Only, up there,
from the shut-off women's quarters, there comes at night the unceasing
clack of the loom shuttle, weaving something (can't you hear it?)—
an endless fabric, with vague patterns, for some vague time,
for vague secret expectations. It could be a forgotten old crone
weaving the last trousseau, for me, the old maid; or again,
maybe it's I myself, waiting for—what?—I don't know.

Ah yes, I waited for someone, once, to come and take
that cloth and its secret weaving—or for me to lay it

upon his knees, as, now, I offer you these words,
as though that alone has meaning.

 Dear friend, I've exhausted you,
and I too am exhausted. Forgive me. Now I can go,
happily weary, with no dreams and no desires,
only that boundless and wonderful urge to seek forgiveness
from all people and things.

 Forgive, forgive, forgive me
in my triviality, whose grounds for pride in achievement
are—nothing. Only this sheer elation in seeking
your pardon—I thank you—and my own final forgiveness
for myself—long prepared, and perhaps even justified.

*It has become dark. Silence. The young woman journalist, clearly
moved, collects her papers. All she says, however, is "forgive me, I've
exhausted you," like a remote echo, and makes a move as though to kiss
the Lady's hand. But the Lady tactfully withdraws it. A pause, and then
the scratch and flame of a match, in a boundless, noiseless void. The
Lady lights the candlestick, and moves towards the stairs. "Forgive me,"
the journalist says again, and tucks the file containing the typewritten
interview under one arm—confident that it had hit the right personal
note. As she goes through the garden, she trips against something long
and soft, and shudders, remembering the rats. In fact it is a length of
rubber hose for watering. The garden benches are bright with moisture
that reflects the starlight. A deep, infinite sky. Private, exhausted
happiness.*

*The aged Lady died on the day the interview was published. Two closed
carriages followed her bier—three elderly relatives, the old gardener,
and the young woman journalist, clutching her paper.*

*In fact the interview made a great impression. It was reprinted as a
separate pamphlet and ran into several editions. Now, very often, on
spring or summer afternoons, you can see young couples or old maids or
even soccer players placing a bunch of violets or a few wildflowers on
her grave, alongside the big official wreaths set there every so often by
various artistic, academic, philanthropic, or political organizations.*

*One morning they found the old gardener lying dead on the stone steps
of the tomb. He was clutching a few white roses, the birdcage with its*

canaries, and a violet umbrella. It seems likely that he had brought the umbrella to keep his Lady's statue from being rained on. The evening before the first rains of the year had fallen, and there were still a few drops of moisture on his cheeks.

GYAROS, LEROS, SAMOS, MAY 1967–JULY 1970

· PERSEPHONE ·

She has returned, as every summer, from the strange dark region, to her
large family home in the country—very pale, as if tired from the journey,
as if sick from the great difference in climate, light, warmth. Something
resembling a layer of protective shadow still covers her face and hands.
She lies stretched out on the old sofa, in a spacious, freshly whitewashed
room, on the upper floor, with the shutters closed on the three windows
and the balcony door. Even so, the glare of the sun shines intensely on
the walls in flickering strips of light. On the floor, a pile of baskets, full
of wildflowers, like those she didn't have time to take with her, then, on
her first sudden journey. We may assume that, shortly before, her
girlfriends have brought them to her as a welcoming gift. Now, only one
young girl remains beside her, wearing a light blue dress, a blue ribbon
in her hair—perhaps her most faithful, devoted friend, the water nymph
Cyane. Next to the sofa, on a chair, a plate of cool water. Her friend,
every so often, moistens in it an embroidered batiste handkerchief,
squeezes it, and places it gently on the traveller's forehead, covering her
eyebrows. Now and then, a drop rolls slantwise down her cheek to wet
the wide multicolored pillow—almost as if she were crying with
another's tears. And her hair is a little damp. Outside, one can barely
hear the sea—calm, smooth—and sometimes a swimmer's voice. Then
the sunlight in the room intensifies. The traveller speaks:

It's true, I tell you—I was fine over there. I've grown used to it. It's here
    I can't bear it;
there's so much light—it makes me sick—naked, harsh light;
it reveals everything, conceals everything; it changes so often—you can't
    keep up; you change;
you sense time slipping away—an endless, wearisome movement;
glasses shatter in the move, are left behind in the street, sparkle;
some people jump ashore, others board the boats—just as when
our visitors came, went, and others came;
their big suitcases sat for a little while on the sidewalk—
a strange smell, strange places, strange names—the house
was not our own—it too was a suitcase containing new underclothing,
    unfamiliar to us—
someone could pick it up by the leather handle and slip away.

We were glad then, certainly. A move then
seemed somehow to be a move upward—something was always
    happening;

and for all that we feared even then that it would be lost, we did not yet
     know
the secret sally of the boat from the other side of the horizon
or of the swallow and the wild goose from the other side of the hill.

The glasses, plates, forks shone on the table,
golden and blue from the reflection of the sea. The tablecloth,
white, well-ironed, was a shining plane; it had
no creases at all in which other meanings, other conjectures could take
     refuge. Now
this light is unbearable—it distorts everything, shows everything up
in its distortion; and the sound of the sea
is wearisome, with its unstable boundlessness, its fleeting colors,
its changing moods. And these ridiculous boatmen
with their pants rolled up, soaking wet, getting angry at you;
and the swimmers, like coal merchants, daubed with sand,
laughing, apparently pleased, shouting only to be heard
as if their own voices were not enough.

                              Over there
no one dives into the water; no one shouts. The three rivers,
ashen, disdainful, as they converge around the great rock,
make an altogether different noise—intense, uniform—
that fixed sound of eternal flux—you get used to it;
you almost don't hear it.

                         When my mother's brother first came to the house
he had an ashen tinge, like those rivers. He had taken sick suddenly.
They put him in the big bed, took him cupping glasses (I believe he had
     caught a chill
from the bright light and the heat)—I remember his back,
dark-skinned, broad, powerful, like a grassy pasture. We were afraid
the hairs would catch fire—the candle was so near,
the candle was white on the silver candlestick. Afterward they set it
on his marble washstand. The room smelled of burnt cotton.
His clothing, still warm, was thrown on the chair. I watched
the candle drip big drops of wax onto the marble.

                                   My uncle
caught my eye. I was ashamed. I wanted to run. I couldn't.

He had turned on his back, put on his undershirt,
and although his chest was dark and his shirt pure white
you still had the impression that an all-black curtain
had covered something very light and dangerous. So my
uncle, with the sheet pulled up to his chin,
smiled beautifully from out of his fever. Beneath the sheet
I could make out his two powerful feet, like roots. I left the room.
I didn't see him again that visit. I went back to the fields.

                                        Three months later
he sent to Mother, from a foreign land, a pile of his old clothes
for the poor. I recognized his body at once. They left one pair of pants
for several days on a hanger in the corridor. I looked at them
for hours at a time, touched them with my hands; I thought of stealing
     them,
of hiding them under my bed, of putting them on. I was afraid. One day,
I stood a chair there, climbed up on it, buried my face in them and
     smelled them.
I fell off the chair. I was frightened. I wasn't hurt. The noise brought
     people running.
I didn't say anything. I felt no pain. Only a taste of deep sin.

They gave those pants to one of our servants.
They fit him perfectly. Servants (you will have noticed)
have a strange, idiosyncratic way about them, their own life, altogether
     apart,
close and conspiratorial, despite all the mute devotion they show,
especially despite all their deference; something hostile and voracious
in their eyes, on their lips, and, above all, in their hands,
strong, hard, adroit, self-confident,
heavy, coarse, like bear paws,
slow to obey, yet nevertheless so nimble, when they rubbed down the
     horses,
harnessed the carriage or cut up an ox,
or nailed together a table or dug the garden—

My God, how slow-witted, how ignorant—and they don't even know
     how handsome they are
with their coarse, sweaty skin, absorbed in their work
amid hammers, nails, saws—a pile of tools

with unknown names—terrifying in their usefulness,
terrifying in their secretiveness, or rather their conspiring,
wood and complex ironwork, honed blades gleaming—

And they all have about them a heavy odor of still water and pine
or milk of figs. They never unbutton in front of us,
not even one shirt button. They never laugh. But you know
that left to themselves they go naked, joke, wrestle
on summer afternoons, in the rooms below.
                                        One day I saw them
through the keyhole. One was asleep, stretched out on the bed;
the others silently stripped him, painted his member with soot,
in stripes, like an erect snake. He woke up, chased after them;
they ran under the arches, around the columns, laughing
great guffaws of unforgettable laughter.
                              I was terrified. I took to my heels. My God,
those stripes, light and dark in turn, like an endless vertical tunnel,
something closed and treacherous. I was suffocating. And I wanted to
      scream. I didn't scream.
I went up the stairs two by two—the staircase hummed, cool, shady,
and outside I could hear the golden sunshine and the boatmen's voices,
far, far away, and dark, like the hair in a male armpit. I was suffocating.
I ran upstairs, to the big room, opened the balcony door;
an odor of pitch and carob reached me, an odor of redness;
Mother's dog was asleep in the shade of the big medlar tree
with its muzzle propped on its two front paws. I shut the door again.

Perhaps because of that I finally chose the shade. Darkness is black—
black, glossy, unchangeable, without variations. You escape
from the effort of making distinctions—but to what?
                                        That servant
was as though created from darkness. When *he* seized me—
      remember?—
we were gathering flowers in a big meadow. Baskets full
of crocuses, violets, lilies, roses, amaranth, hyacinths—I had bent
over a strange flower—it was like a narcissus—a narcissus
never before seen, with a hundred colors, with a hundred stalks;
on it dewdrops sparkled. And I was dazzled there,
bent over as if doubled within myself, as if leaning over a well,
to see my form (almost self-sufficient), I was in love

with the rosy shadow on the edge of my lips,
with the fine-skinned, ivory hollow between my breasts.

Above my back the sunlight snapped like a flag;
it burned my hair; thousands of the most delicate stars twinkled,
one on each strand of my hair, with five-pointed colors. I saw them
in the cool water (or in that narcissus? I do not know), countless
they sparkled around my face, as if I had caught fire and wanted
to fall into my watery image to quench the flames.

                                        And suddenly
I saw, rearing in front of my eyes, his two black horses
as if blinded by the light (I saw them, too, in the water). I cried out,
not from fear but from wonder, as if that flower had swallowed me,
as if I had fallen into the well, as if I had suddenly taken in one leap all
    the stairs
down to the servants' rooms; and I felt on my naked sole
the splendid glissade of the lower hemisphere. I barely had time
to see them fall into this chasm—your baskets of flowers,
the garden fountain, the stone lion, the bronze tortoise.

I remember an austere internal density, and above it
I heard you all calling my name;
and my name was strange; and my friends were strange;
strange the upper light with the square, pure white houses,
the fleshy, multicolored fruits, pretentious and insolent,
the delicate, greedy stoma of the corn. I wasn't afraid at all.

I scarcely felt the loss—only at the edge of my lips,
which suddenly grew dry—they could not shape sound or the
    articulation of sound,
only the distant, dark freedom, the meeting—
body with body—I and it—one inwardness with another—an incredible
    body.

And then I felt his arm coiled around my waist—
rough, hairy, muscular—to overcome my resistance—what resistance?—
I was not I—no fear of humiliation, then; everything
had become fixed in an infinite clarity
of consummate impossibility.

"Are you afraid?" he said to me
(how weak the most powerful are—they are always afraid—
perhaps we do not fear them as much as we should—the handsome
    ones, unsuspecting
in their childish arrogance). "Yes," I told him, "I'm afraid,"
and he pressed me closer to him, so that I felt the hairs on his arm
enter into my pores as if I were bound to his body
by thousands of delicate roots—not confined at all, since I had been
    freed.

There, the houses are underground, the rivers underground, the sky
    underground;
a few poplars only, ash-gray in the underground garden,
black cypresses, sterile willows, wild mint,
and some pomegranates.
                    He washed a pomegranate for me with his own hands.
His fingers grew still blacker. The pomegranate seeds gleamed dazzlingly
like glass phials filled with blood. He fed me from his palm
amid the great jars and the stone stools, lest I forget
and not return to him again. How could I not return? This sea
shakes its glitter at you, splinters of glass in your eyes, your mouth,
your shirt, your sandals.
                    "Keep me,"—I said to him—
"let me be only one—even half—the whole half (whichever it is),
not two, separate and unmingled, for nothing is left to me
but to be the cut—that is, not to be—
only a vertical knife-slash and pain to the core—",
nor will even the knife be your own. "I can't resist," I said to him—
    "keep me."

He is the great, dark certainty—the only one. Always gloomy,
with his heavy eyebrows concealing his eyes,
so erect, and yet as though stooped over,
shut into himself, inside his hairiness, almost invisible,
biting a leaf or smoking his clay pipe
and the small flame lights up his nostrils from below
like a far-off flash of lightning in a deserted fleshy landscape,
an absorbent landscape—it absorbs me.
                            On the blind wall of the underworld
two bronze rings were hung. They shone

182 • PERSEPHONE

with a secret light, blackish green—perhaps someone was stripped here
or some handsome young man strung up. I liked to see them—
two holes to nowhere—I took my fill of them.

                                    Remember
that statue we stared at one afternoon in high school,
decorated with gold, silver, lead, bronze, and tin,
painted a dark color (now I realize how much it looked like him)—
I think it was a Serapis—the work of Bryaxis the Athenian—
ah, *he* knew a thing or two. We loved it, with the laurel wreath on its
        forehead,
so handsome, with a superb weariness diffused throughout the body
like the victor in the pentathlon who appears after the contests,
naked, just before he goes to the bath, in a close circle of his friends
(victors always have few friends, or none).

                                    He was standing
somewhat at a loss in the midst of his victory, not knowing how to
        respond,
obliging and unapproachable. Then a cloud, rosy, I think,
obscured the whole amphitheatre. His large thumbnail
slowly widened (I watched, but kept it to myself; I didn't tell you)
like an uninhabited shore, spilling over with
the infinite melancholy of heroes. And there, on one bench,
was an empty lemonade bottle, reflecting
with apparent intimacy something rigorous and completed.
It is strange, now, to speak and to hear my voice. Before, I was afraid
I would give myself away. Only to myself I said, repeated
slowly, deeply, his name. At night I would call to him silently
"Nocturnal One, Nocturnal One," turned toward the wall.

                                    How is it
that they all came together, down there, under the low sky, where
        sometimes
the sound of a bird pierces through?—the servant, the statue, my
        uncle—
all silent, of flesh and shadow.

                            Here, an odor of warm resin
and burning barley pursues you. Islands, scattered
in the brightness of the sea, always have something to enhance you,
take from you, or forbid you. Here, the noontimes
are like dead spas, congealed in light. A frenzied woman

runs naked, crying out amid the whitewashed, locked-up houses,
in the yellow air, and the sea shines like marble
with masts and motionless flags. The woman runs
madly—now her passionate cry can be heard on the hill,
and now the sound of her panting, here, outside the shutters.

                                                        Over there
nothing disturbs the silence. Only a dog (and he doesn't bark),
an ugly dog, *his*, dark, with crooked teeth,
and two large, ambiguous eyes, trusting and strange,
dark like wells in which you cannot discern
your face, your hands, or his face.
                                        And yet
you *can* distinguish the darkness, total, dense and transparent,
complete, consoling, sinless. He pretends he doesn't see you
but he smells everything, unerringly.
                                    When I dream
I suddenly feel his breath steaming under my chin
or across my temples, as if to track my thoughts,
fears, desires (and I, too, see them). I feel all my movements,
even the quietest and most simple—when I comb my hair, when I
        wash—
reverberate in the pool of his breathing
making endless circles down to that great depth,
as unfathomable as nonbeing. Every word unspoken,
every gesture postponed, goes into his own space,
his own sovereignty—he inhales them.
                                        Sometimes,
when I walk absentmindedly in the garden, beneath the poplars,
or wash a shirt in the stone basin,
or let my hand rest on my bosom,
or hold a flower, with a solitary tenderness all my own,

I feel suddenly naked, nailed to the wall,
or to the trunk of a tree, or the metal mirror at the entrance—
there above all, to the mirror, doubly nailed,
doubly visible, with no hiding place, without a leaf,
in a condensed transparency, illuminated from within and from without
by the two searchlights of his breathing, blasted
from his narrow, suspicious nostrils,

his prophetic, sensitive, sacred nostrils.
                                "Go away, go away,"
I told him once, nailed there, furious,
in an indefinable guilt and innocence, not having
anything more to hide—free in my weakness. Only my hair
swarmed over from here to there, entered, emerged from
his nostrils, like roots perpetually in motion, casting light
all around me like feathers and waves. I watched it. It gave me back
a different pride—my own—an independence
in the face of the dog and his master.
                                And besides
from whom, and for whom, did he guard me? For his master perhaps?
    For me? One evening, in the garden
he jumped up and squeezed me at the waist with his front paws. On my
    right thigh
there remained something damp, tepid. Then I was afraid. And indeed
the great snake stood erect before me, with its tongue out. Perhaps
it was from that he guarded me? From whom, and for whom, did he
    guard me?

The stain is still there, on my thigh, gleaming, milky,
like new skin closing over a wound. Ejaculate, maybe,
or perhaps a tear? Dogs, too, weep—I know it—to that extent
    sometimes
I pity him—when he looks at his ugliness in the river
at evening, by moonlight; when, docile, he lets me thread in his rough
    coat
flowering asphodel, daisies, mint—so ridiculous
in his clumsy servility—he takes on something of human weakness.
                                But surely he too
was once vanquished by man? They dragged him out into the light, they
    mocked him;
a crowd of children and evil old men looked him over—right at midday,
right in the middle of the road—his dark muzzle, his crooked teeth,
his dusty black coat, where one of my daisies
still remained.
                I don't want him banished.
He too is a companion—always he lies in wait for me,
obliging me to lie in wait for myself, to find myself.

Up here, a jumble of voices and reflections, from opposite sides,
    summon you, divide you,
as when we used to go to the stadium—remember? scorching
    afternoons,
hot marble—it burned our feet; the benches were shimmering; we didn't
    know
which one of all those naked bodies to single out—an endless tension;
our eyes got huge, encircling our faces
straining to see in a circle, around the bodies. They held the javelins
    poised;
one foot jerked in the air; the discus gleamed;
thousands of flying soles glittered; a chest dripped with sweat,
panting, breasted the tape—you couldn't catch him.

We're never equal to our desires. Desire isn't enough. What remains is
weariness, resignation—a felicitous near-loss of will,
sweat, distraction, heat. Until, finally, night comes
to erase everything, to mingle it with one solid, incorporeal body, your
    own,
to blow damp from the pinewoods or down from the sea,
to submerge the light, to submerge ourselves.
                                        Outside the window
you can hear the strolling violinist pass, the lame lamplighter,
those silent, slow wayfarers holding in their hands
oak boxes tied with red bands, and the others
fallen face down, striking the ground with both palms.

You can hear, too, the horses in the stable, and water falling,
as when worshippers lift up two clay vessels,
one to the east and one to the west, pouring hydromel
or barley water infused with wild mint
over a grave with laurel, as they murmur
ambiguous words, prayers and exorcisms. And Mother's voice
saying something about "pure golden grain, harvested in silence." Nor
    does night
refresh—an endless passageway, secretive,
with monstrous statues, painted curtains, masks, mirrors,
optical illusions, metal objects, crystals, doors, rocks,

one in darkness, the next in light—the stairway the same,
one step golden, the next black.
                              "Rend her," I said to him.
And the three women always there, with rounded backs,
with covered faces, bent over the empty well,
speaking incomprehensible words; and the echoes multiplying
their inexplicable voices from out of the well. I can't bear it here any
     longer.

This light is resurrection, death. Draw the curtains.
Vast, implacable, inimical summer. The sun
seizes you by the hair, dangles you over an abyss. Who or what defines
     me?
Does he? His dog? Mother? Each one
for some purpose of his own that concerns me, and that I do not know.

Endless days. Darkness comes late. And night is like day—it doesn't hide
     you.
The sea sparkles brilliantly, even at midnight, rosy or golden green.
The salt grinds, crusting the rocks. A boatman
pisses into the sea from his caïque. The sound can be heard
amid a muted groaning of hawsers
tied to metal grapples—a tug-of-war
between water and land in the same landing place. Above the shore
the road runs between two rows of dusty oleanders. A thorn
trembles deeply in the field, like a column capital ready to fall.
The whine of a mosquito shifts around the room
giving erratic signals, describing swift rhombuses,
exhausting your attention with acute and obtuse angles. The air
smells strongly of resin and sperm. You can't breathe.

After midnight, footsteps are heard, perhaps the servants; someone
tossing old iron castoffs at the far end of the garden. Little by little
the nettles choke them—an aluminum plate, a spoon,
a broken figurine, a zinc table. With the beginning of autumn
they appear again—the wheel, an oar, the tiller,
that axle from the old-fashioned wagon—things of memory,
our own things, useless, ill-treated, rusty,
and yet almost round still, like buried jars or like stars.

Then comes a great calm—soft, gentle, moist,
reaching beyond the garden to the peak of memory, as if autumn had
    suddenly arrived.
Somewhere, in the background, sharp blows can be heard, in distant
    woodworkers' shops,
as of nailing long planed planks. The underclothes
spread out in the dust of the courtyard take a long time to dry.

That's the time when hares come down to the road. Their eyes gleam
in the lights of the last wagons. A great stillness,
level, spread out—you can't fold it;
one corner of it's moistened in the river,
the second is lifted southward, out beyond, toward the sea,
the third disappears in the island opposite, in the woods,
the fourth in the moon with its yellow grasses.

Things are beautiful in autumn. I can breathe. The sun loses
its sovereignty, its terrible arrogance. Everything calms down;
everything turns in on itself, so much so that I think
death is our own truest self. The western star
rises higher, crystalline, translucent; it glitters
auspiciously over the black woods, like a tiny
drop of the purest water, shining
very near, as if pasted to the windowpane, yet at the same time
infinitely distant—a white gleam, a tear
filtered, entirely clear, a self-contained and joyful emptiness—
a silent, deep certainty of the end and the whole.

Then is the time for me to return to his side, almost set free—
or rather to find freedom in his shadow. Draw the curtains. Look—
a bee has settled, motionless, on my ring,
still humming—do you hear it?—a sounding ring-stone.

So, close the curtains. I can't bear it here any longer.
This light pierces me with a thousand arrows,
it blinds my eyes. I can't bear it. Draw the curtains, I tell you.

*Her friend does get up to draw the curtains. But she herself starts up
from the sofa. The damp handkerchief falls to the floor. She reaches the
window in two steps, grasps the cord, and stands there, hand raised.*

Then, suddenly, she opens the shutters wide. She stays that way, in the blinding light, like a statue slowly coming to life. She moves her hand, gestures toward the outside. A boatful of young swimmers passes. They call out, greeting her. On the shore road, shimmering from the heat, a large black dog passes (maybe that *one?) holding in his teeth a basket of multicolored fruit. He looks vaguely toward the window, as if blind. A handsome, sunburnt swimmer, passing beside him, kicks him in the belly with his bare foot. The girl at the window laughs. The dog goes on his way. The young girl turns back in, rings the bell. A servant, with gray and black striped pants, which fit him very well (perhaps her uncle's), appears at the door. "Set the table," she tells him. He goes away. The two friends open the balcony door and the other two windows. The room is flooded with light. The flowers in the baskets smell sweet. The sounds of the sea are more clearly audible, mingled with the clatter of plates and cutlery below in the dining room. The damp handerchief remains on the floor like a small, secretive white bird, tame, perhaps, and obedient. Little by little it dries and the dampness evaporates.*

ATHENS, ELEUSIS, DHIMENIO, SAMOS, DECEMBER 1965–DECEMBER 1970

· ISMENE ·

*A young officer of the guard has asked to be received by the Lady of
the Palace. His father, who has worked on the palace estate since
boyhood, has become something very like the man of the house. Now,
old and ill, he is sending his son, with a basket of fruit and a pot of basil,
to convey his respects, and his farewell, to the last surviving scion of the
great family. Permission granted. The young officer, in his well-fitting
uniform, is vigorous, handsome, with that bright Greek warmth
characteristic of his country origin, but also with a clear if indefinable
sensuousness—doubtless developed through his contacts with city folk
during off-duty hours away from the barracks. He appears personally
touched, flattered, almost erotically aroused in the presence of this
aristocratic lady who, though heavily made up and tightly corseted, still
preserves the faint charm of a remote and burnt-out beauty. He
awkwardly deposits basket and pot on the floor, as though the gesture
were somehow unbecoming, and passes on his father's message. She
offers him a chair, facing the window. She asks after his father's health,
and about the estate. He talks nonstop about life in the fields, about
crops, trees, watercourses, horses, cows. Though less than attentive, she
affects tremendous interest in everything, eyes fixed on his strong,
clumsy hands, now resting on his knees. It is a fine late afternoon in
spring. The light that enters by the open window is pale pink. Later it
changes to orange, violet, purple, midnight blue. Birds can be heard in
the garden. Now and then a reflection from the heavy jewelry she wears
catches the furniture, the big mirror, the windows, or the young man's
face. Suddenly he falls silent. Night is closing in. An unexplained lull, an
expectant pause. Perhaps because of that she now begins to speak, as
though filling the void—or to fend off the approach of something
indecorous yet inevitable:*

Your occasional visits give me great pleasure. Up here
time moves slowly; nothing comes or goes any more
except this inured decay in the wood of the furniture,
in the roofbeams, the floorboards, the stairs,
in the plaster, the fittings, the curtains, the hinges—
slow decay, a silent rusting, above all in hands and faces.

The big wall clocks have stopped—nobody winds them;
and if I sometimes stop in front of them, it's to see, not the time,
but my own face reflected in their glass,
strangely white, plasterlike, impassive, as though outside time,

while against their dark background the stopped hands,
directly behind my image, are a still lancet
that can no longer open a wound, no longer
strip me of anything—hope or fear, expectation, anguish.

This slow austerity increases the distance between
me and myself, between one action and another,
one memory and another. It can take an entire month
to move from one room to the next. An invisible mist
permeates everything. Often, on winter mornings
I sit here behind the window and gaze amiably out; on occasion
someone will chance to be passing in the distance, mist-wreathed,
a faceless, fleshless blur—you don't try to identify them,
nor do you care where they're going—here or there—it makes no
     difference . . .
                  The trees
are equally insubstantial. At such times, if a woodman
tried to fell with his ax a willow or a cypress,
no sound, no wood, no ax.
                   This fine indeterminacy
is the one true reality—it makes a stranger of me,
distant, almost invulnerable, like that blur in the mist,
and I'm glad of the lightness, though, yes, I fear it a little.

If I take off these bracelets, if at night I let down my hair,
if I untie my sandal laces, above all if I remove
these heavy necklaces, which clasp my throat like chains,
I feel I'll float up, become airborne. I wouldn't want that.
Perhaps that's why I wear them. They anchor me in some way,
though they're often a burden—I even wear them when sleeping, as
     though
I were a dog that I myself had tied to a fallen door.

What you called a moat of silence surrounds this house, to be
respected or not—I wish it were gone. Somewhere here, perhaps even
     inside me,
there's a long narrow passageway without skylights,
without lights at all, without doors—it leads nowhere, it smells
of dust, rotten boarding, mildew, roaches, ancient time;

men pass silently, carrying broken chairs,
large wooden boxes, picture frames, antique mirrors—

Sometimes a crystal falls, a tack, or the pallid hand
of a field marshal in an oleograph, or a bunch of violets
from the transparent, delicate hands of some painted lady—
nobody stoops to retrieve them; besides, they're not noticeable
in this soothing eternal shadow, where everything's passed
into the sphere of the unexploited, the inexpressible,
whether of silence or even of mice.
                                All that can be heard
are the footsteps of mice (not any gnawing—
things no longer have density, nothing to gnaw on), only
their scrabbling steps on the walls and on our bodies
or rather within our bodies.
                                And it's a fine occupation
to observe this soundless collapse
in so deep a void (bottomless, infinite)
that engenders within you a feeling of boundlessness,
something like those vast ideas we so proudly identify:
freedom, immortality, eternity, and the rest.

Well, not collapse, really (since such things have nowhere to fall from or
        to), but rather
an unfettered uplifting, something winged, almost, like birds
that dart up and down or sit still folded in their wings; I'd have called it
a motionless flight amid an absolute, noble futility,
a final equilibrium, the ultimate lightness of all
matter—and so of death too.
                                That's why you find me so joyful—
if joy is the word for this: the lack of all purposefulness,
of any ambition—a magnificent hibernation
with a total awareness of cold, above all a sense of pity
for those who feel pain from the chill, who discuss the chill,
who huddle in heaps of flannel, overcoats, blankets
to protect themselves. Oh, this ridiculous concern with our protection—
protection of every kind, from cold, heat, hunger, thirst,
from sickness, from error, from death; and our mind never grasps the
        fact

that the chill comes up from within us, that in the end you can't escape
 it.

Of course, in winter, a little fire in the grate is worth something—
I was always intrigued by the flames, with their supple dancing
 movements,
their many-hued, insubstantial angels, the shadows they cast
on the ceiling and walls—the shadow of the great loom or the spindle,
the shadow of a guitar hung from a column; and, most of all,
if there are naked bodies—the shadows of their limbs, enlarged,
on their own bodies, like another body,
black and red: the shadow of breast under breast
with the nipple highlighted; the shadow of mouth in mouth;
that terrifying physical certitude, that exquisite enmity
as limbs straighten up, and then their elegant bending
in a deep act, not of abasement but of contrition. That bending
is the measure, I think, of true stature. Those who are always frightened
(for example my sister) lack the strength to stoop, so that
their height is nothing but a frozen rigidity.
What sort of pride do they have, then? What kind of innate virtue?

Oh, my sister settled all questions with *It's either right or it isn't,*
as though she were a precursor of that future creed
that divided the world into two (the here, the hereafter), the human
body in two, threw out all below the waist.

I felt such compassion for her it almost hurt. If they'd so much respect
 for her
that was because she freed them from doing what she'd done. In her face
they honored their own dead opposite, forgave themselves,
were exonerated, at peace.
                              If she'd lived, ah yes, there's no doubt
they'd have come to detest her. All she thought about
was death. And now I can say it: since she knew
there was no way she could avoid it, rather than going slowly
and with leaden feet to that meeting, or grovelling to no purpose,
she chose to preempt death, to challenge it, in the name
of a sly and impertinent magnanimity, turning round the fear
of a lifetime, of her own longing for heroism, turning
her own ineluctable death into a cheap immortality,

yes, yes, *cheap*, despite its blinding luster. My God, how could she stand
    it,
she who was so eternally frightened, even to the point of anger, eternally
    scared
when faced with food or light, when faced with colors,
even when faced with cold, pure water?
                                                    Never in her life
did she let Haemon touch her hand. Always indrawn
as though scared of losing something, folded in on herself,
with one hand thrust into the opposite sleeve,
with her back stuck to the wall, her eyebrows drawn together,
eager only to participate in every misfortune,
proudly aware, perhaps, of her own misfortune—but what misfortune?

She never wore any jewelry; even her engagement ring
she stuffed away in a chest, promenading
her somber arrogance in the midst of our schoolgirl parties,
brandishing over our laughter that scowling gaze of hers,
like a naked sword of futility.
                                            And if, once in a while,
she consented to help at the table, to go get a plate or a jug,
you'd think she was cradling a naked skull in her hands
to set it among the pitchers. No one got drunk any more.

One night, boys and girls were playing together, dancing, and someone
had an inspiration: let's change clothes, make the boys wear the girls'
    dresses
and let us have their male attire. There was a strange fulfillment, an
    awkward freedom
in this exchange—we were like strangers to ourselves, yet
at the same time real and honest. Only my sister
stayed in her own black dress, in the corner, turned to stone,
reproving and repugnant. We rushed down the stairs,
streamed out into the garden, scattered. The girls
in their male clothes were bolder than the boys. And there was a moon,
a big moon like a round tin dish. From the windows came
music filtered through the foliage.
                                            Haemon
was wearing my dress, and was so much a part of me
that I danced in under the fountain, let the water pour down

on my hair, my shoulders, my cheeks—
as if I were crying, he said—till I got chilled through and felt
I'd become a gilded statue of my real self, lit by the moon,
facing my father's blind eyes. That chill still comes back to me.

That was when my sister vanished for three days.
I think she'd run away to your father's place. He brought her back home
riding a mule. From the packsaddle hung, upside down,
two white hens and a dappled rooster. I remember being impressed
by how relaxed they looked in this upside-down position—exhaustion
    maybe?
or resignation? quiet acceptance of the inevitable? *She* didn't even see
    them.

My sister, you see, was also ashamed of being a woman. Maybe that
was her real misfortune. And perhaps that was why she died. Perhaps
    each one of us
would like to be something different. Some bear it, more or less,
others not at all. Fate binds us, they say, on the wheel of the
    inachievable,
leaves us circling the well in the depths of which there awaits us,
closed in, dark, unresolved, our own face. My sister
refused to confess, to submit—hopeless and unyielding.

But one noontime in summer, when the whole house was asleep
and I crept barefoot down the stairs, I saw her
by the dining room pantry, a bowl of syrup in her apron,
wolfing down huge spoonfuls of bread pudding. I turned and fled.
At once the chirr of cicadas in the garden filled my ears. She had not
    seen me.

I never mentioned it to her. She didn't know. I felt so sorry for her.
She too could be hungry (and knew it). Perhaps she even felt love. What
    she couldn't bear
was to yield to her own desires, which were not, of course,
her own acts, her own choice. It was only her death—no, rather
it was only the time, the mode of her death that she could choose.
And indeed, she chose them. And those words of hers, "unwept,
    unbefriended",
above all, that "unwedded", were her only admission,

her first fine humble gesture, her sole act of feminine daring,
her final, unique flash of honesty, some sort of vindication
for her embittered arrogance. In my eyes, that excused her.

And that other thing—once when we opened the syrup jar
and found it half-empty (a sight that caused everyone amazement),
a red flush crept up her cheeks. I looked away. Through the windows
the day was bright and arduous, so much so that I prayed, fiercely and
     silently,
for a general blindness to everything. A few unnoticed roses
looked in past the sill from the garden. And I felt, for the first time, that
     death
isn't black, but white—you can't hide. Two servant-girls
were punished for that theft. I think from that moment
she'd decided on her death, was watching and waiting for it.

Her trifling offense—what kind of offense was that?—had scared her,
     maybe
because it's wrong to consent to our desires? Never, never
had my sister looked so lovely as when she was dead. All by myself
I made up her cheeks, heavily (perhaps I also remembered
that blush of hers in the dining room, faced with the syrup jar),
painted her lips bright crimson, made her eyes look deep black, huge,
with black burnt cork (she never made up herself). I hung
five rows of necklaces on her to hide the scars round her throat,
plus those earrings with two naked lovers, rings and bracelets,
and a broad gold buckle for her belt. Made up and adorned this way
she'd acquired a curious resemblance to me.
"How like Ismene she is," a girl whispered. Now
she'd renounced her frightful decisions, her moral principles,
all those stupid male goals and obsessions. By dying
she'd at last become a woman.
                              And beside her, her suitor,
naked (how does it happen that we discern the body's beauty
with such exactness in the very midst of death? perhaps because
the orange blossom with which they'd sprinkled them smelled so sweet)
—and this bridal youthfulness, complete, unprotected—impregnable—

Almost no one bothered with Eurydice's corpse. The women
were taking their time enshrouding Haemon, they insisted

on washing him so carefully, over and over, bit by bit,
toes and fingers; armpits, breast, limbs,
and the flaccid motion (as they turned him) of abandonment,
or rather of surrender, made me think of that night in the garden,
and the big moon, and the water that drenched me—I'd have liked
to dress him in my clothes again, but hadn't the courage. A butterfly,
orange with black stripes, came in through the window
and perched on his sex. Then the women at once began their keening
and quickly enshrouded him. Then he really became a corpse.

From the courtyard outside came the sound of Creon's wild groans,
and the clang of his sword, emphasizing his guards' silence.

I wonder sometimes if the sole, the only reason for our being born
isn't just to acknowledge the fact of our coming death. Yet in moments
     of respite
from this useless inquiry our life moves on.
                              Haemon
had become remote from us all, he no longer belonged to my sister,
nor to his friends. A great peace, a sense, almost, of contentment—
that irreparable physical deprivation—a calm certainty:
no one any longer can take from us what's nonexistent;
memory holds it entire in a deep exclusiveness,
especially when adjusting it, on occasion, to others. You have something
     of Haemon—
that modesty bred of strength and integrity; above all, the chin
with its central furrow.
                         Evenings when I sit here
I don't know why the birds are still twittering in the garden—
maybe because of the ploughshare's new furrow—
                                   The dead, you know,
always take up a lot of space; however small and unimportant,
they grow bigger at once, they fill the whole house, you can't find
a corner to put yourself in. Even Mother,
decorous, taciturn, eternally self-controlled,
has now acquired an inviolable authority over
the flowerpots, the kitchen utensils, the linen,
the tightly drawn curtains, in that time before evening
when it begins to rain, and her long darning needle
emerges glinting from that ancient workbasket—

this is Mother's place, Mother's style,
her attitude, her concern—all, now, belong to the dead.

Sometimes I stand in front of a mirror
to comb out my hair. The whole of the glass
is taken up with their bodies. Only beneath one armpit,
as they spread their great arms in a gesture of prohibition,
do I glimpse, briefly, a small squashed bit of my face,
or one eye, as though I were monophthalmic. Every morning
the steps were marked with dust-covered footprints made
by their naked, enlarged soles. It was a real problem
to go up or down without treading on them.
                                        Until, one day,
I heard our new gardener come up the steps, two at a time—
"Madam, Madam, the carnations have bloomed," he called out,
      breathlessly,
on the very verge of tears. His hair glistened
with fresh drops of moisture. It was May. I went rushing down.

The carnations had bloomed indeed, right by the fountain.
We set the canary cages out on the garden wall,
we washed their feed cups, changed their water, gave them fresh
      birdseed,
breakfasted under the trees. The day had warmed up.
I stuck a carnation in my hair. The bread was delicious.

Perhaps those carnations, too, were a gift from your father. He knew
how much I loved flowers. All his life, when he went to the city,
he'd bring me back, in his handkerchief, a mass of damp earth
full of wild cyclamen bulbs. He would help me bed them out. I suppose
they're still flourishing up at the top of the garden. If you'd like
we can go up sometime and see.
                                  Be sure to tell him
that I always remember him; nothing's changed inside me,
nothing, I tell you—and that's hard, at a time when all else
outside and around us is changing: carriages, houses, hands, faces,
weapons, hairstyles and dresses, the hats we used to wear—

I remember the afternoon drives we took then, in the carriage—
those hats all covered with flowers, wax cherries, grapes,

and those long ribbons that fluttered about behind us,
now and then flicking our ears like friendly bridles
that the wind tugged gently, making us hold up our heads,
and drawing the skin of our cheeks right back as well
in a big smile (we might also have been copying
the carriage horses, quite without meaning to)—ribbons blue, pink, and
        yellow,
roots of all colors, as though we were heavenly trees,
trees free and free-moving.
                            And Mother's scarf
fluttered out further still, like some great blue diaphanous bird.

When the evening star came out, it seemed to me as though—
how, I don't know—the rustle from the scarf at once changed,
becoming somehow ill-omened. I was scared
that it might twist round her throat and choke her, might wrap round
        her entirely
in the way they once swaddled corpses.
                                    We'd drive back home,
hasten to light the lamps, to do something, anything.
The two lamp brackets at the entrance guarded the gateway. Later,
when the moon came out, it was like the buckle of an invisible belt,
and above it trembled a swan's shadow, or maybe Mother's scarf.

My small brother had a passion for buckles; he'd assembled
a whole collection of them, from different periods, women's, men's,
from wide military baldrics or exquisite antique girdles—
strange patterns, strange designs, strange representations
of men, gods, birds, monsters.
                            One time he showed them to me.
They twinkled and glinted in that autumnal sunset.
I understood nothing. He kept explaining, explaining to me
as though anxious to hide something; and something, for me, did
        remain unexplained,
and that was precisely what pleased me. Perhaps he wanted it too—
I mean, to stress the inexplicable. The dominant luster
was a deep cherry red, like blood, or the coppery green
of human entrails. But the thing that stayed with me most
was a sense of vigorous bodies, naked, after the impatient movement

of stripping off their belts. When I told him this, he got cross. (But is there
anything in the world more baffling, more elusive
than the human body, so tangible—maybe that's why—so full of
    variety?)

He was the one who went over to the Argives. My sister had a weakness
    for him.
He and she both were uncompromising, touchy, wrong-headed. What I
    mean to say is
they cherished a highly personal notion of justice, never perceived
others' rights, or injustice in general. That's how they
and the others were destroyed. But I still keep those buckles—the only
remembrance of him left me. And as I found out later,
he'd collected them from the belts of corpses. That discovery
didn't change my first impression one bit; enhanced it, rather.

How strange that amid all those changes, upheavals, *rearrangements*, as
    they say,
the one thing to survive, standing clear from all those deaths,
is the human body—exposed, unsuspecting, obstinate, splendid. I
    believe
the only beauty is innocence, the sole virtue, youth—
yet how great is its power? or ours? It's renewed, you'll tell me,
in the generations to come. Not for us, not for us. Then—what kind of
    renewal?

I remember when they swept the scraps from the table—bones, crusts,
    pits—
my eyes would covertly follow (you know?) those golden coils
of orange peel, so flexible, so enticing, as if they
wanted to regain their shape. A primitive shout, "*No, no!*"
rose in my throat. I said nothing. I watched. They tossed the skins
over the courtyard wall. Don't you sometimes feel like that?
A suppressed shout. And the nights smelled of orange peel.

Please thank your father from me for his beautiful presents, give him
my best wishes for his recovery. We had good times on the estate—
our only enjoyable summers. It was there we got acquainted

with horses, plane trees, brooks—with the stars too, I may say. It was
      there
we learned the names of plants and birds—tomtits, goldfinches,
      blackbirds.
Once they brought me a partridge in a basket; a few days later it died
as inexplicably as a man will. I buried it
under the two apple trees. My tears wouldn't come. I heard the shouts
of boys bathing in the river. Soon, bare as they were, and dripping,
they mounted their horses, bareback, and vanished into the forest.

Maybe you too were among them. Me they left behind.
Me they taught riding separately, in a fenced-off meadow
full of nettles, thistles, mallows. Things were just fine then.
I loved the vintaging too. The whole place smelled of must—
house, air, water, clothes, windows. I would gaze
at the feet of the grape-treaders, red, bright red,
as though washed with blood in the course of some mock battle
that nevertheless preserved a splendid savagery. "Their wives,"
I said to Mother, "should lick off their feet to stop
all that must going to waste." And Mother laughed.

Those evenings stretched out for ever. The whole of creation
smelled sweet, like thick must jelly. A myriad stars
sprinkled the cisterns with fine powdered cinnamon. A horse
whinnied in our dreams.
                              Haemon's horse, you know,
never budged from his graveside after his death.
I took it fodder and water, offered it sugar lumps in my palm—
it never touched them. In a week it too was dead. Afterward everything
      quietened down.
We gave away their clothes, locked their rooms. No one
spoke their names any more. We even covered their mirrors.

Your father may have told you of the difficult times we went through.
What did they learn, my God, what did they gain? Troubles, troubles,
      duties,
pointless heroic acts; great doors they opened, closed on the same
      darkness;
masks of plaster, bronze, gold, velvet,
flattery, tricks, disguises—to hide from whom?

from themselves? from others? from fate? And that gluttonous taste for
   glory—
I think each reputation rests on endless misunderstandings,
and in any case on the denial of life—what, after all, can you do with it?

A man kept calling from the rocks down below—perhaps it was just in
   our heads—
calling, calling; no one listened, they were in a hurry
to be off—where? to do—what? They had no time to themselves
for undressing, lying around, dreaming in their own body,
looking in a mirror, looking *at* one another;
they looked in each other's eyes only—what did they hope to see there?
perhaps what they hoped for, certainly not what they knew.
                                                          One day
a bird flew into the dining room. General confusion. People
didn't know how to react, though no one was asking them; they got
   cross:
"Get it out! Get it out!" they shouted, jumping up from their chairs,
   gesticulating.
They broke two glasses. The bird flew out of the window.
The maids stooped down and swept up the glass shards. I watched
   them.
They were the only ones smiling—they knew the bird. I winked in their
   direction
and smiled too. The innocent always (don't you think?)
have an air of guilt about them. You know this yourself, I'm sure.

The fear never left me that one day they'd put me on the throne.
Only those scared of themselves pursue honors, or, rather,
those who hate life and mankind. I would get no joy at all
from being a public figure, from having no shadow, no place of my own
in my own private region, where I could kick off my sandals at night,
play with the keys to my armoire, let them dangle from a carefree
hand when I was in bed.
                        My poor father—I think of him always—
had a face like a clenched fist, clutching
a great black curtain, to draw it; indeed, as I've sometimes said,
perhaps it was good he was blinded, perhaps that way at least
he could see inside himself, remember bit by bit
all that he'd never seen; and thus maybe really see it, since till then

he'd viewed his autocratic person (much flattered, of course) through the eyes
    of his frightened subjects. We felt so sorry, from childhood on,
for him and them both.
                          An unbearable burden, I feel,
that of ruling and giving orders. And always, in the last resort, each
one of us is ruled by what he rules—not counting that boundless
    suspicion
of everything, everybody—let a bird's shadow but flit haphazardly
into a room at sunset, it's a quivering knife
fashioned from soundless metal. This is why tyrants
become daily more wholly tyrannical. When the world fears you
or needs you, you never know what to expect from it.

Better then (but how?) to neither rule nor be ruled—
sufficient the rule that stamps us before our birth; sufficient
the death that lurks in wait for us—you know something about that.
The years between lose their edge in the end, the body goes slack,
color leaches from hair, windows, eyes;
the hand loses its grip, that once had palmed and held
a large, hard, golden coin, while our entire life
was an effort to keep this coin, a terror
of dropping it, losing it; one hand became useless,
useless one half of our life, our entire life.

Now my hand has unclenched itself, given up;
the coin dropped, they took it from us. Only in my palm
there remains, deep-etched, the mark of that endless pressure. The flesh
has grown softer, smoother. At last you can move
both your hands freely. You can walk
swinging empty hands in the empty air without alarm—
an idle, frivolous rowing in the acme of pointlessness, till
they cast in your teeth another, copper, coin.

Lies are bad—so your father, too, used to say. Inside this softened body
desire persists; harsh as ever, unyielding—along with the sense
of an inexcusable slowness. At such times women often
embrace statues, kiss their stone mouths, have dreams
that they're sleeping with them. If you've ever happened to notice
statues' lips wet, it's from the saliva of passionate women. Of course,

206 · ISMENE

memory's some sort of refuge. Yet it too is being drained;
it's needed for new images, be they casual or alien.

This is my favorite window. Curled up here, half in, half out,
I watch and remember. No duties. A great calm.
I'm beginning once more to study trees, birds, colors,
the feet of hunters trudging homeward at nightfall. I feel so free.
They have something to tell me, a secret to reveal. At times I'm ashamed
of this new tenderness of mine—childishness rather—
that descends on my lips despite myself, in some sense like
a swallow perched on a tumbledown roof.
                                        Odd, really,
the way that noise quieted down (it hadn't let you hear anything else),
the way it faded into the distance. Am I really, was I ever, myself?
      People
went and down then, whispering to one another, jerky movements—
politicians, soldiers, diplomats—what revolting people, my God,
like walking rote memories, calculated, repeated. You didn't know what
      hour, month, or year it was.

Wars, revolutions, counterrevolutions, the same again and again,
ashes heaped in the squares from the fires they lit
for great festivals, or the dead—the ash is the same.
Sometimes they even burned those whom a little before they'd called
      heroes.
The bay leaves had completely lost their meaning.

You shut your eyes as you'd shut a door in a strange house,
so as not to see, not to think. Intrigues, bribes, betrayals;
those with the most pliant backbones always stood the tallest:
Thebans, Argives, Corinthians, Spartans, Athenians—which of them
      really
ran things? A secret power seemed to be pulling strings from a distance;
masked men came out at midnight with powerful torches,
a face you knew changed suddenly into white lightning or thunder,
people seemed to melt back into fear.
                                        One afternoon,
high up, from a poor student's garret, came the sound of a flute. The
      women
gathered below in the street, knelt, wept. The madman,

shirt unbuttoned, kept beating his breast with a stone, groaned
    "Mother, mother,
mother, I want to die," groaned "I want to die."
A covered truck went past. They all scattered. The flute fell silent;
the madman pissed in midroad. People parted once more
unrecognized, jostling, strangers.
                            But I was young then,
so young I didn't understand. Forgetting was easy. In that window
was left hanging, aflutter, tied with string,
one little rose. Just that. It too withered.

The bells rang, were still. People arrived, left, went running.
Sometimes it rained in torrents: the cisterns inside the houses brimmed
    over,
you'd think the water would bear everything down to the sea, wash it
    away.
Then the sun came out again; things dried; nothing had changed. The
    garden
played innocent; the carnations gleamed. Up beyond the garden
printing presses and typewriters rattled. The same men with different
    masks,
wound up or run down, entered the halls, sat down
at large black polished legal tables;
their hands were huge insatiate lymphatic spiders
unwinding scrolls. They read, wrote, sealed; sent off for
yet other documents; gestured; opened their mouths wide.
But no shout, or sound, emerged—a black hole in the air;
maybe they shouted "Long live—" or "Down with—," but I couldn't
    make out a thing;

one fear alone stood out, though I didn't know why then; it baffled me
    how
mere equipment could be rigid with fright, tables and chairs,
the open chimney flue, half-finished wine in the glass,
a roast chicken on its dish, a fork poised above the plate—
motionless, frozen.
                    Some fine messengers showed up;
they too opened their mouths, but again, not a sound emerged,
though otherwise they were themselves—they panted, and we were
    pleased

by this panting of theirs; their tongues, too, were visible—red,
a bright red, like summer, high summer, with streams and trees.

Then they sent word and summoned the blind old prophet. A sweet little
      boy
led him by the hand. Majestic, conniving, handsome,
with his long beard down to his knees, with his huge vacant eyes
(I thought he was acting blind, that his beard was false),
with his staff of authority—he breathed calm, serenity, wholeness;
knew—it was said—the tongues of birds, fire, silence, winds;
a dove perched on his shoulder.
                                        My sister feared him,
would hide behind his back, or slip out to the next room,
and from there, I'm convinced, would eavesdrop. I loved him. One day
he took me by the chin and lifted my face. "You'd be better looking," he
      told me,
"if you were a boy." "I am," I said. We both
laughed like conspirators. The others got cross with him,
as though he were to blame for all that awaited them. He rapped his
      staff and left.
Behind him lingered some wisps of down—black, white, reddish gold.

For a while a great silence fell, as though everything had lost
its weight and significance. A tranquil relaxation
crept round the back of one's knees. No one chased off
the cat that had climbed on the table and was gnawing a fish. Light
      poured
diffuse and near-pure white through the windowpane. The next moment
drums began to beat wildly. One trumpet call from the ramparts,
another across in the olive trees. At night beacons
flared from hilltop to hilltop. Torchbearers passed by,
in the darkness a vast hole opened, chaos made visible. Then
night vanished in night again. Everyone vanished. I understood nothing.

Sometimes they made us recite poems in front of strangers.
We were children, we didn't want to. We cried. Sometimes they made us
      take
a bouquet to some ugly, feeble old man with false teeth. Sometimes
they'd drag us out onto the balcony with them, to wave to the crowd.
      Sometimes they hid us

down in the cellars with the big jars. We'd watch the spiders;
the wax candle dripped, we took the hot blobs and shaped them
into hares, ploughs, boats, or naked figurines. Sometimes they sent us,
at night, with an escort, out to the estate, to your father.

We scarcely had time to take off our sandals, stroll round the lawn,
pick one apple each for ourselves, before they took us back.
The flags changed on the battlements, over the public buildings. Who
        won, who lost?
The cavalrymen sprang from their horses, removed the saddles,
lugged them into the hallway. They sat on stools, took off their belts,
took off their boots. Their feet were enormous.
They smelled of pinewood and goatstink. The women feigned head
        colds,
kept grinding the coffee mill by the window till moonrise.

That, I think, was the time that the wolves and foxes came down
from the forest. The whole night shone as though freshly whitewashed.
The streams held still, didn't flow. The rocks were white.
In front of their beds gaped the huge boots of the horsemen.
The smallest one felt hot, stripped stark naked,
stepped behind the curtain. The curtain glowed bright.
Golden leaves rained on the terraces. Birds called.

It was just about then that Father was blinded. Suddenly everything
turned red, vivid red with green spots, even the dishes
red, with a hole in the middle. Somewhat later
trumpets were heard once more. The men were torn from their sleep,
strapped on swords, leaped on their horses. An enormous shadow
was left behind in the courtyard—perhaps from the dawn moon,
perhaps from the winged marble lion on the ancient tower.

The place where they'd lain on the beds stayed warm for a little, then
        grew cold.
The women rolled themselves up in their bedclothes and wept. My sister
lost weight from day to day, became harsher, grew pale,
avoided Haemon and me. Afternoons, she went out alone—
perhaps as far as the gates of Thebes, perhaps to hold converse
with that lion-bodied woman. Her eyes would nail you

with two frozen questions, and you'd wish she were looking anywhere
   else.
Clearly she was waiting for something extraordinary. She never slept at
   night.

The sheets fell on the floor. Often I'd pretend to be sleeping,
watch her as she lay there, so still and tense. One night
the moonlight had entered our chamber, bathed it halfway across;
I saw her move her bright fingers like a dancer, a priestess,
as though weaving an unseen rope, as though writing figures in air.
She was adding up something—her years perhaps (or the lack of them?),
and then she grasped her throat, let her silvered fingers linger,
and began, suddenly, shaking, as though in terror. She rose,
took Mother's white lace umbrella, opened it,
sat beneath it, hunched on the bed, as though to protect herself
from the moon, or the night's shadows. Posed thus she looked
as though tattooed all over with minute silver-blue meanders.

But perhaps meanwhile I'd fallen asleep. When I opened my eyes,
the beds' sturdy cast-iron feet struck me as hirsute, bestial.
I heard the jugmaker going by to his work. I looked out the window.
In the street were empty cigarette packs, paper flags and napkins,
   cartridges.
Behind the cypresses gleamed the wall of the marble workshop
with a great bronze horseman. One day we heard
a terrifying, unfamiliar noise. There in the dining room
the huge chandelier had fallen, smack in the middle
of the breakfast table. After that, you could expect anything to happen.

Nothing was left but fragments of crystal and luster. In the doorway
stood two hugely tall cripples with crutches.
The maidservants chased them away. The menfolk had vanished.
From that instant everyone idled. The women wore no make-up.
They slouched around late in slippers, forgot to light the lamps,
crossed themselves behind their loose hair. Nettles grew in the gardens.
They'd hidden the keys in the ivy. Father's horse, now very old,
vanished one evening and never came back. They hung up
one of its old shoes on the storeroom door. Its tether
they strung up between two trees as a line for the washing.

At moments, amid the general confusion, there descended
a marvellous silence, so transparent it scared you. Everything took on
a new look, a new sound, a fresh attraction,
that loaded sense of indifference. You saw things straight, really heard
    them.
The hens ran loose in the graveyard, scratched about all day;
they laid huge eggs just anywhere, among the daisies,
under the rosemary bushes, in the road, on chairs. An invisible hand
removed, one by one, the big rusty nails from the doors.
The flies woke early, drummed on the windowpanes.

Outside the walls the dead multiplied. I was always curious
about corpses—not an attempt to win familiarity with death,
or reconciliation either. Sometimes I'd dodge the watchful eyes
of my mother and tutors, scramble up to the battlements, peer
out through the embrasures. They'd be moving the dead on handcarts,
    stretchers, ladders;
others still lay sprawled on the plain, in elegant postures,
quiet, youthful, handsome, beside their slain horses. I saw them
without the slightest distress—handsome, as though ready for love.
Until our own dead came; and all at once we grew up.

I saw my sister at daybreak in the courtyard—marked by fate—
so very pale. Her hands, her clothes, her hair were dusty all over.
The dawn frost chilled us through. We shivered. Daylight descended
in infinite whiteness, riddled with black crows.

What did they learn, my God, what did they gain? The rest you know.
Nothing was left. Only the stony Sphinx on her rock
outside the gates of Thebes, indifferent, undistracted—
she no longer poses questions. The vain hubbub subsided. Time fell
    vacant.
An endless Sunday with shut windows. Incredible
that on summer evenings they still water the gardens.

A moat of silence—just as you said. Look, the moon's come out.
You can hear the fountain outside too. Don't you hear it? Your hands
still keep those beautiful calluses from fieldwork. I hope
you don't stay in the army for ever. When your term of service expires
go back to the estate, near your father. This door

leads straight to my apartment. The passage facing south
is never guarded. Knock seven times. At midnight, I'll let you in.
I'd like to give you some little things for your father.

One of those suits of Haemon's—I've kept them in the closet—
should fit you beautifully, I think. And his new sword,
with its ivory, gold, and rubies—he never got around
to strapping it on. It's a beautiful night. Mind the stairs.

*By now it is dark. She retreats to her apartment while the young officer's
footsteps can still be heard on the stairs. She fumbles for the matches on
the little table, and lights the three candles in the candlestick. She strikes
the hanging gong, and the Nurse appears. "I won't want supper
tonight," she says, "I won't be needing you any more, you may go to
bed. Oh yes—bring me a glass of water. And wind up the wall clock in
the hall, we forgot it. Take away that basket of fruit, too. Put the
flowerpot in the window." After a moment the Nurse returns with the
water, then goes. All is still. She locks both doors. The tick of the clock
is now audible from somewhere nearby. 9 P.M., 9:15, 10, 10:30. She
stands facing the mirror, removes her make-up, undresses. Sagging
breasts. Marks on her belly where the corset pinched her. The
fingerprints of time on her thighs. 11 o'clock. She strips off her
necklaces. The skin under her chin is slack, pendulous. 11:15. She
grasps the candlestick in her left hand, and goes right up to the mirror.
With the ring finger of her right hand she draws down the skin beneath
each eye. The eyeball is blurry, with a faint network of red veins. Now
she moves her fingers to her dyed hair. The roots are white. An
expression of nausea invades her immobile features; the corners of her
mouth are drawn down. 11:30. She begins to make herself up. She puts
on a red dress, puts her jewelry back on. Then she relaxes in the red
velvet armchair, opposite the mirror. She closes her eyes. Midnight.
Seven discreet taps on the door. Silence. Then seven further taps, a little
louder. Silence. And yet again. Then, nothing. A vast stillness. The glass
gleams. She rises, goes to the mirror, makes herself up again, plaster
white, her eyes huge, black-circled. A plaster mask. She takes off her
dress, puts on one of her sister's—full, pleated, buttoned-up, brown. She
adds a belt with a broad buckle. She opens the drawer of the nightstand,
takes something out. With her back to the candlestick and the mirror,
she drinks the water in a series of small, separate gulps, as though*

swallowing aspirin tablets. She sinks back on the bed, fully dressed, and still wearing her sandals. Motionless. At peace. She closes her eyes, smiles. Has she fallen asleep? From the hall nearby the tick of the clock can still be heard.

ATHENS, SEPTEMBER–DECEMBER 1966; SAMOS, DECEMBER 1971

· AJAX ·

A huge, powerful man lies prone on the floor, amid smashed crockery,
stewpots, slaughtered animals—cats, dogs, chickens, lambs, kids, a
white ram tied upright to a stake, a donkey, two horses. He wears a torn
white nightshirt, covered with blood—a little like an ancient chiton—
which leaves most of his muscular body uncovered. He seems
exhausted, as if perhaps he's recovering from a night of drunkenness.
On his face, a look of illness and distress, quite incompatible with, and
especially ill-suited to, his physical dimensions, the bulging muscles of
his arms, his thighs, his calves. A woman, with foreign features, pale,
sleepless, frightened, and perhaps secretly angry, stands silent in front
of the door. Her pose is somehow odd—as though she had a small
child hidden behind her. It is an hour since dawn. Outside it must be
broad daylight. Here, a feeble reflection spreads over the walls from the
closed grilles. In the street can be heard the voices of fruit vendors, knife
grinders, fishmongers, and a little further down, on the shore, the sound
of sailors scrubbing and tidying ships at their moorings. The man is
motionless on the floor. You can't tell where he is looking, what he sees.
He speaks slowly, wearily, and sometimes feverishly or even a little
fearfully:

Woman, what are you staring at? Shut the doors, shut the windows, bolt
    the yard gate,
stop up the cracks, bad things are getting in—insects, lizards,
huge flies, secret laughter. Look, on the wall,
a black fly, black, black, getting bigger, blacking out the day,
sniffing black air—cover it with your hand, kill it,
I can't bear to look at it. Why are you so petrified? Come on, look at
    me—

I am the mighty one, the invincible one—you've heaped praises upon
    me,
weighted me down, stifled me—one by one, you and all those with you
hanging around my neck—stifled me. This is your doing. Welcome it.
    No one
can tolerate my being tired even for an hour; no one
can tolerate my being sick. As for you, all your own
slightest troubles you unload, magnified, on my back—
all your grumbling and whining: one maid's been seduced by a sailor;
another wears a silk blouse, makes up her big eyes,
paints her nails cyclamen pink; the third, the little one,

put her hair up in a chignon, forgot the soap in the washtub;
the lettuce has wilted; the coal supply is down; all your troubles
you trot out in order at dinnertime, that time of tranquility
when battles and quarrels have ceased, and everyone is looking
for a drop of oblivion, turning to his basic bodily needs
among the plates and glasses shining calmly beneath the lamps—
and you with your constant grimaces, puffing, waving your hands,
opening a vast mouth, gulping down air, stars
and one cunning little starlet, like a silver chick pea, and me saying:
Now it'll stick in her throat, she'll cough, choke, be silent.

Even when it was time for making love, at night, in bed, suddenly
you'd get mad that they left the clothespins in the yard
and the damp would rot them. Ah, you stupid creatures, that's how
you drive us out of bed, out of the house, out of the world,
out of your practical, clever brains, that are so taxed
with recipes for cooking, sweets, drinks, drugs; out
of life itself with its small, sacred daily incidents,
with its small, tangible objects that give relief from the great intangibles.

None of you've ever asked me where my brain and eye are turning, what
        fears,
what wrongs, what jealousies I face (the fearless one, you see) or even
if I've got a toothache or a headache, just as though I didn't myself
have teeth or a head, only stones or mere air. What are you watching
        like that?
Shut the doors, shut the windows, bolt the yard gate.
And the black fly—look at it there, sharpening its nails on the ox horn!

So here I am, then, the mighty one, the invincible one—look at me. No
        one
ever asked for a share of my troubles. You, the innocent ones,
the deceitful, the desperate and cunning, felt nothing
for me but self-interested respect, not affection at all,
only an exacting respect. What's more, you feel a superior anger
at any sickness of mine, as if I'd betrayed you. And in fact I did,
since I've betrayed myself. Here I am, in a heap on the floor; and my
        enemies
laugh at me, laugh in secret. All last night

they lay in wait, surrounded the house, watched me. They peered
through shutters, curtains, keyholes, from the cupboards—
I heard the floor creak, scraping on the wall. When I went out
they hid behind trees, lay in wait for me. A white moon,

white as cotton, enormous, rose over Ida; a white frost
covered my eyes; I've forgotten—what was it?—a white handkerchief
when we played blindman's buff as children on Salamis; you can't make
    out
who's calling you, or from where, in a disguised voice, as if you were
inside a big, gloomy church in bright sunshine, and the pallid
lofty icons were whispering about you to each other—
a huge snake, a lion with a thorn in its pad,
a severed head on a tray, two frightened eyes,
one great solitary eye, beards, blood dripping
from the point of a spear, smoke, burnt laurel, tiny bells. I said I'd go
    back—

What's forward? What's back? The moon had whitewashed the road;
the whole road shone and I looked enormous; they watched me
from every side. How could I go back? Even my shadow
had abandoned me—had melted away in the glare of the whitewash—
unless it was salt. Huge octopi, dry, crucified
on bamboo skewers hung from the walls. My sword
now expanded, gleaming, too heavy to lift, completely lighting me up,
now shrank almost to nothing, like a child's pared fingernail.
Shut the doors, shut the windows, bolt the yard gate.

All the houses shut—they'd shut me out. Copper rings
shone on the doors. Great barrel hoops
rolled down from the hills—they ensnared me. The enormous moon—
    round, round—
opened a dry well for me to fall into. I could neither
walk nor stand still. And my steps could be heard
on the cobblestones, strange, persistent, treacherous, till from down in
    the harbor
came the sound of an anchor chain being raised, and everything fell
    silent.

Then all the passageways shut me out; frayed ropes, disguised noises;
up there in the camps the fires had died down; all around, the enclosure
    walls
gleamed with little clay pipes. Huge masks
hung in the air—and it was *they*, in the neighbors' courtyards,
they, with cardboard masks of oxen,
donkeys, horses, sheep—they could no longer escape me;
they walked on all fours, pretending to be animals—they didn't fool me;
they crawled on the ground like monstrous babies. The silence curved
above me like a glass bell—I was afraid I would break it. And suddenly
I heard them from a thousand secret corners hideously calling my name,
my name, over and over, roaring in the pipes, in the empty jars,
in the toilet bowls, in the chimneys; my name—
some far off, with women's voices, and others nearby, with a voice of
    thunder,
mimicking my own voice, "Ajax, Ajax, Ajax,"
with such stupid arrogance, "Ajax, Ajax,"
that I hated my name forever—oh, more, I wanted never to hear it
    again,
for no one ever to pronounce it again; to be anonymous, forgotten,
tied under the belly of my horse. Then I couldn't stand it any more,
I raised my sword, struck, penned them all in,
dragged them in here—look at them—and they were these animals.
Shut the doors, shut the windows, bolt the yard gate.

Woman, what are you staring at with that look? That fly—kill it.
Am I not human too? Why, then? All night
you too lay in wait for me behind the door, yes, with my child—
you showed me to the child, so he could see my collapse—no, no,
you covered his eyes with both hands, so he wouldn't see me. All night,
bronze arrows lodged in the walls, every sound reechoed,
rippling out endlessly—my step, my breath, my pulse,
my clothes brushing against my knees, my chest—how to escape them?
What do you guard against first? My enemies had planted the arrows,
hidden antennae, to keep a watch on my movements. I caught them. I
    grabbed
one by the ear, pulled hard. I wanted to look at him. His rubbery ear
stretched, stretched as I pulled, while he still stayed out of reach.

Another sank his teeth into my thigh—a mad dog—these crafty sons of
　　Atreus!—
and Teucer missing somewhere in the mountains. I called out: Teucer,
　　Teucer;
my voice didn't reach him. I called out again. Beneath my feet I lost hold
　　of the earth. I had nothing,
nowhere to hold on to, not even my own life—
as if I were rummaging for it blind. I knew, suddenly, that it had been
　　cut short
and instead of it holding me, I held it in my hand
like the flayed tail of some unknown, improbable animal.
Shut the doors, shut the windows, bolt the yard gate.

This night is over. I am calmer now. Don't be afraid, woman.
I came back out at dawn. I saw you standing sleepless in the doorway.
I went down to the shore, before the sailors were awake,
took water in my cupped hand and splashed my temples. How small,
　　my God,
how small we are in the face of the infinite cosmos awaking,
in the face of that serene, immortal light. And suddenly, I was aware
of all the accursed terror of the night shrinking, becoming *this* small,
　　huddled
among the rocks, with a beautiful, silent grief,
a sorrow for my own self—aware of myself watching the still ships,
looking again, and knowing I could see—could hear—the joy of it!

One boat had a red stripe all around; its reflection
in the water redder still and cool like a burnt-out fire;
and I said again: "like a burnt-out fire"—a sweet exultation
made my teeth and my knees clench over that "like"—that I could
once again set one thing next to another, speak, make transformations—
"like a burnt-out fire," and I didn't burn myself. What a day, when one
　　heard
only the creak of planks and ropes with the breathing of the water—
　　calm
creak of invisible oars and oarlocks, a secret rowing
bearing me far away, forgotten, with no weapons at all.

Then near me a flock of gulls rose up—they covered me with a white
trembling arch—peaceful, weightless, generous wings
stirred in the air like an affirmation—great friendly palms
silently applauded the silence, clapping me on the shoulder
with renewed confidence—yes, a new confidence. So then, don't grieve.

I assure you I'm calm now—I long neither for the death of others
nor for my own. I care nothing for
the deceit of the gods and my own self-deceit, nor for the derision
of my fellow fighters—I am far away, it doesn't touch me. What can I do
     with them,
the useless plunder and the great shield and spear?
From what do you need protection? And in what way? It's not the
     Trojans who made me give in—
fear of the enemy is nothing compared to fear of a friend
who knows one's hidden wounds and aims right at them. I lay on the
     shore
watching the pale and shadowy dawn, without the burden
of any expectation or hope. The heart of man
is a moist root in the earth—patient, hidden
so deep—spring is near; it can begin to throw off shoots again.

I saw the tents shining with morning dew—a gray and rosy
gleam advanced like convalescence on the rocks. I remembered
other mornings, far away, unsuspected, full of haste and the sounds
of anchors, oars, cauldrons, tackle-blocks, while the sailors,
awakened too early, were pissing on the shore, all in a row,
and that rosy glow, on the horizon, on the coast,
on their hands, their faces, their cocks, trembled as if enchanted
as we bent involuntarily to the water to see our reflection
and once more fell in love with our bodies in their unfettered virility
until the sun's ghost emerged gigantic from the sea
and we lost ourselves once more amid vain boasting and battles.

I don't want any of these things—what use would they be?—let them
     go.
My former exploits seem like fictions. All the prizes
that belonged to me the others appropriated
by fraudulent lots and bribes; while I, as the fate of the Greeks was
     being decided,

threw into the helmet, not moist clods of earth
but my large, distinctive wedding ring, and was the first to go out
in hand-to-hand combat against the enemy. And when once more
they burned the ships, and smoke and flame rose to heaven,
so much you'd have thought the sea was on fire, when Hector
was charging furiously over the trenches, again I
was the first to stand against him. The Atreidae perhaps don't remember
    these things;
they care only for plunder and prizes. So, let them share them out
with trickery, fear and deceit—until when? One day
they too will stand naked before the night and its long road;
the stolen shield—however beautiful and big—will no longer be of any
    use to them.

A little further up from the shore, in hill-high piles
the clothes of dead fighters lie rotting; their shoes warp, their buckles
    are rusted
from the heavy dews and the rains; little by little
a deep soft bed has formed; at the coming of spring it blossoms
with thousands of many-hued wildflowers—perhaps they take their
    colors
from the clothes of the dead. If you walk over them you'll feel
a certain deep, calm softness—not that of decay and dissolution, no,
a different softness, of something finished and nonexistent. You bite a
    leaf
and it has no taste. You pluck a flower, look at it;
you see, inside its petals, a transparent landscape in the color and shape
of the flower—all is hollow, in a deep hollowness; with one step you can
cross to the other side with its tranquil poplars and white river.

Those who fled circle silently near us, down the nearest streets,
up on the olive-clad hills, out in the vineyards—
I saw them on my way back to the house. They beckoned to me. The
    chimneys
were like black statues above the roofs. They passed—
dark, dark and dumb, like hillside trees drawn
on a luminous fragment of water. A white moon
stands above them all day long—it casts no light on them. They cross
    the road,
gaze into the general store at caramels covered with muslin,

at cardboard puppets with strings, at cigarettes, matches,
tweezers, newspapers—they don't read even the headlines. They see
    themselves
in the darkened bakery window. Like dry weeds
their hair falls over their cheeks, their chins, their shoulders.

Their hands are long and withered—they can't keep hold of
shields and bows—not that they try to; nor can they control
the speech from their slack lips. Unchecked, invisible,
with that delectable austerity proper to their position, attuned
to their beautiful movement, to the absence of all concern,
to their leisurely, endless time. Unassailable creatures. I envied them.

On the bridge they crossed paths with a band of gypsies. No one
could tell them apart. Only that the rustling of yellow dresses
suddenly stopped, and the coffee mills flashed unexpectedly
with reddish gold sparks. The seven deep-black horses
bent their heads to the ground, perked their ears. Only
the huge bear with the rings reared up on her hind legs
right in the middle of the bridge, blocking everyone's passage.

She didn't want to move away from there. She looked back sniffing the
    air—
a scent of sulphur and incense and grapes. Her eyes
huge, black, impenetrable. They had to pull
several times on her strap; they flourished whips at her too. She went,
turning her head back every so often, looking where I looked.

At that moment, the shadow of a bird passed before my feet—I didn't
    life my eyes—
remote sympathy and forgiveness. And I prayed silently
for a little calm—not faith, not faith. Take away these slaughtered lambs
    and oxen—
lambs and oxen, yes—and let my unharmed enemies mock me.

Take them far away from here—I can't bear to look at them. Ah, that's
    always the way it is,
all my strength wasted fighting phantoms, winning
wholly imaginary victories, conquering golden cities—
illusions, illusions, illusions. So, lambs and oxen. Nothing else.

All last night you, too, heard their pitiful bellowing.
Look at this white ram—what serenity, what sadness
in its eyes, my God—a little St. John—they taught me
the meaning of calm humility. Let them laugh as much as they want, the
    Atreidae,
at my reckless "exploits", and at those other real ones
I performed once for Greece and for the Greeks—one day they will
    remember me.

Let them not remember me. What does it matter after all? Sufficient for
    me
that which I found, losing everything. In a little
I'm going down to wash in the river, to wash my sword. It would have
    been nice
to preserve all these animals—the white ram especially—
but how could we keep its expression? In its eyes shine
the shrunken door, morning, two leaves
and one small bright bean—perhaps it's also the fountain
where Achilles' horses drank. Throw them out of here—what are you
    still keeping them for?
Shut the doors, shut the windows, bolt the yard gate.

Listen—they're laughing again in the courtyard. Aren't they? Hush.
    Hush.
Woman, I'm cold. Fetch a blanket. Cover me.
Isn't it cold? Aren't your teeth chattering too?
How good it would be for you to shrink, shrink, shrink,
quite still, all curled up, covered over, hidden
under your fallen shield, it too corroded by rain and salt,
with its old heroic images all obliterated, and from inside
to tighten its strap, pulling it toward the earth till you become one with
    the ground—

Ah, to lie in wait too, all ears the whole time in case someone passes
or kicks the shield by mistake; and the metallic echo, next to your ear,
clang, clang, a great clangor; your blood will suddenly drain, in your
    veins
will run only that dreadful clangor, sounding interminably deep within
    you,
clang, clang, making your contortion audible to all, making evident

the shape of your abasement—I hear that sound, it masters me
like the betrayal of my own self by my own self,
the same self that I had trained and toughened
with the illusion and vanity of invincible courage—what courage,
when from deep within our strange life and our strange death rule us?
No, this is no humility. If I was vanquished, I was vanquished
not by men, but only by the gods. No victory, no defeat is ours alone.
Shut the doors, shut the windows, bolt the yard gate.

Ah, nothing is our own—whatever we do, and are, remains
a gift—given and to be taken away again—from someone else, a
    stranger, and without our will.
And this fly keeps buzzing, buzzing—kill it! Some stranger's foot
just knocked once more against the fallen shield. Do you hear it? *Clang,*
    clang—the shield—
clang, clang—it's stopping, it's stopped. It was nothing. And take this
    blanket. I'm not cold.
It's just this noise here, at my temples, and the shadow on the wall—
turning, gear turning, gear—round and round again.

I want to remember something good—a sun-drenched day on Salamis
when they were caulking the new slipways on the shore, and in the air
floated the smell of planed wood, and higher up, in the small pine wood,
the cicadas went mad. I want to. I can't. Memory's severed at midpoint,
all is submerged in that void; only the ugly things rise clear—
the enemy's flashlight in your eyes when you are sleeping,
the irons on your legs, the knife at your temple, the screams of the
    wounded
at night in the valley, with the jackals, and my own scream
reaching my own ear from far away. I can't. I look all around. I can't
    see.

I want to see over the backs of these slaughtered animals. "A tree," I
    say;
"A tree," I reply. Just that. Nothing else. The tree is missing. It wasn't
    there.
And I find even my own body unacceptable, I don't want to touch it—
a sense of disgust—it's strange, unfamiliar; a goatish smell—what *is* the
    human body?
passages, holes upon holes, lying down in slimy darkness;

coarse hair, like burnt ropes; behind the ropes
rots a great unrecognizable carcass with strong jaws,
naked jaws, bleached already, powerfully clenched
in a grimace of general dissatisfaction and comic menace. And that
    tightening
of the white jaws with their huge teeth, is the only
sign of pride and honor in this slack, spineless world.

What good are they any more to you—honors, prizes, commendations?
    They are nothing.
Failure and derision are nothing either. They too are a waste of our time.
Never in my life did I seek slaves, admirers, underlings. I want one man
    only
to talk things over with as my equal—where is he? Only our death
is the equal of each one of us. All else is easy glitter,
compromises, excuses, willful blindness.

Returning here, I noticed the traces of old fires in the meadows—
charred branches, ashes, cinders, soot; scattered nearby were large spits
from open-air feasts and sacrifices. Piles of large bones
lay whitening in the dawn with the silver-white
of memory or of the yet unborn—infinitely calm and with a certain
    dauntless
pride, proper to a distant memorial for the missing—that is, for
    ourselves,
and the grass was yellow up there, although further down
the sea sparkled mindlessly rose pink, imposing once more
one motion from the beginning—its motion, our motion.

Then I remembered Salamis—ochre mornings with mist and drizzle
that blurred all in the midst of time—boats, anchors, wineshops,
    fishmongers,
and only the road shone silver, all alone, going forward vaguely
    somewhere,
turning every so often, and turning again to evade invisible obstacles,
or for its own delight, with that silver whiteness.

At home, I found Mother seated in the dining room,
bent over, concentrating, stringing pearls on thin thread,

white, turquoise, silver. "What will you do with them, Mother?" I said
   to her.
And she: "I'm going to throw them down the well." She smiled. "But
   then," I said,
"why are you stringing them?" I looked at her. She kept her eyes down.
   "The woman who will wear them
prefers it that way," she answered. And suddenly I realized
that within every well, and within us, is a beautiful drowning woman,
a drowning woman who doesn't want to die—and I don't know what
   that signifies—
enduring, enduring, below the clamor of the horses, the carts, our
   chariots.

Open the windows, open the doors, unbolt the yard gate.
It's nothing. I'll go out for a little to wash in the river. Tell Teucer—
Actually, where is Teucer? Teucer, Teucer! And take away these
   animals.

I'm going to wash myself, wash my sword—perhaps also to find a man
   to talk things over with.
What a beautiful day—O sunlight, golden river—Farewell, woman.

*He leaves. The woman remains immobile beside the doorway. A noisy
clanging is heard, as if a hammer were striking a metal gong hanging in
another room. Perhaps an invisible foot struck the fallen shield with its
seven impenetrable layers. The noise persists. Servants enter. They
gather up the slaughtered animals. Including the white ram with the
sorrowful eyes. A tall, big-boned servant girl enters silently with a big
broom. She sweeps up the broken dishes, cigarette stubs, trampled
coffeepots. Her loose black kerchief hides her face. She leaves. The room
is now empty. All at once it seems much bigger. The metal gong has
fallen silent. Now the voices outside in the street can be heard very
clearly, and all the activity in the harbor—cranes, windlasses, anchor
chains. Suddenly a sailor comes running: The master, he exclaims, the
master's dead—his sword's through his ribs— The woman stands still in
the doorway; so does the tall servant girl, at the end of the corridor,
upright, petrified, both hands resting on the wooden handle of the big
broom.*

LEROS, SAMOS, AUGUST 1968–JANUARY 1969

· PHILOCTETES ·

A summer afternoon. On a deserted island shore—Lemnos perhaps.
The colors are fading slowly. A boat at anchor in the rocky cove. The
voices and laughter of sailors can be heard, a little way below, as they
bathe, exercise, wrestle. Here, outside a rocky cave, transformed into a
home, sit two men—one handsome, bearded, mature, with a virile
intelligent air; the other a robust youth, with burning, searching,
passionate eyes. He has something of the characteristics of Achilles, only
a trifle attenuated, as though he were Achilles' son, Neoptolemos. A
thin, obscure moon moves vaguely, slowly, somewhere in the sky, silver
amid the lengthening rose and violet refractions of the sunset. It seems
that the older man, after years of solitude and silence, has been speaking
at great length to the Youth, his unexpected visitor, who arrived scarcely
two hours ago, and now he falls silent again—inscrutable, sated, weary
from a new, similarly futile, yet human, sense of weariness and sorrow.
A vague remorse clouds his broad forehead. Nevertheless he still studies
the Youth's striking face, as though it were something he has been
waiting for. At the back of the cave, from time to time, his weapons
catch the light—the great shield, finely worked, with representations of
the labors of Heracles, and his three famous spears—the only ones of
their kind. The Youth, as if coming to a difficult decision, begins to
speak:

Respected friend, I was sure you would really understand. We younger
    men
who were called in, as they say, at the last minute as though to reap
the glory already prepared with your own weapons,
with your own wounds, your own death,
we too have knowledge of it and acknowledge it, and we have, yes, we
    too, have our wounds
in another part of the body—unseen wounds,
without the compensation of fame and of the honorable blood
poured out visibly, in visible battles, visible contests.

Such glory we'd be better off without—which of them ever wanted it?
Not one hour could we call our own, paying
the debts and obligations of others. Not even if we were in time
to see one early morning a quiet hand open the window across the way
    and reach out
to hang a canary cage from a nail in the wall,
with the solemnity of any useless and indispensable gesture.

All the speeches of great men, about the dead and about heroes.
Astonishing, awesome words, pursued us even in our sleep,
slipping beneath closed doors, from the banqueting hall
where glasses and voices sparkled, and the veil
of an unseen dancer rippled silently
like a diaphanous, whirling wall
between life and death. This throbbing
rhythmic transparency of the veil somehow comforted
our childhood nights, lightening the shadows of shields
etched on white walls by slow moonlight.

Along with our own food they prepared
the food for the dead. At the hour when we ate
they took from the table pitchers with honey and oil
and carried them to unknown graves. We made no distinction
between wine jars and funeral vases. We did not know
what was ours and what belonged to the dead. The tap
of spoon against plate was an unexpected
reproving finger touching us on the shoulder. We turned to see. Nothing.

Outside our bedrooms drums and trumpets,
crimson sparks and mute hammers in secret forges
where day and night they beat out shields and javelins,
and other hammers in workshops underground
for busts and statues of martial gods, martial men—no athletes, no
        poets,
none at all—together with hundreds of tombstones
with beautiful, naked young men, always standing,
masking, with their vertical poses,
the eternal horizontal of death. Only, sometimes,
there was a tilt of the head, a slight curve of the neck
like a flower at the edge of a cliff; and the cliff was not to be seen—the
        craftsmen
had learned (or perhaps they had been ordered?)
to leave out cliffs and things of that kind.

There was a long, white gallery (it never changed)
lined its whole length with funeral stelae. And they never let
our gaze linger even a little on their shapely limbs
or the marble curls that sometimes fell on their foreheads

232 • PHILOCTETES

like puffs from the lips of a sudden, perfumed wind
in a golden, summer afternoon—I think, yes, that it smelled
of lemon blossoms and sun-warmed willow. Such high standards
they bequeathed to us—who asked for them? Why couldn't they have
  left us alone
in our littleness, our own littleness; we don't want
to be measured against their standards—besides, what good did it do
  you, or us?

I understand you own gallant withdrawal, respected friend,
with a commonly accepted pretext—a wound in the body,
not in the mind or the spirit—a good excuse
that serpent's bite (perhaps the serpent of wisdom?)
to let you stay alone and exist—you, and no one else—
or even not exist, coiled in a circle
like the serpent biting its tail. (Often I too have wished it.)

And perhaps to meditate, in your solitude, on some revenge,
some recognition of yourself or, at least, the recognition
of the importance of your weapons. And see how you've been
  vindicated—
I make no secret of that—it's for them I have come, as you guessed—
they will give victory to the Greeks at last,
(the oracle's clear): your weapons, with my own hand.

I nevertheless came primarily for you. And I wouldn't accept your
  weapons
in exchange for my recognition or in exchange
for the deliverance that I offer you: that I will take you with me, on my
  ship,
with all your incurable wounds, with all your solitude—what kind of
  deliverance is that?
Such words are much in fashion now—we've learned them—
what can we say?—No one has time any more to see and to speak.

Torchrunners race through the night. Their torches gild the streets.
For a moment the statues of the gods shine out, pure white,
like doors opened in gigantic walls. Later
the shadow of their stone hands falls covering the street.
No one any longer can distinguish anything. One evening I saw

a frenzied crowd lift one man onto their shoulders
cheering him. A torch fell on him.
His hair caught fire. He did not cry out.
He'd been dead for some time. The crowd scattered. The evening
was left all alone, laurel-crowned, with the golden leaves of the stars.

The choice, I think, is impossible—and between what? I remember
when I was a child—from the guest rooms of our house
the splendidly masculine voices of the guests would reach me
just before bedtime, when they went to undress—and, surely,
at that time they would forget schemes for war and contests and
       ambitions,
physical in their nakedness, erotic and innocent,
as though they'd touched their own breasts, perhaps by mistake,
and they'd linger for a while at the end of the bed with legs apart,
forgetting their knees cupped in their warm palms,
until they had finished a small, enjoyable tale
embellished with their laughter and the creaking of the beds.

I heard them then from the corridor, as I stealthily examined
their gleaming swords and shields
propped against the wall, secretly reflecting the moonlight
that shone on them through the glass door—and I felt so alone and
       confused
as if that were the moment when I had to choose for all time
between their laughter and their weapons (which were both their own). I
       was afraid, too,
that Father would get up in the night and find me in the corridor
touching these strange weapons—most of all
that he would realize I had heard the laughter, would realize
my secret dilemma. I never went near the guest rooms;
I only heard the guests' voices
as they went from passage to passage—one in shade
and the next in light—often drowned out by the clatter
of the horses' hooves outside in the courtyard. Once, indeed, I was
       terrified
by a great shadow that fell right in front of my feet—a horse
stopped at the glass door and peered in
casting a shadow over the hammered images on the shields.

That's how big my father's shadow was, too; it darkened the whole
   house,
blocked windows and doors from top to bottom,
and sometimes I thought that in order to see the day
I would have to put my head under his legs—
this scared me especially—the feel of his thighs on my neck. I preferred
to stay in the house, in the rooms' benevolent half-light,
amid the docile furniture, the obedient feel of the curtains,
and at other times in the deserted hall with its statues. I loved the
   kouroi.

There coolness and silence reigned, at the hour when outside,
in the olive groves and the vineyards, the cicadas went mad
in the burning golden noontime. On the floor
the shadows of statues crisscrossed, calm, harmonious,
forming diaphanous blue rhomboids; and once
a tiny mouse, made bold by the stillness,
walked slowly across the feet of the kouroi, stopped,
stared with two drops of oil, all suspicion, at the oblong windows,
pointing the tip of its nose, like a soft dart, toward the absolute,
in the name of all petrified things—their small associate.

Father did not like the statues. I never saw him
pause before any one of them—perhaps he was already himself
his own statue, the image in bronze
of a proud, unapproachable horseman. And only
that friendship of his with Patroclus
brought him at all close to me, when he came down
with broad strides off his pedestal
and they disappeared under the trees. It seemed strange to me
that I never heard any creaking
from the joints of his bronze knees.

And Mother, too, was a shadow, a diaphanous shadow,
ethereal and remote—a tender presence
amid her enduring absence. The men,
on their way back from hunting, just before they reached the house,
saw, behind the trees, the western window,
which seemed to be hanging from the branches, in midair, by itself,
and there, in its darkened frame, Mother

as if she too were suspended, staring
far off at the sunset, as though gilded. The men believed
it was for them she waited, hungrily watching the road. Much later
we realized she was gone, that she was indeed hanged.

On her face, the shadow of the rope was just barely discernible.
The moment she heard the hunters down the road
she'd composed her expression, brushing back with her hand
a black ringlet that perhaps had fallen into her eyes,
swept aside the shadow of that rope. It was later we learned the truth,
when the last horn was heard over the lake, in the twilight,
when a little plaster fell from the facade of the house without a sound
and the whole field was hazy, rosy and golden, with the blue ghosts of
        the trees,
and the dogs, nearly exhausted, their tongues out,
howled wildly as if they would mount to heaven, in ecstasy.

Soon the evening was filled with bright, dappled wings
of slaughtered birds, there on the stone table outside,
with dishes full of grapes—dark blue, amber, red—
and cool well water. And Mother smiled sadly:
"Did you see how you wanted to be a bird for me?" she asked me,
and commanded the servants to pluck the birds for dinner
in the back courtyard, where already the shadow of the mountain
fell like sunlit, sparkling iron, and the giant cypresses,
austere, gloomy, and solitary,
took a mute, inexplicable initiative.

It was then that the men, sweaty, dusty from the hunt,
with bits of thistledown in their hair,
with stains of pine pollen on their shoulders,
had gone into the bathhouses, and from outside could be heard
the sound of water falling, and the scent of soap mingled
with the smell of the garden—warm resin, geraniums, mint, rosemary—
cool fragrances, deeply refreshing. And the gardener set down
his big watering can on the stone bench, taking the occasion
to say a humble, cheerful "Good evening" to his respected mistress
mixed up with names of flowers, habits of seeds, and something
about diseased leaves and fruit, about caterpillars and insects.

Above the eucalyptus, thousands of birds shrilled glorias,
insanely, as if proclaiming a trade fair, while below them
the servants were plucking the other birds. And evening came,
calm, slow, irreversible, filled with light green-golden down feathers,
at their roots a fleck of imperceptible red. Sometimes
a down feather like that would catch in my mother's hair
and shade her completely. Then, tactfully,
getting close to her for a moment, I would remove it—I couldn't bear
to see Mother shaded by alien sins. A small exclamation
escaped her involuntarily, as if they'd pulled a knife from her chest.

Another evening—I remember—she had put her hands round the lamp
to protect the flame from the wind; her hands
became transparent, pink, like two great rose petals—
a curious flower, and the flame of the lamp
an implausible pistil. Then, I saw
her keys left on the stone steps,
next to the bags and the bows of the hunters; and I realized:
those hands would never again be able to unlock anything,
hands that were so singular, so remarkable, locked for all time
in their particular transparency. When she talked
it was as if she left the most important thing unspoken; and her lips
     hardly seemed to move
in the shadow thrown by her long eyelashes.

I still remember one midday: as she drank water under the trees,
I stared again at her hands, more transparent
than the glass she was holding; the shadow of her glass
fell on the grass, a pale, luminous circle; then
a bee settled in the circle's center, its wings faintly lit up,
as though it were besieged by the sense of an inexplicable happiness.
It was the last summer before I too was called up with my class.

I have told you a lot about Mother—perhaps because I discerned in your
     hands, my friend,
a hint of that light in hers. Whatever she touched
suddenly turned into distant music, no longer tangible,
audible only from then on, or not even that. Nothing was left—
a forgotten echo, a vague sensation—no certainty.

The light changed after that—camp fires, naked bodies,
red, intense red, flushed from the flames, as if stained with blood,
as if stripped of their skin—more carnal and bestial,
more shameless and sensual, like some great sacrificial beast
whose entrails and testicles hung from a hook through the night
among the stars, drained of color by their light,
while in the trench nearby ran
blood, sperm, urine, excrement, filthy water,
and the shadows galloped far away in the red glow,
until the moon rose soft and moist like the sex of a woman;
then began remorse and repentance and creation.

Then one could hear the babble of the river under the trees—
an echoing coolness—and not ask where it was going.
The fires died down little by little. Great birds, asleep
above in the branches, now and then half-opened their eyes,
and faint moonlight filtered through onto the leaves.

The men picked lice from their chests and legs;
the youths, almost hairless, bashful when touched,
felt every so often two strong jolts in their nipples
as though stabbed by two delicious arrows in the night
and their belly muscles tightened like ropes at their waists. The sentries
took off their sandals and rubbed between their toes,
amassing black, greasy little lumps of dirt, which they kneaded for
     hours,
malleable and restful, like secret little statues,
then hurled them silently into the night. Later,
smelling their two fingers, they'd sniff at them for a while,
handsome, rough, drowsy, until sleep overtook them.

The great shields, left on the ground,
gave off a slow, metallic sound, as though being struck
by the distant spearpoints of the stars. In their hollows
commands of generals congealed unseen. Above the tents
sparkled the vast naked herringbone of the Milky Way. And it was once
     more
almost as it had been, in summers long ago, a dread
of some unknown, indefinite thief, or even of the usual thieves,

lest they jump into our rooms through the open windows, from the
    balcony—
we didn't know how to guard against them then (or now)—we were
    distracted
by the buzzing of a mosquito, the hum of moonlight,
the arches echoing with clandestine kisses.
A woman, trusting in solitude, excreted calmly in the field,
feeling on her buttocks the sharp pricking of the weeds and the stars.

This sensation of eternal thieving, or rather pillaging—
mute, concealed, and constant. And suddenly the curtain of the
    bedchamber
made three dancing leaps over the heat
with the clear aim of transferring our attention
to the gold-embroidered hem of a woman's gown; and later
hung motionless, dull blue in the still air, covering a statue,
perhaps a granite statue of night, or one of theft in red stone,
and again that seductive sawing of crickets
and those soothing voices of frogs
or the dry rustle of a cockroach's circular progression inside a helmet.

We didn't have time to make certain. Before we had finished
the first count of the stars, we fell asleep. At dawn
a blind owl fallen in the underbrush felt its way,
while its milky eyes explored another country,
and the shadow of Oeta drew away from the plain
like a huge tortoise drawing in its feet.

Then the sun resounded on the horizon. High in the air
gleamed the sixty-four-fold hooves of his horses
and, below, the bullock carts gave off an answering glow. The gates
    opened.
A crush in the marketplace—fruit vendors, tradesmen—
mountains of fruit and vegetables, and the country folk with their
    donkeys.

Some philosopher who woke too early was strolling silently
between two rows of butchered oxen. Potters
set their pitchers in order beside the road
like a fantastic clay army. At the gymnasia,

still cool from the early morning dampness, in slanting light
the first runners emerged from the dressing rooms and tried a few
short laps, almost like birds in the air. Soldiers
filled great field kettles in the barrack yards.

A few women with uncombed hair shook improbably pure white sheets
out of the windows. Metopes of temples
and the upper tiers of the stadia gleamed bright. Such brilliance,
blind, blinding precisely in its self-display,
as though it hid something from us—and indeed it hid us—
perhaps this was the theft? And it was also
the huge jars in the gardens and the cellars
and the gold masks with their vacant, searching eyes.
A momentary silence; the same vague feeling; a common conspiracy.

Beards grew, hair, nails, organs;
and always notions about corpses and about heroes, and again about
       heroes;
great bones of horses on the slopes amid the dry broom;
the breathing of unwashed bodies quickened. A woman, once,
walked far into the evening with a water jug on her shoulder.
The air closed, blocking the way behind her. The evening
folded at the tip of a banner. Some star
suddenly shouted an inexplicable "No", and later
the galloping of the horses faded away during the long night
leaving the stars more silent above the river.

No one any longer had time to remember, to reflect, to question—
a permanent displacement; everything cut short, worn out, unfinished.
The lamentations and the cheering took on, little by little,
the same tone, as did the faces of enemies and friends—
       indistinguishable.

Only at night when the horizontal silence fell, when the fighting
       subsided,
one could hear amid the rocks the prolonged groans of the wounded,
and the moon was like the dilated eye of a slaughtered horse—only then
did we ascertain that we were not yet dead.

240 • PHILOCTETES

Then, a thousand-eyed cunning glittered in all the corners of the night,
encouraging us to take back all they'd stolen from us, steal it, even.
        There, below,
on the moonlit shore, our ships, dark,
motionless, turned to stone, were meditating on another journey—
and if sometimes a wet oar gleamed for a little, it would quickly echo
        the beat
in the pulse at our wrists. Light-footed messengers
hurried to and fro, swooping like bats, and perhaps there remained
a tell-tale sign in the white pebbles or the thorns—
a black feather, part of a sandal strap, a silver buckle—
and next day, at dawn, we'd have to get rid of them.

And it was as if we already heard the secret axes in the forest
chopping wood. We heard the great thud whenever a tree
crashed to the ground, and the frightened silence
hiding behind our shoulders. And it was as if I saw already
the Wooden Horse, hollow, huge, gleaming dangerously
in the starlight, almost divine, while its shadow
stretched out, mythical, over the walls. And I felt already
as if I was there inside the hollow of the horse, with the others,
entirely alone, in an uncomfortable position, in the horse's neck,
and watching the glassy night through its vacant eyes
as if suspended in the void, knowing
the mane that rippled above my neck
was not my own—nor, of course, the victory. Meanwhile, I readied
        myself
for the great, useless leap into the unknown.

Thus, in this position, high up there in the planked throat of the horse,
I felt swallowed up, yet still alive, with a view over
the enemy camps, the fires, the ships, the stars,
all the intimate, awe-inspiring, incalculable wonder—as they say—of the
        world,
as if I were a lump caught in the throat of infinity and at the same time a
        bridge
arching from two shores, both precipitous and unexplored—
a false bridge, certainly, made of wood and bitter cunning.
(It was from up there, I think, in the midst of such a nightmare,

that I gazed for the first time upon the soothing brightness of your
   weapons.)

Other times, at high noon, during a pause in the battle,
or on the march, when a halt was called, we knew at once that we were
   thirsty—
nothing else: we were thirsty. We gave no name to water and our thirst;
we only bent down, embarrassed, to quickly retie our sandals,
and thus, bent over, we looked out, retaining
an inverted image of landscape, men, people like ourselves,
a deceptive image, forgivable, transparent, broken,
as if reflected in water. And there was no water. We were thirsty.

That road was laid waste to its furthest end. On both sides
were covered wells, polluted with corpses. Stone cracked
from the great heat. Cicadas shrilled. The horizon
was whitewash and tongues of fire. In the pitiless sunlight,
on the coping of the walls, vertical slivers of broken glass sparkled,
dividing companions, friends, allies. But for all
the sharp-pointed, glorious glitter, nothing was hidden. I saw gallant
   men
throw ashes on their hair, and I saw the ashes
mingle with their tears, black furrows
scored in their beards, down to their chins.

Those who once, stark naked, washed their horses on the shore
and rubbed their manes with light oil, both horses and men
gleaming in the brilliant mornings, these same ones
who danced in the evenings above the fires, their naked heels
glowing the deepest purple, now cringe
among the rocks, grow angry, grumble, place their hands, palms down,
in front of their legs, are ashamed, hide,
as if they are to blame, as if they are all at fault. And perhaps they envy
the young warriors for their beautiful innocence, for their daring,
their enthusiastic parroted eloquence, and perhaps most of all
for their heavy, shining hair, bursting with health and love.

And yet they too set off once with charming naïveté
and the secret vainglorious ambition to change the world. They set off

all together, yet each one apart, and they knew it and they saw it: each
    one
for his own reasons, a private ambition, covered by
one grand idea, one common purpose, a transparent roof
under which they could more clearly distinguish each one's share,
the misfortune and meanness of all. How, dear friend, could you have
    put order
into this confusion? How could you stay near them? Now I understand.

Nights in the ships, when the weary private soldiers
lay down, heaped like sacks on the deck,
adorable in the guilelessness of their youth,
in their ignorance, their animal purity, their physical beauty,
strong from their exercise at useful work, in the fields, in workshops, on
    the roads,
obedient to necessity and facile hope,
with the eloquent generalizations of their own innocence, like cattle
led to the slaughter for the profit of others, and yet
smiling in their sleep, muttering, snoring,
cursing a dream cow or, half-naked, murmuring over and over
a woman's name to their nocturnal erection,
spilling the secret perpetuity of oceanic starlight—these nights,

I heard, amid the splashing of oars, the voices, the squabbles
of the commanders, over booty they had not yet taken, over titles
they had not yet decreed. And I saw in their eyes
hatred for all, the savage suffering of the eminent;
and deep inside, like a feeble firefly in the depth of a dark cave,
I saw their loneliness too. Behind their beards
glittered their fate, stripped bare, as behind a forest's naked branches
a parched plain in the moonlight, sown with white bones.

And this knowledge was like a blessing, a release,
a soothing admission, an inert delight
at the touch of eternity and nothingness. For a few moments,
despite all this, I could still enjoy the privilege
of distinguishing behind or among the shields and the spears
a bit of sea, a little twilight, a beautiful knee,
and of having—yes, despite everything—a tiny justification to give me
    pleasure,

and all my countless unknown terrors were dissolved completely,
a deep and joyful cloud, in mythic infinity.

I remember one night when we sailed with a full moon. The moonlight
set a gold funeral mask over every face;
for an instant the soldiers stood and stared
as if they didn't recognize one another or as if they recognized one
      another
for the first time; and suddenly, they all turned
and stared up at the moon,
all motionless, above the ever-moving sea,
silent, bewitched, as if already dead and immortal.

Then, as if they felt vaguely guilty, as if they could not endure
this infinite, light burden, they began to yell,
joke, make vulgar gestures, compare their organs,
smear themselves with grease from the spit, leap, dance, wrestle,
pretend to read in rams' scraped shoulder blades facetious omens and
      dirty stories,
perhaps to forget that moment, that understanding, that absence.

Perhaps you too, on such a night, amid the countervailing
voices of your fellow warriors, could hear, clearly,
the absence of your own voice—as I did, that time with the full moon.
Yes, I heard myself not shouting; and I stayed there
immobilized among them all, all alone
among even my best friends, all alone
in a great lonely circle, on a very high threshing floor,
and I could hear with terrible clarity the voices of the others, and at the
      same time
I could hear my own silence. From up there
I observed for a second time the brightness of your weapons. And I
      knew.

Perhaps it was at a similar moment, respected friend, that you too
      decided
to withdraw. Then, I suppose, you let the snake at the altar
bite you. You knew, in any case, they only need
our weapons, and not ourselves (as you said).
But you are your weapons, the honors won

through labor, friendship, and sacrifice, a gift from the hand
of him who strangled the Seven-headed one, who killed
the guard of Hades. And you saw it
with your own eyes, and you asked for it: your legacy
and your perfect weapon. It conquers on its own. Now,
please show me how to use it. The time has come.

Perhaps they will say that the victory is mine only, and perhaps they will
    forget
the weapon's possessor, the expert—this no one would wish,
but what does it matter to you?—you will win
the final victory, and (as you said) the only one,
this honeyed and terrible knowledge: that there is no victory.

Alone, you hung your empty shirt in a tree
to deceive passers-by into saying: "He's dead";
and you, hiding behind the bushes, heard
how they believed you were already a corpse, so you could live
through the whole range of your own senses; and then you'd be able
to wear once more the shirt of your feigned death
until you became (as you have become) the great silence of your being.

An old spear, dipped in blood, retired from battle,
solitary, smooth, useless,
resting upright against the rocks, with its bronze tip
pointed straight at the moon, broken by moonbeams,
will curve like a tolerant finger
above a lyre—the eternal lyre, as you said. At this time,
I believe that I understand what your thankfulness has in view.

Now I remember a glorious twilight on the ocean—a stillness
forgotten, incredible—the naked boundlessness
of sky and water; no headland, no islet,
only the shadowy triremes, sailing or rowing
in a deep mythic rosebowl; the oars
silent, uniform, like broad, diagonal, wet rays. A sailor
tried to sing, and he stayed that way
with his mouth open like a hole,
and within it appeared once more the sparkle of the sea.

Then I too loosened my belt and sensed
my own movements, peaceful, inevitable, incomprehensible,
with that authenticity of the metaphysical. And it was as if I'd untied
an age-old noose from around my neck. I held my belt for a little
then put one end of it into the water, watching it trace
a smooth line through the boundlessness, while at the same time,
in my fingers, reverberated the motionless pulse
of a rare lightness. Then
I drew my belt out of the water and, wet as it was,
I firmly tightened it around me once more.

Sometimes, the light of twilight is an enlightenment—is it not?—
reflected so abundantly on the water, joined
with its own image, autonomous
in relation to night and day—a quite independent synthesis
of night and day. That gleam,
so brief, and yet immortal—a breastplate, all gold,
securely around our chests; above all
that invulnerable, thinnest layer of air
between the breastplate and our flesh, which returns to the center
the outward movement of our breathing. Sometimes,
at a very deep indrawn breath, we feel the points of our breast
secretly touch the breastplate's metal, cooled by late afternoon,
with the supreme pleasure of the nonexistent, in erotic contact.

I can show you the mark of the belt on my body—
the print of a small wheel—the impressed trace of the buckle.
Oh, yes, freedom is clamped tight always, it's a vise
that grips the whole body—and the heel, always, without fail.
Besides, the tightening of the belt forces the chest to expand.
This deep and painful withdrawal, which little by little calms down.

Still, let the gods guard us from becoming captives
even of the most beautiful revelation yet, lest we lose forever
the tender artlessness of metamorphosis
and the ultimate achievement of speech. Perhaps this would have
    frightened you alone
in your complete solitude—and the lack of objects, I think,
not for your use, but for touching, comparing, describing,

for the fraternal relating of the infinite, the calculation of the
    incalculable.

For this, at least, come back with us. The proud pain
of your celibate sanctity—that I will not reveal to anyone.
No one will understand it, nor will anyone be alarmed
at your unalloyed delight in your freedom. The mask of action
that I have brought hidden in my sack will hide
your transparent, remote face. Put it on. Come.

When we get to Troy, the wooden horse I told you about
will be ready. I will hide inside it with your weapons. This will be
my own mask, and one for your weapons as well. Only in this way
will we gain victory. This will be
my victory—and yours too, I mean. It will be the victory
of all the Greeks together, and their gods. What's to be done?
Only such victories exist. Let us go.

The ten years have already passed. The end draws near.
Come see what you foresaw. Come see for what plunder
we have exchanged so many of our dead, the way we've exchanged
our ancient enemies for enmity among ourselves. Amid the ruins,
where columns of smoke will rise straight toward the sun,
amid the slain, the fallen shields, the chariot wheels,
amid the groans of vanquished and victors, your own
knowing, gentle smile will be a light for us,
your own forbearance and silence a compass.

Come. We need you not only for the victory but, above all,
after the victory, when those of us who are left go aboard the ships once
    more, returning
with Helen, older by ten years,
with a changed accent, with a different look in her eyes,
concealing in long, gold-embroidered veils
her foreignness and her aging, concealing
amid her veils and our own foreignness the remorse, the despair,
and the great, inescapable terror of her love:
why did we come, why did we fight, why and where are we returning?

I believe that even the most beautiful women, when they age,
become a little like mothers, all acquiescence and bitter endurance,
all tenderness and affection, and this disguised
as the seemingly formal justice of necessary errors,
necessary losses, ten necessary years. Then, the women
grasp the keys at their belts with their palms,
with one identical gesture as if a sharp pain had struck them in
    midbody—
beautiful women, aged, mythical mothers,
in a final gesture of simple sanctity:
lest we see that the keys will never again open anything.

How will we endure Helen's gaze,
behind her dark, glittering veils,
amid the sweet shining of the stars, the unexplored night,
while the rowers keep silent and the oars beat
the secret, oceanic drums of return, to the rhythm of the irrevocable?

For now, at least, stay near us. We need this
even more than your weapons. And you know it.
Here is the mask I brought you. Put it on. We are going.

*The serene bearded man takes the mask and lays it on the ground. He
does not put it on. Little by little his face is transformed. It becomes
younger, more positive, more present. As if copying the mask. Great
suspense and expectancy. A star falls. The Youth feels a small breeze on
his face, and his hair parts evenly in the middle of its own accord, as
though separated by a light, golden comb. Below, on the shore, the
sailors' singing can be heard—a straightforward popular song, full of
ropes, masts, rowers, stars, much bitterness and manliness and
endurance—all the dark, glittering sea, all the boundlessness, reduced to
human measure. Perhaps it is the same song that, on another journey,
the Hermit too had heard. And perhaps because of it he makes his
decision. He rises calmly, fetches his weapons from the cave, surrenders
them to the Youth, lets him go ahead, and follows him toward the
beach. As he advances between the rocks and the tall thistles he sees his
weapons, moving ahead of him, shine in the starlight, and hears the
sailors' song reverberate on their metal. And thus it is as though he were
following, not the Youth, but his own weapons, marching in the*

direction toward which their gleaming, well-sharpened tips always pointed—the quarter of death. And the mask remains up there, on the rocks, outside the cave, bright too amid the mysterious blessedness of night, with a strange, incomprehensible affirmation.

ATHENS, SAMOS, MAY 1963–OCTOBER 1965

· HELEN ·

The dilapidation is already visible from way off—unplastered,
crumbling walls, faded shutters, the balcony rails eaten with rust. A
curtain stirs outside the upper-floor window, yellowing, its lower edge
ragged. When he gets nearer—hesitant still—the same neglect is
apparent in the garden: plants running wild, with great fleshy leaves, the
trees unpruned, the few flowers choked by nettles, the fountains dry and
cracked, lichen growing on the fine statues. A lizard squats, motionless,
between the breasts of a young Aphrodite, warmed by the last rays of
the setting sun. So many years ago. He was very young then—twenty-
two? twenty-three? And she? You could never tell. There was this great
radiance she gave off—it blinded you, pierced through you, you no
longer knew what existed, if it existed, if you yourself existed. He rings
the doorbell, and hears it sound inside, a lonely echo, in a room he once
knew, unknown now because differently arranged, with unfamiliar
dark-colored side passages. They are in no hurry to answer the door.
Someone peers down from the upstairs window. Not her. A
maidservant—very young, who seems to be laughing. She withdraws
from the window. Another pause. Then footsteps on the stairs inside.
The door is unbolted. He goes in, climbs the staircase. A smell of dust,
rotten fruit, dried lather, urine. This way now. Bedroom. Wardrobe.
Metal mirror. Two broken-down ladderback chairs. A small zinc-topped
table with coffee cups and cigarette butts. And she—? No. No. It isn't
possible. Old. Old, a hundred, two hundred years old. Even five years
ago—no. No. Holes in the sheet. There she is, sitting on the bed,
hunched up, absolutely still. Only her eyes—still huge, imperious,
penetrating, vacant.

Yes, yes—it's me. Sit with me for a little while. No one comes any more.
    I've nearly
forgotten the use of words. And I've no need for them. I guess summer
    must be almost here:
the curtains stir differently, they're trying to say something. Such
    nonsense. One of them
has already got out of the window, it's straining to break loose from its
    rings,
to fly away over the trees—perhaps already it's trying to uproot
the whole house, take it somewhere else—but the house resists with all
    its corners
and I too with it, though I feel, have felt for months now, freed
from my dead, and indeed from myself; and my very resistance,

incomprehensible, involuntary, strange, is my sole possession—my link
with this bed, this curtain—but also my fear, as though my entire
body were controlled by this ring with the black stone that I wear on my
    forefinger.

I stare at this stone now, hour after hour in the night—
black, no reflections—it grows and grows, is brimming
with black water, the water rises, floods; I sink down,
not to the lower depths, just to an upper level, from which
I can make out my room below me, myself, the wardrobe,
the slave-girls silently bickering; I see one climb up
on a stool to strip from the window that photograph of Leda,
with surly vindictiveness; I see the duster leaving
a dust trail of tiny bubbles that rise and burst
with a silent poppling around my knees or ankles.

I see you too, your face thunderstruck, confused, broken up
by the black water's slow currents—your face now widening, now
    elongated
with yellow stripes. Your hair rises toward the surface
like an inverted medusa. But then I say: "It's only a stone,
a small precious stone." Then all its blackness contracts,
dries out, is concentrated on one tiny point—I feel it,
here, just below my throat. And there I am, back
in my room, on my bed, beside familiar flasks and bottles,
that look at me, nodding agreement, one by one—they're my only help
against insomnia, fear, remembrance, forgetfulness, asthma.

And what about you? Are you still in the army? Take care, don't be too
    concerned
with heroic deeds, high position, glory. What use are they to you? Do
    you still
have that shield with my portrait engraved on it? You were so funny
in that lofty helmet of yours with its outsize plume—so young,
so shy and reserved, as though your handsome face were hidden
in the back legs of a horse, and its tail hung down
over your naked back. Don't get angry again. Stay a little longer.

The time for rivalries is long past, the desires have dried up;
maybe now we can look, together, at the same scene of futility,

where, I believe, the only true encounters happen—indifferent
perhaps, but always soothing—our new identity, solitary, quiet, empty,
without displacements or contrasts—merely raking over the debris in
    the hearth,
sometimes building fine tall ash mounds with the cinders,
or, seated on the ground, beating the earth with soundless palms.

Little by little things lost their meaning, grew empty; or could it be
that they'd never had any meaning? Sagging, hollow;
we stuffed them with chaff or bran to give them shape,
body, solidity, to firm them up—chairs and tables,
the beds we slept on, words—always empty, fill them
like those canvas bags and sacks that merchants use, their contents
identifiable even from outside:
potatoes or onions, wheat, corn, almonds, flour.

Sometimes a full sack will catch on a nail on the stairs
or on an anchor fluke down at the harbor, tearing a hole
through which the flour trickles, a small stupid river. The sack slowly
    empties.
Beggars scoop up the flour with their cupped hands, to make
flat bread or porridge. The sack sags. Someone
picks it up by its two lower corners, shakes it out in the air,
so that a cloud of white dust envelopes him, whitens his hair,
especially whitens his eyebrows. The others watch him.
They don't understand at all, they're waiting for him to open his mouth
    and speak,
but he says not a word, just folds the sack into fours, strides off
all white still, incomprehensible, no explanations, like a person
in fancy dress, like some naked lecher draped in a sheet,
or a clever corpse, resurrected in its grave clothes.

So, no meaning to past events, or things; and it's the same with words,
    even though
we use them as names, at random, for those things we miss, or those
we never saw in our lives—the ethereal, we say, the eternal—
words: innocent, seductive, consoling, ambiguous always
in their pretense of accuracy. What a sad story,
giving a name to a shadow, saying it in bed at night
with the sheet drawn up to our throat; and, hearing it, we suppose

in our folly that we rule the body (it rules us), that we're holding out
      against the world.

Now I forget the names I once knew best, or confuse them one with
      another—
Paris, Menelaus, Achilles, Proteus, Theoclymenus, Teucer,
Castor and Polydeuces—my brothers, moralists both; I think
they turned into stars (so it's said), guides for ships—Theseus,
      Peirithoüs,
Andromache, Cassandra, Agamemnon—sounds, mere sounds
without substance, without their image cast on a windowpane,
or on a metal mirror, or on the coastal shallows, as then
one still and sunny day, with a bristle of masts, when the battle
had slackened off, and the snap of damp sheets in the blocks
dominated the world, like the lump of a sob held fast
in a crystalline throat—and you saw the lump glitter, shiver
without becoming a cry, and suddenly that whole scene, ships,
sailors and wagons, sank into the light, into anonymity.

Another submergence now, deeper, darker—from those depths
occasional sounds drift up—when hammers struck wood
trenailing a new trireme in the little shipyard; when a big
four-horse chariot passed on the stony road, picking up the strokes
of the cathedral clock in another age, as though the hours
were far more than twelve, and as though the horses were forced
to go round and round in the clock until they were tired; or, one night
when two handsome youths under my window sang
a song for me, without words—one was one-eyed, the other
had a belt with an outsize buckle, it shone in the moonlight.

Words now won't come to me of themselves—I search for them, as
      though translating
from some tongue I don't know, yet can still translate. Between the
      words,
or even in them, deep holes remain; I peer through these
as though through the gaps where knots have dropped from the boards
      of a door
that's been nailed shut for ages. Nothing. I see nothing.

Words and names I no longer distinguish, a few sounds only—a silver
    candlestick
or a crystal flower vase sound of themselves, then are suddenly silent,
acting as though they know nothing, as though they didn't ring, as
    though no one
had touched them, or even come near them. A dress sinks softly
from chair to floor, transferring attention from
the previous sound to the simplicity of nothingness. And yet
the idea of a silent conspiracy, though dissolved in air,
floats densely, almost palpable, up to a higher plane,
just as in the very lines and wrinkles deepening round your mouth
you see the presence of an intruder, taking your place,
making *you* the intruder, here, on your own bed, in your own room.

Oh this foreignness of ours, inside our own aging clothes,
inside our own wrinkling skin; while our fingers
can't grip things any longer, can't hold even the blanket
around our body—it lifts up of itself, dissolves, vanishes, leaving us
naked to the void. And then the guitar hung up on the wall,
forgotten for years, with corroded strings, begins to tremble
as the jaw of an old woman will tremble from cold or fright, and you
    must
put the palm of your hand on the strings, cut short
their contagious shivering. But you can't find your hand, you have no
    hand,
and you sense, in your gut, that it's your own jaw trembling.

In this house the air has grown heavy, mysterious, perhaps
from the naturalness of the presence of the dead. A wooden chest
opens by itself, and out rustle old clothes—they stand up,
move around silently. Two gold bits of fringe are left on the rug. A
    curtain
is thrust aside. No one is visible, yet someone's there; a cigarette
smokes itself in the ashtray with regular puffs; whoever
left it there is in the next room, a somewhat awkward figure,
back turned, inspecting the wall, perhaps a spider
or a patch of damp—like that, facing the wall, so one can't make out
the shadowed hollow beneath his jutting cheekbones.

HELEN • 257

The dead no longer bother us, and that's strange—isn't it?
not for them so much as for us—this neutral familiarity of theirs
with a place that's rejected them, and in which they contribute nothing
to the cost of its upkeep, the worry about its decay,
but are simply themselves, consummate, changeless, only seeming a little
    larger.

That's something we're sometimes surprised by—the abnormal
    expansion of the immutable,
their silent self-containment. They're not haughty at all, not anxious
to burden you with their memories, to please you. The women
let their bellies go slack, leave their stockings fallen; they take
tacks from the silver box and hammer them one by one,
in two neat straight lines, into the velvet of the sofa; then they collect
    them
and start all over again, with the same polite concentration. Someone
    very tall
comes in from the corridor; his forehead smacks the lintel above the
    door, yet he makes
not the slightest grimace, and the blow remains wholly inaudible.

Yes, they're just as stupid as we are. Only quieter. Another one
lifts his hand in a formal gesture, as though to deliver a eulogy,
cuts a crystal from the chandelier, and places it in his mouth
very simply, like a glass fruit—you think he's going to chew it, reactivate
some kind of human function; but no, he just holds it between his teeth
so that the crystal glitters with idle brilliance. A woman
scoops face cream out of its round white jar
with a practiced movement of two fingers, and writes
two big thick capital letters—E and Θ, perhaps—
on the windowpane. The sun warms the pane, the cream melts, drips
    down the wall—
this has no significance whatever—in two short greasy tracks.

I don't know why the dead stay here when no one pities them; I can't
    think what they want,
traipsing from room to room in their fine clothes, their fine shoes,
well polished, smooth and silent—as though not treading the ground.
They clutter the place, they flop anywhere, in the two rocking chairs,

down on the floor, in the bath; they leave the faucets running,
leave the perfumed soap to melt away in the water. When the maids
pass among them, sweeping with their big brooms,
they don't even notice them. Only, sometimes, a hint of constraint
will show in one maid's laughter—it doesn't float free, out the window,
     it's like
a bird with a string tied to its leg, jerked down by someone below.

And then the slave-girls get cross with me for no discernible reason,
     throw their brooms
here, into my room, take off for the kitchen—I hear them
heating coffee in the big pots, spilling sugar on the floor—
the sugar crunches under their shoes, the smell of coffee
creeps down the corridor, fills the house, can be seen in the mirror
like a stupid swarthy insolent face, with uncombed kiss-curls,
with two blue earrings—cheap imitations; its breath blows in the
     mirror,
clouds the glass. I feel my tongue searching my mouth,
sense that I've still some saliva. "A coffee for me too," I call out to the
     slaves,
"a coffee—" (I ask only for coffee, I want nothing else). They pretend
not to hear me. I call out again and again, without resentment
or anger. They still don't answer. I hear them slurping their coffee
from my porcelain cups with the gold rims
and that pattern of tiny violets. I fall silent and stare at
one particular broom thrown down on the floor, like the rigid corpse
of that lanky greengrocer's boy who, years ago,
showed me his big stiff cock behind the garden hedge.

Oh yes, sometimes I laugh. I hear my husky laughter rising,
not from my chest now, but far lower, from my feet, or lower still,
from beneath the earth. And I laugh. How senseless it all was,
without substance, permanence, purpose—wealth, wars, grudges,
     reputations,
fine jewelry. Even my beauty.
                              What senseless tales,
of swans and Troys and loves and deeds of valor!
                                        At sad evening parties
I met my former lovers again, with white beards,

white hair, distended bellies, as though they were already
pregnant with their deaths; saw them, strangely voracious,
wolf down roast kid, without a glance at the shoulder blade—but what
    was there
to look at? a flat shadow filled it with tiny white stains.

As you know, I still held on to my former beauty
as though by a miracle (though also with dyes, herbs, lotions,
lemon juice, cucumber water). The one thing that scared me was seeing,
    in their faces,
the passage of my own years too. Then I'd clench my stomach muscles,
set my jaw in an artificial smile, as though I were
shoring up, with one thin prop, two walls on the point of collapse.

So enclosed, tensed, taut—the fatigue of it, my God—
tensed every moment, even sleeping, as though I were inside
an icy suit of armor or a wooden body corset, or
my very own Wooden Horse, treacherous, cramped, aware already
of the futility of deceit and self-deceit, the futility
of fame, the futility—and transience—of each victory.
                         A few months
    ago,
on the death of my husband (months? or is it years?) I abandoned
my Wooden Horse forever, down there in the stable, with his ancient
    nags,
for the spiders and scorpions to explore. I no longer dye my hair.

Great warts sprouted on my face. Coarse bristles
appeared round my mouth—I can feel them. I don't look in the mirror—
long, rough bristles, as though someone else has settled inside me,
some malicious impertinent man, and his beard
is pushing out through my skin. I let him be. What else can I do?
I'm scared that if I get rid of him, he'd drag *me* off as well.

Don't go. Stay a little longer. I've so much time to talk.
No one visits me any more. They were all in a hurry to go,
I could see it in their eyes—all impatient for my death. Time drags
    slowly.
The slave-girls hate me. I hear them at night, opening drawers,
helping themselves to lacework, jewelry, gold bars—who knows

if they've left me even one good dress for a special occasion
or a single pair of shoes? They stole my keys, too,
from under my pillow—I didn't stir, pretended to be asleep—
they'd have got them some other way in the end. At least I'd rather they
        didn't know I know.

Yet without them what would become of me? "Patience, patience," I
        say,
"patience," and even that's a tiny victory,
when they're reading old letters from my admirers
or the verses great poets devoted to me. They declaim them with crass
pomposity, countless errors of emphasis, rhythm, accent,
syllabic stress. I don't correct them. I pretend not to hear. At other times
they take my black eyebrow pencil and draw giant moustaches
on my statues, or adorn their heads with an antique helmet
or a chamber pot. I watch them calmly. They get furious.

One day, when I felt a little better, I asked them—the first time in ages—
to paint my face. They painted it. I went and found a mirror.
They'd painted it green, with a black mouth. "Thank you," I told them,
as though I'd seen nothing odd. They were laughing. One of them
stripped naked in front of me, put on my golden robes, and then,
barefoot, with those fat legs of hers, began to dance,
sprang up on the table in a frenzy, danced, danced, curtsied,
mimicking (I think) my own forgotten gestures. High up on her thigh
I saw a bite mark made by strong, even, male teeth.

I watched them as though I were at the theater. No humiliation or
        distress
or outrage—what was the point? I just kept whispering to myself,
"One day we will die," or rather, "One day *you* will die," and that
was an assured revenge and dread and consolation. I stared
straight at everything, with an indescribable, impassive clarity, as
        though
my eyes were independent of me; I stared at my own eyes,
stuck there a yard in front of my face, like the panes
of a distant window, behind which someone else
sits watching what's going on in an unfamiliar street
with cafés, camera shops, perfumeries, all closed,

and I had the sensation that a small fine crystal flask
had broken, and the scent had spilled in the dusty shop window.
    Passers-by
stopped short uncertainly, sniffed the air, recalled something pleasant,
then disappeared beyond the pepper trees or the end of the road.

At moments I still catch a whiff of that perfume—remember it, rather;
isn't that odd? Things we normally call important have melted, are
    gone—
Agamemnon's murder, the slaughter of Clytemnestra (they'd sent me
a fine necklace of hers from Mycenae, made up
of miniature golden masks, linked by rings put through
the upper part of their ears—I never wore it.) They are forgotten
though other things remain, unimportant, insignificant—I remember
    one day
seeing a bird perched on a donkey's back, and that inexplicable
incident seemed to explain, if only for me, some mystery.

I still remember, as a child, on the banks of the Eurotas, by the warm
    oleanders,
hearing the sound of a tree's bark peeling off; the fragments
fell softly into the water, sailed like triremes, drifted away,
and I waited, stubbornly, for an orange-striped black butterfly
to perch on a strip of bark, puzzled at moving while sitting still;
and it amused me to think that butterflies, for all their mastery
of air, don't know the first thing about water travel, or rowing. And it
    came.

There are odd isolated moments, almost funny. One man
strolls out at noon with a basket on his head; this basket
completely obscures his face, it's as though he were headless, or
    wearing
a marvellous eyeless, many-eyed mask. Another,
wandering in a reverie at nightfall, stumbles somewhere, curses,
turns back, searches, finds a small pebble, picks it up, kisses it. Only
    then
does he remember to look around him. And slinks off, guiltily. A
    woman

thrusts one hand into her pocket, finds nothing, pulls her hand out,
raises it, looks at it carefully, as though it were powdered with the dust
     of the void.

A waiter has trapped a fly in his fist. He doesn't squash it.
Then a customer calls him, he's distracted, he opens his fist, the fly
buzzes out, alights on a glass. A scrap of paper drifts down the street
hesitantly, pausing often, without attracting attention
from anyone. That pleases it. But every so often it gives off
an odd rustling sound that belies its indifference, as though it were now
     seeking
some incorruptible witness to its shy, secret progress. And all these
     things
acquire a desolate, inexplicable beauty, a deep compassion
from our own strange and obscure gestures—don't they?

Everything else if gone, as though it never existed. Argos, Athens,
     Sparta,
Corinth, Thebes, Sicyon—mere shadows of names. I pronounce them,
     they sound like ruins
that collapsed still half-built. A pedigree dog, lost, stands outside
a cheap dairy's shop window. A passing girl eyes it;
it makes no response, its shadow spreads over the broad sidewalk.
I never learned the reason. I don't think there is one. All that remains
is this humiliating, forced (by whom?) gesture of approbation
as we nod in assent, as though greeting someone with incredible
servility, though nobody's passing, nobody's there.

I seem to recall that someone else told me, one evening, in a totally
     colorless voice,
the events of my life. I began to nod off; inwardly I prayed
that he'd finally stop, that I'd be able to close my eyes,
to fall asleep. And while he was talking, to do something, hold sleep at
     bay,
I counted, one by one, the strands of the fringe on my shawl, keeping
     time
with a silly children's song for blindman's buff, until
all sense was lost from his story. But the sound remains—

shouts, thuds, creaks—the sound of silence, an odd wailing,
someone scratches the wall with his nails, scissors fall on the
    floorboards.
Someone coughs (hand over his mouth, so as not to wake the other
person sleeping beside him—his death, perhaps), then stops. Afterward
silence comes spiralling back from an empty, covered well.

These nights I can hear the servants moving my heavy furniture,
hauling it downstairs—a mirror, held like a stretcher,
reflecting the worn plaster moldings on the ceiling; one panel
bangs on the banisters, but doesn't break. The old overcoat on its
    hanger
lifts empty hands for a moment, then stuffs them back in its pockets.
The settees with their tiny castors squeak on the floor. I feel,
here, in my elbow, that scrape on the wall from the wardrobe's sharp
    corner, or the corner
of the big carved dinner table. What will they *do* with them? "Bye now,"
    I say
almost mechanically, as though bidding farewell to a guest who's still a
    stranger. Only
that vague sound lingering in the passage, as though from the horns
of ruined master-huntsmen, amid the last spring rains, in a burnt-out
    forest.

And really, such a mass of useless objects, gathered with such greed—
the whole place was cluttered up, we couldn't move, our knees
would bump into other knees, of wood, stone, or metal. Of course, we
    badly need
to grow old enough to become just, to attain that gentle
impartiality, that sweet altruism in comparisons and judgments,
when our own part exists no longer save in this peace.

Ah yes, all those stupid battles, heroics, ambitions, arrogant gestures,
sacrifices, defeats, more defeats, more battles, for objects already
determined by others, in our absence. And men, quite innocent,
blinding themselves with hairpins, beating their heads
against that towering wall, well aware that the wall wouldn't collapse
or even splinter, yet at least trying to see through a crack

to a little blue, unshadowed by time and their shadow. And yet—who
    knows—
maybe there, where someone holds out without hope, maybe there what
    we call
human history is beginning, and the splendor of humankind,
amid rusty fetters and bones of oxen and horses,
amid ancient tripods on which a little bay still burns,
while its smoke rises fraying in the sunset like a golden fleece.

Stay a bit longer. Night's fallen. The golden fleece, yes. Oh, thinking
comes late to us women, it relaxes us somehow. But with men it's
    different,
they never stop thinking—perhaps they're afraid, perhaps they don't
    want
to look straight at their fear, recognize their exhaustion, rest—
no, into the dark they rush, vainglorious, cowardly, bustling. Their
    clothes
always smell of smoke from some conflagration they've gone
through or past without noticing. They undress so quickly, throw
their clothes on the floor, sprawl on the bed. Yet even their very bodies
smell of smoke, it makes them drowsy. In the hair on their chests
I found, while they still slept, some small burnt leaves
or gray-black down from slaughtered birds. These I collected, laid
away in a casket—sole proof of this secret contact—I never
showed them to *them*, they would not have acknowledged them.

Oh, at certain moments, yes, they were handsome—when naked, for
    instance, surrendered
to sleep, quite relaxed and open, with their great strong bodies
damp, slack, like brawling streams that have tumbled down
from the high hills to a peaceful plain, or like abandoned children. Then
I loved them, I really did, as though I'd borne them. I watched their long
    eyelashes
and wanted to take them into myself to protect them, or in this way
to couple with their whole body. They slept. And such sleep compels
your respect, since it's so rare. These things too are gone. Forgotten.

It's not that my memory's lost—I still remember—just that memories
are bare of emotion, don't move us; are faceless, tranquil,

HELEN • 265

clear, to their bloodiest backwater. Only one
still keeps the air about it, can still breathe.
                                                        Late one afternoon,
surrounded by the unending cries of the wounded,
by old men's whispered curses and their amazement, amid
the stink of a common death that, from moment to moment,
gleamed on a shield or spearpoint or on the metope
of some neglected shrine or on a chariot wheel, I climbed alone
to the top of the high walls, and walked there.
                                                        Alone, completely alone,
        between
Trojans and Achaeans, feeling the air mold my finespun
robe against me, caress my nipples, unclothe my entire body,
leaving it stark naked except for a broad silver band
that held my breasts up high—
                                        so lovely, inviolate, tested,
while my two rival lovers were battling, and the outcome
of that interminable war was being settled—
                                                        I never saw
Paris' helmet strap severed, only a glitter of bronze,
a circular flash, as his opponent, enraged,
twisted it on his head. A dazzling nothing.
                                                It wasn't worth watching
        at all.
The result had been fixed in advance by divine decision, and Paris,
minus his dusty sandals, would shortly turn up in bed,
washed by the goddess's own hands, smiling awaiting me, maybe
        wearing
a strip of pink sticking plaster to hide a sham wound in his side.

I saw nothing else; I hardly even heard their bloodthirsty war cries—
high on the wall as I was, above these mortals' heads, airy, sensual,
belonging to no one, needing no one, as though
I, in my self-containment, were the whole of love—released
from fear of death and time, with a white flower in my hair,
with a flower between my breasts, and one more in my mouth, to hide
my smile of freedom.
                                They could
have shot me from either side.
                                        I offered an easy target,

strolling along the ramparts, clearly outlined
against the gold and crimson of the evening sky.
                                    I kept my eyes shut
to make any hostile gesture by them easier—though knowing at heart
that no one would dare it. Their hands shook in wonder
at my beauty, my immortality—
                            (perhaps I can add, now, that I didn't
fear death, I felt it was so remote from me).
                                    Then
I threw away the two flowers from my hair and breasts—the third
I still held in my mouth—threw one to each side of the wall
with a totally evenhanded gesture.
                            And then the men, inside and out,
hurled themselves one at another, foes and friends, to grab hold of
these flowers, to offer them to me—my own flowers. I saw
nothing else after that—only those bent backs, as though they all
were down on their knees on the ground, where the spilt blood was
        drying in the sun—perhaps
they had trampled the flowers already.
                            I didn't see.
                                    I waved,
stood on tiptoe, and vanished—letting
the third flower, too, flutter free from my lips as I went.

One thing's still left to me—a reward of a sort, a remote justification,
        and perhaps
it really *does* survive, somewhere in the world—a momentary freedom,
illusory, too, of course—as a plaything of chance, of our ignorance. The
        sculptors
tried, as I recall, to fashion the last statues made of me
in exactly that pose—the statues are still out there in the garden,
you'll have seen them as you came in. Sometimes (when the maids are in
        a good mood,
and carry me across by the armpits to that windowseat),
I too can see them. They gleam in the sun. A white warmth
reaches up to here from their marble. I don't think about them any
        more. After a little
this too exhausts me. I prefer to watch a stretch of the road
where two or three children are playing with a softball, or a teenage girl
lets down a rope with a basket from the balcony opposite.

Sometimes the slave-girls forget I'm there. They don't come and put me
    back in bed,
so I stay there all night, watching an old bicycle, parked
in front of the lit-up window of a new confectioner's store,
until they switch off the lights, or I fall asleep on the window ledge.
    Every so often
I imagine I'm wakened by a star gleaming in space
like saliva from an old man's open, toothless mouth.
                                                            Now
they have leisure to carry me to the window. I stay here in bed,
sitting or lying—that I can do. To pass the time
I take hold of my face—the face of a stranger—feel it, trace its contours,
measure hairs, warts, wrinkles—what's inside
this face of mine?
                        A sour taste rises in my throat—nausea and fear,
the fear (so stupid, my God) of maybe losing even this nausea, too. Stay
    a bit longer—
there's a little light from the window, they'll have turned on the
    streetlamp outside.

Would you care to ring the bell and have them bring you something? A
    little cherry
or orange preserve—maybe there's something left in the big jars,
crystallized by now, solidified—that is, of course, if those gluttonous
slave-girls have left any. These last years I've become a solitary
sweet-eater—what else is there to do?
                                            After Troy, our life in Sparta's
so dull, boring, provincial: shut up indoors all day
amid the piled-up booty of all those wars. And the memories,
faded and troublesome, creeping behind you, there in the mirror
when you comb your hair, or there in the kitchen, seeping out
with the rich steam from the cooking pots; and you hear in the boiling
    water
a run of dactylic hexameters from that Third Rhapsody, while
somewhere close by, from a neighborhood henhouse, a cock crows
    strangely.

You know, too well, the monotonous life we lead. Even the newspapers
are all alike, same shape, same size, same headlines—I no longer read
    them. Now and again

there are flags on the balconies, national ceremonies, military parades
regular as clockwork toys—only the cavalry keeps a touch of the
    impromptu,
the personal; because of their horses, maybe. They kicked up dust in
    clouds,
we used to shut the windows. Afterward you'd sit there dusting, one by
    one,
the vases, cups, picture frames, porcelain figurines, mirrors, sideboards.

I no longer went to these ceremonies. My husband would come back
    from them all sweaty,
hurl himself, smacking his lips, at his food, chewing up with it
old boring glories, stale exhausted grudges. I used to contemplate
the buttons of his waistcoat, straining as though they'd burst—he'd
    become very fat.
Under his chin a broad dark birthmark flushed and faded.

Then I'd take hold of my own chin, still eating abstractedly,
feeling inside my grasp the shifts of my lower jaw,
as though it was severed from my head, and I held it, naked, in my
    palm.
Perhaps that's why I too grew fat. I don't know. Everyone looked
    frightened.
I saw them, sometimes, through the window. They moved about
    crabwise
as though limping a little, or with something hidden under one arm. In
    the afternoon
bells tolled for a funeral. Beggars knocked on doors. In the distance
the maternity hospital's whitewashed facade, as twilight deepened,
    looked whiter still,
more far off and incomprehensible. We lit the lamps quickly. I made
    over
one of my old dresses. Later the sewing machine broke, and they took it
down to the basement, along with the old sentimental oleographs,
all commonplace mythical scenes—Anadyomenes, eagles and
    Ganymedes.

One by one our old acquaintances departed. Correspondence dwindled
    too.

Nothing, now, but a brief postcard on the odd feast day or birthday—
a typical view of Taygetos, jagged peaks and a wide blue sky,
a shot of the Eurotas, white pebbles and oleanders, or the ruins
of Mistra amid its wild fig trees. But most frequent of all
were telegrams of condolence. No replies ever came. Perhaps
the recipient, too, had died meanwhile—we never discovered.

My husband no longer travelled, never opened a book. In his final years
he'd become very edgy. He smoked constantly. At night he'd pace
    around
in the big drawing room, wearing those frayed coffee brown slippers
and his long nightgown. Every day, at the lunch table, he'd rehash
Clytemnestra's treachery or the justified act of Orestes
as though he were threatening someone. Who cared? I no longer listened
    to him—and yet
when he died, I missed him a lot, I especially missed those stupid threats
    of his,
just as though they'd precisely defined my immovable place in time,
just as though they stopped me from aging.
                                    Then I would dream
of Odysseus, ageless too, with his smart three-cornered hat,
putting off his return (man of many wiles!) with the most fantastic perils
as an excuse, while he (supposedly shipwrecked) put himself in the
    hands
now of a Circe, now of a Nausicaä, to scrape the barnacles off his
    chest, wash him
with small bars of scented soap, kiss the wound on his thigh, rub him
    with oil.

I believe he too got home to Ithaca—that graceless fat Penelope fooled
    him, I'm pretty sure,
back into wedlock with her web trick. Since then I've had no news; it
    well may be
that the slaves tear up his letters, but what need of them now? The
    Symplegades
have been moved somewhere else, more internal—you get the feeling
    they're softer,
unmoving, more fearful than ever—they don't clash together now,
just squeeze tight in thick black liquid from which no one escapes.

You can go now. It's dark. I feel drowsy, I want to close my eyes,
to sleep, not to see either without or within, to forget
the fear of sleep and the fear of waking. I can't do it. I jerk up,
scared that I'll never wake again. I remain sleepless, listening
to the snoring of maids from the drawing room, to the spiders on the
     walls,
to the cockroaches in the kitchen, or the deep and heavy breathing
of the dead—as though they're asleep, as though they've found some
     peace.
I miss my dead now, too. I missed them before. Going, going, gone.

Sometimes, past midnight, I hear from the road below
the rhythmic clip-clop of horses, drawing a late wagon, as though
returning from a dismal show in some tumbledown local theater
with plaster fallen from the ceiling, with peeling walls,
with a huge red faded curtain, down now, but shrunken
from repeated washing, so that through the gap below it
you can make out the bare feet of the stage manager or the electrician,
maybe rolling up a forest backdrop before dimming the lights.

That crack remains lit up, though out in the pit
chandeliers and applause have long since faded. In the air
the breath of silence hangs heavy, and the hum of silence under
the empty seats, along with sunflower seed husks and crumpled tickets,
a button or two, a lace handkerchief, a twist of red string.

. . . And that scene on the walls of Troy—perhaps I reached back to the
     truth
when I let fall from my lips—sometimes even now I try,
lying here in bed, to fling my arms wide, to walk
on tiptoe, to walk on air—the third flower—

*She falls silent. Her head drops back. Perhaps she is asleep. Her visitor
gets up. He does not say good night. It is now quite dark. As he goes out
into the passage he sees the maids, ears glued to the wall, eavesdropping.
They don't move an inch. He goes down the central staircase as though
descending into a deep well, with a sense that he won't be able to find
the front door, or any door. His clenched fingers are already searching
for the door handle. He imagines his hands to be two birds gasping for
air, though at the same time he knows that this image is not quite the*

comforting one we normally invoke against vague fears. Suddenly he hears voices upstairs. Lights go on in the stairwell, along the corridor, in the rooms. He goes back up, confident now. The woman is sitting in bed with her elbow propped on the little zinc-topped table, her chin resting on the palm of her hand. The maids scurry in and out, screaming and shouting. Someone is telephoning in the corridor. Women from the neighborhood begin to arrive, keening, hiding objects under their skirts. More telephoning. The police are already on their way up. They send the maids and the neighbors away. The latter, however, have already had time to carry off the canaries in their cages, a number of exotic potted plants, a transistor radio, and an electric heater. One has got hold of a picture in a big gilt frame. They lay out the corpse on a bier. The police chief seals the house—"until the heirs are found," he says, though he knows very well that no heirs exist. The house will remain sealed for forty days, and after that its contents—or what's left of them—will be sold at auction and the proceeds turned over to the public treasury— "for the mortuary," it says on the catalogue. The laid-up car and its cover are removed. Suddenly everything vanishes. Absolute silence. Only he, the visitor, remains. He turns and looks. The moon has come out, shedding misty light on the statues in the garden—her statues standing there alone beside the trees, outside the sealed house. And a peaceful, seductive moon. Where will he go now?

KARLOVASI, SAMOS, MAY–AUGUST 1970

· PHAEDRA ·

TO YANNIS TSAROUCHIS

. . . It's natural,

when the gods so will it, for mortal men to err.

EURIPIDES, *Hippolytus* 1433–34

A spring afternoon: very peaceful. The usual kind of peace, and yet somehow overlit, overstressed, at times by the call of a bird, at times by the sound of a nail being knocked into wood or of a chisel striking marble—that indefinable solid peace, as though heralding, at any moment, the final completion of an extraordinary statue, naked, mourning; as though a rope were hanging pointlessly from the branch of a tree, while on the cover of a book, forgotten since midday on the garden seat, and warped by the sun, there was crawling, absurdly, a round insect with its wings folded in under its hard, gleaming black shell. In the big whitewashed east room a woman, perhaps over forty, sits in a wicker rocking chair, rocking herself gently, pressing the tips of her feet on the ground at regular intervals. The precision of the rhythm hints at an iron self-control in danger of breaking. Even her toes, visible outside her sandals, are strictly symmetrical. She keeps her eyes shut. Her hands, crossed on her breast, caress her nipples, at first through the material of her dress, but later directly, flesh to flesh. Yet the rhythm of her rocking never changes. Thin white curtains at the windows. Between the two open balcony doors (also curtained) a large mirror. A marble table. Settees. Two armchairs. Two ladderback chairs. The light, though sunset is imminent, remains bright and diffused—perhaps by the curtains. Suddenly, out in the courtyard, a clatter of horses' hooves, the barking of dogs, a young, authoritative voice. At the same moment the mirror, the table, the curtains, the wall all take on a reddish glow. The woman rises, in an abrupt movement entirely different from her previous rhythm. She goes out into the corridor. Her voice can be heard; perhaps she is giving orders to the Nurse. She returns. The room is now an intense red, and she also. She resumes her original seat—but now without rocking. Immediately there enters the youth whose voice was heard shortly before out in the courtyard: handsome, perspiring, with long golden hair. It is clear that he has just returned from hunting. He greets the woman respectfully, but also with a certain degree of awkwardness. The woman eyes his shapely legs, reddened rather than tanned by the sun, a reddish white, and covered with crisp fair hair. There is a short silence. She indicates the chair opposite hers. The light in the room changes from red to a golden violet. All the time she keeps her eyes on his legs, not on his face—scrutinizing his calves, laced in by the thongs of his sandals, and the shining, even toenails, with a light ring of dust highlighting the fleshy substance of each toe. The woman, with an inexplicably provocative gesture, lights a cigarette. The youth

represses a grimace. Perhaps it is the first time she has smoked in his
presence. She blows out smoke from nostrils and mouth. Then she
begins to speak:

I sent for you. I don't know how to begin. I'm waiting for nightfall,
for the shadows to lengthen in the garden, till those
of the trees and the statues move indoors, conceal my face and hands,
conceal my words—still hesitant, these, not fully articulated; words I
     don't know
and am afraid of.
                  I sent for you (all unready yourself) before you could
     catch your breath,
before you go for your bath, with all the dust still plastered
over your handsome face (you turned red, the sun's caught you—you
     didn't listen to me,
you never wore that March ring I wove for you) and all the down
from the forest thistles in your hair.
                     Look,
there's one bit like a ball of fluff—how light it is! and that one there
you might say resembles the tiny jaw of some apocryphal animal—it's
     biting the curl
right over your eyebrow—here, let me remove it. The day's well
     advanced;
it heated up early—you can feel it on the fabric, on the wood of the
     furniture, on your own skin
like a sad postponement.
                 The clack of the loom
sounds odd, lacks space in the room; spreads out to the road—
everything looks outward, is diffused; even I,
though I remain in the house, though I keep my eyes shut
in order to concentrate—I can feel it: I'm not self-sufficient, I gaze out
through my eyelids as though they were glass. I see you so clearly in the
     forest, I see
the slide of your throat when you drink at the spring; no, I tell you,
     rather
outside things get into us—an admission as general as fate—
we're suddenly crammed to choking, we comprehend the previous void,
     this void

that's no longer bearable (and where can you find fullness? Suffocation).
    The sanctity of privation—
wasn't that what you said? I don't really remember (was it privation you
    said, or denial)? What thoughtless words—
the victory of will, you said—what will? what victory?—
something harsh, unforgivable—a dark hill after sunset,
darker than the bed of a blind man.

                    Sanctity prior to sin
is something I don't believe in—I call it sickness, I call it cowardice—
sacrifices to the gods, pretexts for dodging suffering—
The gods are invisible; they offer no proofs; that's probably what we're
    seeking:
no, not our own sanctity—just a shadow to hide in. I know that you
feel love for yourself alone when you're alone, in front of the mirror;
I've seen the traces on your sheets, I've smelt them—it's then we forget
    about the gods.
                    By the way,
how did your hunting go today? I could never understand
one thing about hunting. And you, unlike the others,
never brought your fine trophies home—no rare birds with fine plumage
    and golden beaks,
no stags' antlers to mount on the walls like everyone else does,
getting a special pleasure from them, one curved pair sprouting over
    another
like the plan of a Byzantine church, like a ladder ascending into a calm,
    serene sky—I've heard
that antlers may be the calendar of a stag's life. Is it true? You've
    brought none back. I have a hunch
you never kill deer—the favored beasts of your Goddess. Everyone says
what a good shot you are. I've not seen it. Birds and deer are all right,
but why not the hide of a wolf or lion to spread by the beds in winter
when the cold's so intense that everything shrivels, and we need
the assurance of some power, especially when we wake
and with feet still warm, sleep-softened, try uncertainly
to stand fast once more in time. How nice it would be then if we could
    tread
on the dried pelt of a wild beast—killed by your hand best of all—and
    perhaps

be warmed by that feeling all too rare, as of a daredevil
horseman jumping a ditch—victors perhaps ourselves in an
      unrecognized battle,
standing tall in what you like to call our *invincible will*.

   At times I've thought of
dressing up as one of your slaves or grooms, to come hunting with you,
to know you in your own territory—see how you run, aim, kill;
follow your fine, untrammelled movements, all directed
to one specific goal, one objective, with that fluency and precision
brought by practice, experience. I so much wanted
to know you through some total attachment, through whatever
passes beyond mere obedience into ecstasy.
                                          I think
that would mean being like a dancer, when he leaps, then hangs still for
      a moment
in midair, delaying his descent, slowing down
the law of gravity. Like a dancer, yes, when he raises
high, high, on one hand an air-light ballerina; then
we catch our breath in case he gives her wings, and she flies
straight into a pure white cloud and never returns—or else casts her
      down
into some unseen abyss, which (to be sure) yawns always
there in front of our feet—and perhaps that's why lovers at nightfall
walk so slowly, so carefully, arms round each others' waists,
along the seashore or under the trees.

                            I tell you frankly,
many times I've dreamed of going to ground in a forest thicket,
and of rattling the branches like a wild beast, so that you would shoot
      me
and I'd be your prize quarry. When you picked me up, afterward, to
      carry me to the cart,
I'd have on my eyes (I tell you) two green leaves, to let you
bend down nearer my face.
                        What do you *really* hunt? Do you maybe
offer your whole catch to Artemis? Even so, I'd love
a deep blue feather for my hat—perhaps you could
dedicate something to me as well? Deep blue, yes,
like my eyes, and yours too—remember? It was

your father who first pointed that out. At the time I was flattered,
and so too perhaps were you; you blushed, that night
out in the forecourt, with the lamps hung in the vine arbor, when you
    first
came to Athens for the festival at Eleusis—unforgettable days! So,
a deep blue feather, that I'll be able to hear blowing
above my forehead in secret whispers, conveying to me
messages from the forest, the springs, the tree roots,
the parliament of birds. Dreams upon dreams. I've often thought about
    it:
each feather hides a bloodstained hole; or maybe
each feather pierces a bloodstained hole in our flesh? At other times
I think that feathers are our bodies' flowering, and only when
thought plucks them does there open
the red hole that never thereafter closes.
                                Because of this
I beg a blue feather of you—but don't get the idea it's for my
    shoulders—
only for my hat. It may be that you too, sometimes,
have ideas of this sort. Perhaps you too know that:

the most beautiful things are those we usually say
when we want to avoid uttering some truth; and maybe
this unspoken truth is what imparts
their great beauty and uncertainty
to these trite alien words—an eternal law
of beauty, or so they tell us.
                            Uncertainty always
bears witness to something deep and certain—tragic, very probably,
    even bestial—a sacrificed desire,
a Lernaean desire—it takes pleasure in hiding
in roseate or shining golden clouds
its new heads; it takes pleasure in playing
with a red string at its fingertips, in setting
its severed heads on a silver tray decked out with colored ribbons,
in pulling the nails from the wall, in setting them upright on the bed,
    playing thus
with our one head, itself being many-headed. And besides—what can we
    do?—
this game gives us pleasure. Sometimes, indeed,

we even play it on our own account (perhaps on our own initiative)—
the same red string, the heads on the tray with colored ribbons,
the nails on the bed.
                    "Our only consolation,"
as my Nurse has a habit of saying, "is to meditate day and night
on our death." But when *is* that? Its soothing certainty
belongs to our future, while
the least instant of our present, whatever its claims,
is more absolute than death.

                    We should never
have come to Troezen. Here everything is yours. The eyes of Pittheus
spy on me in the darkness lest I snatch some part of your purity—
a blue feather, as I said. In Athens
things were different; I had my own space.
And you were awkward then; nervously shy
and courteous all at once. You never opened the icebox
by yourself for a couple of cherries, a peach, a small piece of chocolate.
    And your manner of speech
had a clipped brevity, you all but swallowed your vowels, as though you
        were trying
to say only half of each word, to finish that much quicker, fall silent,
as though expecting the answer from somewhere else, not from where
        you were looking. I was delighted
by this ignorance of yours, this expectancy. I thought
it was directed at me—and perhaps it was. One evening
when I greeted you on the stairs, before we'd yet lit the lamps, your
        hand trembled
and for a moment you raised your head to my shoulder level.

                                                    Here
you are the master, with your slaves, your dogs, your horses,
the statues of your gods. I find your ease suffocating.
I don't open the icebox myself, either. When I set the table
I feel that I'm spreading a white sheet over a corpse, that I possess
rights over neither corpse nor sheet.
                    This house
is filled with your shadow. The house is body—I touch it, it touches me,
it presses down on me, above all at night. The flames of the lamps
lick at my thighs and waist; they linger, with a tiny shiver,

below my left ear; they nibble my nipples;
their saliva gleams, burns me, cools me, reveals me.

I have nowhere else left to hide. I shut my eyes tight
and shine all over and am visibly
gleaming, slippery, immovable.
                      The house is body:
is your body and mine together. I begin to walk
and the sheets trail from my feet as though after the act; I go to put
a glass or a plate on the table, and from my fingers
hangs that familiar chain of yours with the tiny cross (the one
they say that the Goddess gave you), the one
that used to hang on your breast, that shimmered from your flesh (yes, I
    stole it from you).

                    I remember
your childish perplexity when you lost it, your guilt, your fury—
how your eyes flashed, how the blood rushed to your cheeks; I saw the
    blood
course under your white skin, rise from legs to breast,
check at your knees, run back to your belly, your thighs,
your arms, the line of your throat, swell out and flush
your nipples and lips—as though your whole torso were in erection—
    one red spot
is still left on your jaw.
               The old Nurse and I both
joined in your search for the chain. We ransacked every room,
the yard, the kitchen, the stables. I watched you
on your knees, hunting under the tables, under the beds, there
at my feet in surrender, for me to observe the lines of your body,
its changes of pose with each movement. I knelt down too, so,
right beside you, both of us on all fours, crawling
like awkward babies, ecstatic when faced with some unknown, expected
    prize,
or like newborn creatures seeking their nourishment in a treacherous
    thicket,
wild from their hunger, with a second, stronger, hunger—
I, the experienced one, the overmastered,
and you, the unknowing, so haughty, delightfully innocent,
adorably innocent.

Another time
you lay face down on the ground to grope under the wardrobes,
low, restless, working your way in as though making love.
                                                    And I
was the floor on which you threw yourself, and I felt you inside me
even while I stood there and watched your every movement,
recording it on my touch and taste. Of course, we never found the
        chain—
the chain I wear at night, in bed, when Theseus is away,
the chain I press to my bosom.
                            Can't you see
its impressions, link by link, scored in my flesh?—
and the tiny crucified figure impressed between
my breasts? I think, if you loved him
he'd truly rise again, though I've learned
my lesson well: resurrection can only be
a solitary act of renunciation, and not
an act of union.

                    Well, as I told you
this stolen chain dangles from my fingers
when I set the plates on the table, it taps at the knives and forks
with tiny perfidious sounds; sometimes it dips right into
a glassful of wine—cross and crucified figure are both completely
        submerged;
I pull back my hand, red drops
spatter the tablecloth, I cover them with slices of bread—
red drops on the bread as well. I no longer know where to look.
Faces, hands, hair, the mirror, the walls
all spotted with blood.

                    But luckily
the blood is invisible; I relax; nobody sees it,
nor do they see the chain; they go on eating (and perhaps, for some
        unknown reason,
with more appetite than before). As for those red drops—
they don't take on me, they make no stains on my skin, since I
am red all over with blood, inside and out,
from this invisible blood—my secret scarlet. I'm only sorry
(glad, too, perhaps) that not even you can see me

—despite my confession to you—with that most dignified,
glorious, universal chain of mine. But I tell you,
even supposing you were able to see me thus
you'd think me dyed all over, from head to foot,
red, bright red, for some idolatrous rite.
                                        Oh, to be sure,
each person sees with his own eyes, and I myself
am no exception. But the worst thing of all
is that even the deepest understanding of the difference between us
makes nothing easier, does not abrogate
our differences and our conflicting claims.

No: I have no complaints against you or my fate. From time to time
only awareness of whatever misfortunes are ours can keep us
above misfortune, in a deep, high space—a soft breeze blows above it,
my tresses stir lightly on my shoulders
like two friendly hands, palms down, like a pair of wings,
diaphanous, soothing, confirmative.
                                        All about me
spreads the compassion of a timeless starlight—my own compassion
for the whole world and (naturally) for my own self. Then

I have not the slightest need to fly,
being there, in the altitude of the dream and my decisive will, alone with
        myself,
released from myself, cut off
from my separate elements, at one with the universe. And the ropes that
        bound me—
hands, feet, throat—now severed,
themselves too now wings—there, I can hear them fluttering,
and the soft brush of their lips against earth and heaven—

I remember a wild white horse, hobbled to a tree. How his tail and mane
quivered in fury, how the muscles of his entire body swelled
under the dazzling white of his coat! I thought
he'd tear his leg off at the root, and, three-legged now, gallop,
proudly limping, into the unknown. (Perhaps
no freedom can be won without some sacrifice on our part.) And in fact
he broke the rope, not his leg; and while I waited, wonderstruck,
for the lightning flash of his flight, the horse

took five slow steps and stopped,
staring solemnly, sadly at his severed rope. That was not how I'd
    pictured it.

Or perhaps I had. I don't know. From up there I watched them
lighting the street lamps below, one by one (the lamplighter went by
with his ladder upon his shoulder). Little by little I recognized
those sad, shut-off streets revolving round themselves,
streets I too had walked (that were saddened on that account),
and I grieved that I'd lost them. Silently I whispered
their names—Academy, University, Stadium, Aeolus streets. The lights
came on in the houses, doorways and windows glowed—the starry
    town,
a terrestrial heaven.
                        I made out
our own house too—the marble stairway lit up
by the two lamps of those naked statues. That's my window, I
    murmured,
that's Theseus's—*but I'm not in there,*
I'm not in there (I repeated), I've escaped. I've broken free
from confinement, mortality. I imagined your expression, perhaps
I imagined your grief (yes, yes, you too will grieve); my fine clothes
hanging empty in the wardrobe or thrown over chairs
or on the bed; my sandals under the bed; on one
lies a dead moth. I shall never wear them again.

    And at the precise moment
when I felt my ribs released, expanding in a deep sigh of relief, a knot
pulled me up short—that miniature crucified figure
impressed on my breast, and the knowledge
that *I shall return*; and I was already *in there, in here*
in my place under the lamp, at table,
staring beyond the glasses, above your shoulders and your indifferent
    eyes
out through the distant window, toward the translucent night where I'd
    escaped for a little,
and from which I'd returned sadder, older, and as though humbled
in a state of angry pride, to measure and test
my actions against your standards—to cut
bread very carefully with the big bread knife

so as not to score the tablecloth or the wood,
nor scratch your little finger, or my own.

My God, I can't bear this pretense. I feel
that my every gesture leaves on wall and floor and ceiling,
or on the furniture, an enormous shadow; the shadow increases,
    spreads,
grows from one moment to the next, reflecting all
my secret, inward stirrings.

                    I no longer know where to stay,
besieged as I am by my shadows, too visible now,
standing out, I feel, in the crowd, betrayed, a sight for all eyes,
a target for slaves, dogs, their master, you, and watching
my shadows' constant changes—they're really more like beasts—
a lion with its claws rips up the scarlet coverlet,
a tigress gnaws the velvet on the sofa, a dolphin
leaps into the mirror with a harpoon in its back, a doe
trails the curtains from its horns like a bridal gown, completely hiding
the fields, the springs, the vineyards and the vintagers' reddened feet; a
    buffalo
bears off the table from the dining room into the garden; a glass drops,
the two servants look up; I grasp the scissors
and try to cut out material for a tunic—from the sound it's as though
I'm cutting the hair of one of my shadows. At the street corner
the basket seller turns and stares.

                    The whole day through
I wait for nightfall to see if my shadows will be swallowed up by
    darkness
so I can fill up less space, be shut in my own kernel, become
like a grain of wheat in the earth. I cannot do it.
My shadows are not absorbed by darkness; on the contrary,
they usurp the whole of the night. And then
I too expand with them, amazed, speechless, submerged,
my whole surface crimped by depth pressure, while my desire
floats naked, gleaming, purest white, upon
the darkness, like a drowned woman with distended belly
and swollen pudenda—a woman with closed eyes, lit by the moon—
no, not drowned, just floating on her back, a pregnant woman.

And then once more I hang on, as best I can, for daybreak, for the
     twitter
of birds in the hedges, for the sounds on the road outside—
the tramp of knife grinder, potter, itinerant greengrocer, fishmonger,
the clatter of hammers in carpenters' or marble cutters' workshops—for
my shadows to separate off, one by one, let me share them, not be alone
     with my lone self.

I can't bear these spring nights. Vapors rise from the earth, condense,
press on you oh so gently, flesh to flesh. A shiver
runs through the air, moves from one room to the next, enters
that third chamber, the rose-colored one, where you sleep. The horses'
     hooves
stamp in their open stalls—perhaps among them that pure
white horse I told you about—lame now (I don't hear the fourth
     hoofbeat)—
What unspoken words are heard, what suppressed screams,
sounds of flutes, lyres, stars. One lone oar in the water—something that
     goes through me
at even-spaced intervals, up to the spasm of pleasure and beyond
to the new spasm, and the next one—inexhaustible.

And the sheets, damp with warm water, sperm, and sweat,
and the garments and underwear thrown around the floor,
and the others in linen chests or wardrobes, wrung out so they drip, drip
small drops that solidify instantly, crystallize, stalactites, stalagmites
in the deep caves within us—strange glass forests,
glass figures of birds, men, trees, beasts,
erotic glass groups in an underground feverish dampness.

Sometimes a green lizard slithers out from there
with suddenly magnified eyes—pure green eyes
that cast a green reflection on the off-white crystals,
on the tall, dim, narrow mirrors. The lizard
observes with perplexed delight, with mistrustful precaution, and
     remains
motionless, turned to marble, drained of its greenness. Or again

a round black insect suddenly pops up from nowhere
with its wings folded under its hard carapace. It explores

the slippery surface with countless most delicate feet,
but doesn't move forward; it sits there—a black eye,
not a blind man's—an extracted eye, cut loose
from the facial nerves; an eye
globular, all-surveying.
                              It sits, stares, deters—a knot
like the knot in your throat that obstructs your speech,
obstructs your vision too—a thing
like heart failure, the end observing the end.

O terror and exultation of finality—the whole thing should have been
     finished,
you and me and our dissension. My God, what ridiculous sentiments,
so exaggerated—and they don't even leave us
the slightest free room of our own to take a step forward
even toward our death. What a childish story: strange, strange.

Really, why are we to blame for all this? Who wanted it this way?
Not us, anyhow. Night and day (my God) are both unbearable. In the
     morning,
when we're scarcely awake (more tired than when we went to sleep) our
     first action,
even before we wash, or drink our coffee, is to reach out a hand
and take our brittle-dry mask from the bedside table
and fix it on our face as though in guilt,
sometimes with flour paste or fish glue, sometimes
with that tacky stuff that cobblers use to glue leather. And all day
     through

you feel the glue drying, coming away
bit by bit from your skin; there's the fear of direct contact
with light, air, water, a hand, or your own hand; and on top of that
you're afraid that the whole mask may come unstuck
from the involuntary contraction of a smile and fall
into your plate of roast chicken, at the precise moment
when you're saying "I'm not hungry at all," so that there'll be revealed,
in utter nakedness, your fierce, unassuageable hunger.

This unglueing of the mask we always perceive
not so much from the outside as from within,

like a gold dental plate in our mouth—we're afraid it will fall out,
this plate that won't let us shout or laugh, confining
our expression within commonplace, proper bounds. The hell with it—
    what can we say?

Evening is drawing on. It's darker. I can't see your face. Better so. I can't
    see
your mask (because you too wear a mask—call it sanctity, call it
purity—a mask). Better so. I can predict, even in shadow,
your look of abhorrence. Remember, you stupid beautiful boy,
those who have suffered much know that vengeance is theirs, although
    they recognize
their own unaccountability, and that of others.
                                        Too bad it's nightfall.
The stars are out. They prick like thorns. It's not
that compassion of timeless starlight—I'd forgotten that. Perhaps it too
was a mask—broader, of course, gold like the burial masks,
    transforming
the red of our blood into ambivalent dew—and for how long? In a little
we hear our bloodstream again, fierier, redder, ascending
to flush not only the face but the mask as well,
piercing holes in the metal, until
our bloody face comes out through the mask, eclipses it completely—
tormented face, with the ultimate arrogance of the defenseless, with the
    daring
to exist for a moment outside its mask, if only
the final moment before, or after, its death.

I have often studied the faces of corpses, so exposed,
no blood in them any longer, but deathly pale,
heavy with sin, indifferent now, an inert weight
on their cold gold mask.
                    Those
that had suffered much and lied much (perhaps to avoid
admitting their martyrdom), they, I am convinced,
are the faces of the Saints.

Ah, don't assume I'm trying to get myself into their company,
or that that's why I praise them. No, no. I was confessing. The holy,

the humble lie—*that* I could not sustain. I cut up the mask
and threw it at your feet; I did not perforate it,
I did not cover it with my face. Yet now, again,
I'd like to repeat to you: sanctity before sin I do not believe in.

I believe in nothing. I understand nothing. Each of us alone,
each proscribed, with the scarlet seal
on forehead or back.
                          From a long way off I hear my footsteps
on winding streets with ancient rusted lampposts,
with cracked doors and waterless fountains. The window shutters
lean ajar on the shoulder of fate. A snake in the road. Two sick cats.
A gimcrack notice board, its nails exposed, a faded
poster tacked on it; a loaf ringed with a chain-twist pattern—from a
    distance
it looks like a gross bald head crowned with bay leaves. Someone climbs
the steps of the belltower, but doesn't ring the bell.

There's also an old, old woman, knitting a huge black sock. This sock
hangs from the castle window down to the old crone's knees. There's
    something this sock,
this old crone remind me of—could it be myself?—and take care
you don't drop any stitches—while from the upper part of town
comes the sound of a flute—the same unfamiliar phrase; and abruptly it
    stops; and you know it.

Someone down in the basement is gesticulating—the shadow of his hand
falls across his body like a severed hand. Someone else
strikes a match, looks at his watch—the watch has no hands.
Someone bangs the garden gate knocker. The gardener's dead. His dog
slinks away under the trees. A flower vase falls
in the dark corridor—your movement to save it comes too late;
and the meaning of this delay spreads through the air. Later
a smell of warm sperm, all night long. I understand nothing.

And this senseless attempt of ours to enter a hole in the wall,
a tiny hole where a nail's dropped out—and to hold
the nail in our teeth for ever, with that special taste
of rust, plaster, and time. So what do we understand? What can we say?

Perhaps you too saw him one afternoon, late, toward evening,
the man with the empty suitcase who pretends to be lame (and is,
      perhaps),
who pauses every so often from the weight of that emptiness,
leaves his case on the sidewalk or on the steps,
wipes away sweat with the back of his hand, and once more
picks up his suitcase, listening to the rattle
of two glass marbles inside it (one yellow, the other blue)
as they roll and strike each other.
                                            This rattling noise
is so plainly, convincingly audible that it seems an easy matter for you
to be dead, or dying. You suddenly go out
through a door you know every inch of onto a balcony
that's quite unfamiliar, high above tall trees, roofs, chimneys,
high above a wide sweep of windows—on their bright-lit panes
move the shadows of those who are dancing in the foreigner's house
while music, quite unconnected, is heard from the other, uninhabited
      side
where the hills grow dark and the wagon bearing the two
murderesses moves off, right under the loneliest star.

Then I, too, eagerly appropriate my death; I distance myself,
observe from inside a kind of temperatureless glass booth
the comical movements and grimaces of the scared, the hopeless, the
      angry,
Theseus's, yours, the slaves'—yes, comical, because I hear
not a sound, not a voice, except for those two glass marbles
in the empty canvas suitcase. Everything's left
completely cut off from the atmosphere and from all causation, divided,
alone, uncoordinated, lacking consequence, continuity, connection.

Beautiful death. Silence that watches and listens to silence. For a little,
      I'm enjoying myself.
I observe unobserved. I rejoice in my own absence.
I no longer need a mask, now that no one can see me.
I remain still in my freedom to move. I see myself as a solitary
corpse by the sea—right by the sea. Until
I suspect I am not a corpse. I suspect my own ruse. I know

that genuine death neither reproves nor judges.
Perfect death, peaceful and terminal,
is blind, deaf and dumb, like pure white. I know it.

Then with the brooch pin from my breast I prick the tip of my left
    forefinger,
suck my own blood, with the deliberate gesture
of a conscious child, so as not to scream, weep, yearn,
being thus closed off—made little, with eyes tight shut, in my stifling
    body—
from a corpse's self-pleasure. And night is deeper inside, further inside.

The night spreads, like a universal suicide, surrenders
bodies, naked, to a gigantic marble mortuary. The dead
no longer worry about concealment—that man with the swollen rotten
    prick,
or the one with the wart on his nose; the two women
with gross flabby bellies and sagging dugs; a youth
lopped of his testicles; a queue of bald, wrinkled old men
with toothless mouths gaping in a rictus of greed; and high above them
a great misty moon like a boiled potato
just peeled by the bony hands, all gnarled and knotted,
of the last old woman. Ah, that insatiable,
ugly hunger, right up to and in the face of death!

Why do you sit there as though turned to stone, in an attitude of
    disapproval,
and perhaps with an expression of mockery, of sullied purity? Away
    with you now
and wash off the sweat and dust of your splendid, monastic hunt! I
    won't
light the lamp. Go now. Oh yes, and tonight, as always,
I'd love so much to take you to the bath myself, wash you
with my own hands—to let my hands familiarize themselves with you.
    Your body
I know so well, like a poem memorized by heart
that I'm always forgetting—the most unknown thing in the world,
the most mutable and elusive is the human body—who can ever learn it?

Even the statues, although unmoving, although
seen and touched time and again, you imagine to be
fluid and wavering—they slip away from you. When you close your eyes
it's impossible for you to remodel them accurately, to reconstruct them.
    The Nurse
has described your body to me countless times, in every detail. Often,
    abstracted,
I sketch you, stark naked, on the back of my cigarette packet. Later
I fill up the sketch with tiny daisies, to hide you,
and it's as though I were covering a beautiful corpse with flowers.

What's the first thing, honestly, anyone will conceal? The sketch?
    Hands? Mouth? Eyes? Always the same desire,
the same uncommitted sin—the game in reverse: the same string,
the same severed heads on the tray, the same nails, and the black
    umbrella
above the steps down which the five children were thrown. Outside on
    the street
citizens jostle, shout, hurry, clutch banners,
soldiers drop to one knee, fire volleys. And I, at the window,

witness the scarlet stream by the sidewalk and am deeply embittered,
not so much for those killed as for that umbrella above the steps
and for those five children, my own,
my fantasy children, more mine than those I bore. Do you suppose
woman's purpose is procreation? Or could her involuntary
purpose be love?—the martyrdom and glory of mankind. You may go.

Listen to the frogs down there in the marshes—they've gone crazy; they
    too must know something.
Perhaps one day you'll learn it as well (what use will it be then?)—
Our own suffering, however slight, torments us
more than the whole world's pain. Besides, what pain
is slight? You haven't found that out.
                        Well,
I shall teach you it—and let them call it wrongdoing. One man's
wrongdoing wars with another's, and sometime wins,
but nature's wrongdoing—how shall I put it?—that's irresistible,
purposeless, unjustifiable (why wrongdoing then?). One's own life
is the only wrongdoing, and death the only

definite justice, even if always acknowledged too late. Perhaps this too
is one of our tricks, a spurious consolation speech—
the final consolation for one who will no longer need it.

So go. Why do you sit there petrified? Off with you to your bath,
go and wash yourself clean of my vile words, vile eyes,
my red, befouled eyes.
                              Perhaps in there,
just for a little, you too will remove your mask, your glass armor,
your frozen sanctity, your murderous cowardice. Begone, I tell you—I
     can't stand
the insult of your silence. My vengeance is set. You'll see. A pity—
you won't have long to remember it. What's up with those frogs this
     evening?
Croak, croak, croak—what are they trying to say? and to whom? What
     are they trying to hide?
What intoxication? What pain? What truth? What a beautiful,
     incorruptible night—
incorruptible, incorruptible, incorruptible—what a beautiful night—

*She is the first to rise. She goes to the middle door, opens it, vanishes.
The darkness does not let us discern the expression of her face or
carriage. The young man exits left—probably to the bathhouse. The
room is completely empty, silent. Suddenly it is flooded with the sounds
of running water, crescendo, as though someone nearby was taking the
ritual bath of purification. This noise emphasizes the silence from the
middle door, which has remained open. After a little there can be heard,
as though in the room itself, the impassioned croaking of frogs—at once
resilient, viscous, sensual, poignant, and disgusting. Then silence once
more. Only the sound of falling water, diminuendo. A little later, out in
the courtyard, a clatter of wagon wheels and horses' hooves. A man
enters right; imposing height, swarthy. Anyone here? He strikes a
match. The flame reveals his thick short curly beard. He lights the lamp,
approaches the middle door. The interior is illuminated: the hanged
woman dangling from the roofbeam. Tucked in her girdle, a large sheet
of paper. He takes it, and reads, aloud: "Your son, Antiope's son, tried
to rape me." A howl bursts from him. Not in lamentation. A curse. The
grim sentence of exile. People come running—slaves, wagoners, the old
Nurse, maidservants. The young man appears from his bath, naked,
dripping all over, with a towel wrapped round his waist. He hears his*

condemnation in silence. He kneels. Outside in the courtyard the lamps
of the two wagons—the one that just arrived, and the other one that has
been prepared at lightning speed to remove the exile—cast the shadows
of the two statues, of Aphrodite and Artemis, in a cross on the body of
the hanged woman.

ATHENS, KARLOVASI, ATHENS, APRIL 1974– JULY 1975

The time we waited, shut up in the large room with the covered
     mirrors,
He came, uninvited, a stranger—what was he looking for?
We did not want to see, to hear, to recognize him.
His pitiful dusty clothes—we were not looking for compassion—
his worn-out shoes demanded sympathy—we didn't have anything to
     give—
a stranger, uninvited, with no share in our sorrow,
he came to feel sorrow for us; behind his dusty beard
glittered the stars of his smile
with that complacency of forbearance, with the assent
of his ancient ordeal, as if to say: "This too will pass,"
like the embroidered samplers on the walls of old houses
blending a housewifely wisdom with many ill-assorted silk flowers,
roses, carnations, pansies (not violets),
and embroidered yellow ribbons all around.
                                        What did he want?

And even if we have anything we don't want to give it. Let them leave us
     at last
to our venerable, respectable grief, to our death,
to our pride, so we don't shrink before the shadows of things; let them
     leave us
to exhaust our posture of genuflection, listening
to the comforting woodworm in the corners of the silence.
                                        Get him out
     of here, we said,
a stranger, uninvited, wily—
acting the poor man to make us confident in our wealth,
so as not to abase us, to bribe us with his orphaned state,
with his gauntness (he was already displaying his naked ribs, his broad
     chest)
to extract from us a smile once more, a new sign of life;
his gaze rang above us like a child's rattle
to focus our attention elsewhere; he turned out
the pockets of his trousers and his coat
to demonstrate his poverty, to convince us—
and from his pockets fell only a little lint, a few limp shreds of tobacco,
as if it were snowing on a small, gray spot, half a yard across,
and his turned-out, empty pockets were

like the ears of gentle creatures that eavesdrop beyond the silence,
or like small wooden steps up to a dove cote,
smelling of whitewash, droppings, and warm feathers.
It was a beginning from a slight tenderness that causes neither shock nor
    displacement;
it was a measured forgetting, to encourage us,
to extend our memory toward things beyond or above.

Where did he come from, this Stranger? What was he looking for? Did
    his road run
from yesterday or from tomorrow? In his unwashed hair
were ashes and dewdrops—clearly he had walked through the night
and perhaps he had travelled from the fire, come down from the
    conflagration. In his voice we recognized
the creaking of the door when they open it to give us a little heat,
when the carpenters' crews in our neighborhood are planing large
    planks
for new buildings, when in the shade of the wall, at summer noontimes,
foremen and craftsmen, laborers and errand boys gather
and talk about the day's work, simplifying time,
rounding out life into two perfect hemispheres, two only,
one light and the other dark; and later in the brief silence that
    intervened
they heard the final leaf from last year detach itself from the tree
and fall with a fearful and incredible din between their knees
and they went on with their neutral conversation about bread and salt
while the Stranger went on further, alone.

Outside the window the wall opposite shone
stark white in the slanting sun; it made us look, made us listen,
we didn't hear our own crying. Those things we lost and are losing, he
    said,
those that are coming, above all those that we fashion,
are our own, we can give them—so he said—
uninvited, a stranger, unacceptable,
and his words were like a row of small pitchers in island windows
strong, stout-hearted pitchers, sweating,
recalling cool water in young mouths—
and though we denied the water and our thirst, they recalled them—

or flowerpots with basil, geraniums, pelargoniums,
at the hour when evening falls and the cattle return from pasture
and time is gentle and boundless, interrupted only by the ringing of
    cowbells
—various metals, various sounds, varying distance,
confirming the boundlessness in every direction,
forward or back, to one side or the other, up or down.

The moment was no more than a wink
but it was the center of an expanse with an infinite periphery
beyond the mountains and the horizon, behind yesterday and tomorrow,
    beyond time, to all time
the dead and the unborn, above
the smoke of evening chimneys that gave off the fragrance of humility,
    patience, moderation, beyond
and above the small lamps that were lit before the stars,
above the stars that were lit before our consciousness and our
    understanding—

Fortunate the stars, calm, auspicious,
without the least premonition of death, altogether without death. And
    the children we then were, he said,
those we are still, yet by now released from the narrowness of our first
    years,
from the acuteness of this narrowness, from the impatience of growth,
from the grown-ups' misunderstanding.
                                        The children cried all alone
in the bushes and no one took them seriously
because their faces were stained with mulberries or blackberries
and their grief was red and laughable.
                                        We are those children,
we keep them now in an ample light, along with the boundless plain,
with the wheat and the poppies, with the vines,
with the wine press and the feet of the vintners, splashed to their knees
    in must,
when the men with torn trousers and torn shirts
hurled insults without reason and without passion—great bare-breasted
    blasphemies,
shaggy blasphemies, whose foolish virility and merriment

sent the girls running to hide
behind the huge clusters of grapes, behind the wide grape leaves,
and the ears of the women were delicate and red like morning horizons.

It is enough that we break the siege of the moment, he said. How? Tell
    us. He did not answer.
It is enough that we remember—the time we cut reeds from the river
    banks and fashioned spears
throwing them over the tall mansions, testing
the power of our arms, wood, iron, stones, wind,
unconsciously augmenting the power of our arms,
learning to control not only the solid but the imponderable too.

The countryside was divided into circles of solitude beside the oleanders,
    the willows, the briars,
the birds for the first time learned their names, as did the trees and all
    things:
the penknife with which you cut the reed,
the little harmonica in your pocket,
the snare, the lime twig, the shepherd's pipe,
the steps of the lamb, the neighing of the horse,
the sound of the river, like another prolonged neigh of a light horse
    through the whole length of the laurel thicket,
the distinct colors and scents of flowers,
wool, cotton, linen, silk,
the hunt of the beekeepers at dawn in the poplars,
the multicolored heaven of kites, string tautening then going slack—
this buoyant bright curve of the string like the deep exhalation
you make to expand your chest once more in an infinite breathing space.

Later they would mingle from within, by themselves, like dense leaves
    on the tree's branches
binding earth, light, and air. Because each sound
had many echoes between the two mountains, St. Elias and the Forty
    Saints,
though the plain was boundless, like an immortality. When we have
    remembered, he said,
the moment of that we remember has never passed. The prickly pears
have not only shape and taste—they enclose
a world of seeds and meaning within their green hairy fists,

they remember our procrastinations, they remember a "later"
like a continuation of our own omissions,
like the hope of recomposing the entire plain
when at dawn the lark trills high in air and its song,
vertical, spiralling, makes the earth spin like a top in our open palm.

Dew-damp oregano, hay, and wild roses scented the air then,
the drivers watered their horses at the spring beneath the plane trees;
the horses broke their ropes at noon and vanished, galloping into space,
the cackling of the hens was a *gloria* in the golden hayloft. So it is not
    absence, then,
this opening of window or grave to heaven. No absence, one horse's
    galloping,
the replacement of withered flowers with fresh flowers in the glass,
with fresh water, the washing of the glass, one gesture after the other—
    what transgression?—
all move more or less in a circle, they return
onto a higher level, we meet them again.

The beams of the house with their double loaves, their pomegranates
    and quinces,
remain always like horizontal columns in the temple of a simple
    recognition—
columns on their sides in the posture of repose, kisses, coition, sleep.

   Then the children
refused to take their siestas,
would not close their eyes for a moment to the miracle of the sun
nor did late afternoon find them asleep; they experienced
the touch and the taste of the ephemeral—in what sense ephemeral?—
    they ran barefoot among the thorns of eternity,
barefoot—not so the grown-ups wouldn't hear them—
only to feel under their heels the warm belly of earth. The children
    stopped, gasping for breath,
stared for a moment at their moving reflections in the river,
pissed into the river, sensing the coolness of the sound above the warmth
    from their running legs
at that moment when cicadas and gypsies were disturbing the afternoon
    neighborhoods. When evening came

the rivers were still, cows ruminated on the history of the world,
wild horses went back to the stable of their own accord,
children went back home,
watermelons crackled in the frosty night,
the scent of spearmint rose as though released by a quick brush
from the wide skirt of a guilty woman. Then they heard from far away
the instruments at the festival in the other village
at St. Demetrius, or further off, at Talanta
and tomorrow's rolling thunder increased amid the bells;
they heard, too, dogs barking in the fields, the vineguard's distant
    footsteps,
the swallows stirring in sleep in their soft nests,
the secret conversations that governed the allotment of water in the
    melon fields,
the thud of the spade on the soft, wet earth, and most of all
the stars that took deep breaths and sighed quietly,
saying one to the other, and to us, "How beautiful is creation!"

   Thus we bored
the first holes in the reed, thus we learned
to walk our fingers along the reed
repeating the sighs of the stars.
The forest guard went downhill in the moonlight with his shotgun
as though he had a small fountain of silver water slung over his
    shoulder, and the mailman
laid down his leather bag as a pillow beneath the trees
and fell asleep on the breast of the world,
while the croaking of frogs vainly bombarded the translucent distance.

Walls, folds, terraces steamed warmly in the night's dampness
for here the warm Greek months had rested their broad backs,
and up on the slope of the hill the small cemetery with its wooden
    crosses hummed
with the growing of grass, wildflowers, nettles,
and glowed all over like a tilted lake in the night. In the shadow of its
    fold
the big boys' chins dribbled at noon as they ate stolen watermelons.
    Now
the cemetery gleamed, quiet and solemn,

like a father's admonishing unshaven face—just as though you found a
     piece of bread fallen on the ground,
picked it up, kissed it in secret, and propped it on a windowsill.

There was a shivering little cry every second
like a bee's wing brushing the cheek of a flower,
and bees were plentiful in the garden
and we were so close to things that we remained remote
and could not connect, in the idea of a bee, its sting and its honey—do
     you remember?—in the days
when it made a difference whether you sat on a stool or under a tree,
on an old millstone or a broken column capital.

Later, time and noise and knowledge expanded
to a return from afar, to the unity of time, here,
where every night the frogs can be found in the field
and the field in the frogs—remember their ancient voices
that filled the ear on summer nights,
the frogs that sat on their soft feet, secretive and garrulous,
ready to jump into the water, ready to jump back into the air,
leaving behind their leap a secret undertow and the echo of their voices
bead by bead in the spinal column of summer—I mean that time
when the stars still appeared supernatural and imaginary
and there had to be a dialectical mediation by silence and time
to let the voices of the frogs and their echoes rediscover their nature,
lost summers, endless nights,
bees and stars in the boundless plain,
the plain and silence and time.

All ours, more ours with our memory—said the Stranger—more
     fortunate,
the secret olive trees on the little hills with their apostolic nightfalls,
the reed awnings of the villagers propped in trees lit only by the small
     eyes of birds,
the osier sheafs we softened for weeks in the brook to make baskets,
the soft dark figs, chilled from the dawn, when we took off our sandals
at the roots of the fig trees and climbed to heaven,
not with a ladder, not through the branches, but on steps of air. Every
     evening—remember?—

that huge star like the eye of the Almighty watched over the sleep of the
    herders and fishermen,
and the feet of the women, when they took off their stockings,
were broad and bright—they lit up the big flat roofs where the black
    raisins were drying,
they lit up the benches and the doors; before the women slept
they combed their long hair with ritual motions
as though dipping their fingers in invisible vertical rivers,
as though conversing with another love, since their husbands had
    already gone to bed
and their rough breathing made their frizzled mustaches rustle
like dry wheatstalks in the field. The women—
large, secret, solitary,
almost self-existent and self-sufficient—continued
an indiscernible conversation, while they combed,
as though proposing an alliance with the high beds of night
ratifying one by one the articles of the stars with a slight nod of the
    head,
an alliance with the tops of the plane trees, eucalyptus, poplars,
with mute springs, with the complex sources of water—
and the frogs in concert on their green banks
spilled over the rim of night
making a deep-shadowed transposition to cover the silence of the
    women,
to cover their glances, their pride, their desolation.

An owl, petrified on the roof, watched them with her two round eyes,
pretending she didn't see them, and they that they did not see her,
but beneath their ancient slavery, through two small underground
    tunnels,
she transmitted to their veins her concentrated light.

Unapproachable women, haughty, self-sufficient, eternal virgins,
lovers of the night, lovers of mute germination,
—they had met with witches in the deep stone caves, full of blind bats,
and when they tossed salt into the food, you never knew what they were
    preparing;
kettle, pot, and frying pan

wore a mask of smoke; they did not reveal the mysteries of the women;
    did not reveal
their hidden herbs, their culinary concoctions, their solitude when they
    mince the parsley,
when they iron in the room until late, and the moon overtakes them
    through the open window
and they are careful not to step in the square of moonlight on the floor
at the hour when the ironed underclothes, piled on the table,
are like uncut pages of books they have read
and they know all the secrets of our bodies.
                                        We do not understand
their incantations when they polish the copper kitchenware with earth
    in the courtyard
and the copper kitchenware shines in the sun like earthly heavenly
    bodies,
and the women shine too, in the triumph of their hegemony
over the mute armies of closed things.

    We do not know
the stubborn freedom of their silence when they refuse to become
    enraged,
their arrogance as decorum lowers their eyelashes,
their multiple defenses, like the tight-layered skins of fresh garlic,
these fragile coverings. What are they after? What are they keeping
    back?

What panoply of virtue are they protecting behind their transparent
    smiles amid the bloodstained autumn evening
when the steps of the Madonna are betrayed by the rustling of straw
    and dry leaves
and the bright marks left the whole length of the road
by the humble footsteps of donkeys, oxen, cattle? And these women
have a round drop of blood on their skirts
and an imperceptible "oh" on their lips
perhaps from the needle that pricked their fingers in a careless moment
    while sewing. What assault
did the silent creatures of god organize amid their solitary affection? We
    do not yet know.

The women
stole seed from men and worked the fields alone,
had their own property, inalienable; paraded
shaking their round bellies in the intoxication of creation
beneath the oranges of spring, as though bearing behind their white
  aprons
small spheres of earth.
                        They did not speak, the women—
they were arrogant, they belonged to the future, they marched forward,
when the men stopped every so often before the plough,
or wielded the scythe like the weary eyebrow of the moon, in the
  obscurity of late evening.

These, alone, in the garden with the tall heliotropes, confidently awaited
  the birth,
and the heliotropes lit up their throats and faces with bright circles
and the first rosy freckles on their broad foreheads
were mystic signs of eternal life
like corms or the bulbs of cyclamen,
like secret roots of trees that work unheard, unseen.

There is always a birth—said the Stranger—
and death is an addition, not a subtraction. Nothing is lost. Because of
  this, men
when they know fear from their work, from decay, from the void, from
  the daily papers,
from the memory of wars, from the crack of their finger joints
or the cry of the sun wedged in between their bones,
seize women as they seize the branches or roots of a tree above the abyss
and swing out high there as though wrestling or playing with chaos,

and the women know it and close their eyes,
they do not say no;
they wait;
and when the men are asleep again they stay awake,
and the men too are their children, like their children,
and they will raise them too, like the others—
they will nourish them at their breasts and with their silence, sometimes
  with their denial,
let them drink again, with their thirst for union; and a huge dark wave

will round out its momentum from the men's side, poised
to smash down full on the breakwaters, to crush them,
till it exhausts itself on the everyday sandy beach, on the small pebbles,
  the weariness, the forgetfulness,
without, very often, being able to strike the rock, to shake the songs of
  praise on high
like the countertorrent of a shattered tension. And again the women,
as if they did not see their wave subsiding, will let them lie,
will busy themselves with the household chores that keep their eyes
  downcast,
kneel before the kneading trough to gather last night's leaven
as though they did not notice the man's helmet that had fallen to the
  ground; they will silently pick that up too
as if it were a clay flowerpot; later they'll plant flowers in it,
small homey flowers, some blue creeping cinquefoil,
will mend their men's socks by lamplight
with that patient wooden egg, will mend
their tattered and threadbare confidence, because men
travel much, suffer much weariness, many fears, much fighting,
and they are fine fellows with their curled mustaches, their wild hair,
  their wild organs,
and are children and do not know their power, all they know
is to pick fights, play the young braggart, because they
never learned the full tally of waiting, month after month, and the next
  year too,
they do not carry life in their bellies, never nourish it with their bellies,
never hear its footsteps starting within them,
they are not the earth, only the seed cast on the earth, and, later,
  weariness and sleep—

a wide deep sleep, without dreams (it's women, again, who have
  dreams), but sometimes
men hear their sleep in their sleep, hear their own steps in their sleep
as if flawless statues were borne in a procession,
as if the stones were speaking, the rivers, the forests,
and their familiar sleep encircles the earth like air,
the earth with its women, children, ages.
                                        This sleep
becomes the familiar of the whole range of our kingdom,

a ladder thrown into infinity,
the great awakening of all our power amid total light

and then the men turn and smile and are tolerant
with the calm attitude of the successful
as if they had just cut, on their knees,
a river with their two bare hands—so serene,
that the women are frightened,
take themselves off to the kitchen, cense the sweepings,
prepare sage tea and cupping glasses,
burn cloves in candle flames,
throw drops of oil into a glass of water,
make the sign of the cross on the bread and on the pillow,

but the shadow of the wooden ladder rises from the ceiling
and the onion braids stir in invisible winds like the sails of the boats in
    which their menfolk serve,
and the hanging coffeepots mirror unknown returning faces of family
    ancestors—

the cross cut in the dough rises,
the lime in the pit in the courtyard begins to seethe,
the cocks crow all night long
as though dawn broke seven times, as though there were no night at all
and the faces of the males, even the smallest boys, gleam in the evening
freckled with white plaster as if they had worked all day building a great
    church
all naked columns and huge windows,
no stained glass, no icons, no sepulchres,
imbued with a high whiteness without shadows, without wounds,
    without death.

And it is like an exodus from time, like a nailing down of time, like its
    abolition
by the swiftness of thought and memory and dreams
and by the endurance of human achievement.
                                        It is union, he said,
of man and woman, of silence and sound, of life and creation,
and the hiss of stillness through the houses' keyholes no longer goes on
    behind your back

and the blowing of night through the holes of the stars is not a sign
for someone else whom you do not see and who alludes to you.

The gates above and below remain wide open. The air blows round with
    candor,
the atmosphere clears, keys of their own accord become useless
and all the ancient countryside, thick bone and gristle,
trembles at midnight in its whole body with the hum of crickets, the
    croaking of frogs, the sawing of the Milky Way,
and the moon rising solemnly from the horizon
is like a new-filled bucket lifting silent water from the nether world.

Then the bones of Greeks, Venetians, Franks, Turks, Greeks,
buried beneath whole mountains, years, and earth-mounds, rejoint
    themselves
from their green-stained armour, their rotted clothes—
naked bodies, sentient, whole,
compact and erotic, amid the first acquaintance with sensations,
not enemies one to the other, not antagonists,
their only weapon the ancient longing of our blood, our memory. The
    hands of the men reach out,
the thumb becomes a great bridge across the ages,
the mountains are like the fertile breasts of women, smooth and
    haughty,
swollen with milk.
                    And the sacred human tools
hang from nails in house or workshop
quiet, serious, tolerant,
as if there were no separation and abyss and absence and loss.
The toothed saw with the oblong shape of a millennium,
the hammer like the statue of a man's fist,
the scythe like the open arm of a lover; and the metal
tacks like stubborn teeth that gnaw at distance and the unknown;
even the wooden tacks they use on shoes
are like little stars thrust into a humble, useful firmament.

The woodworm suddenly stops his work and eavesdrops
on the laden lattice-work of the grape vines,
on the seeds that open their cracked doors; and the black ant that was
besieging the red leaves of the pomegranate falls to the earth

and the roses flare up in the gardens. At that moment the men
take on a new familiarity with the stars; just as when, bare-chested, they
    lean out the window as though
they had cut up melons with their penknives
and were tossing the damp seeds down into the night. And the creaking
    of the old boards
beneath the bare soles of the women who got up at midnight
achieves a sincerity and simplicity, as though the floor were saying:

"You can stop walking on tip-toe. The children are sleeping quietly.
    Their fever has gone down." And the women
smile again all alone in the wisdom of their endurance
and the children smile in their sleep
as if they had suddenly learned the secret of architecture within their
    own secrecy
from the wasp's earthen ramparts with their many fathomless holes
and the waxen hexagonal honeycombs of bees.

Perhaps this way we too learned later, from the children we once were,
from the women, the bees, the stars,
from memory, action, desire,
the order and economy of nature, the household, the office, our bodies.

All our own, said the Stranger. All of this world—
and we carry our dead within us
without their taking space, without our being weighed down—
we continue their life from the deep passages and lonely roots,
their own life, our own integrity in the sun. At that point precisely there
    comes into being
a great calm, a great translucency,
and far off blue islands are visible and islets that never appeared till now
and the chorus of young girls is clearly audible on the opposite shore,
young girls who departed early, leaving
half-finished their first conversation with a daisy.

Well, I told you death does not exist, concluded the Stranger—
calmly, simply—so much so that we smiled without hesitation,
had no fear of the covered mirrors. A triangular sun on the opposite
    wall
had lengthened; the whole of the northern room was lit up

with a steady reflection. We caught the scent
of fruit brought down from the mountains to the greengrocers' shops,
heard the hammering from the nearby blacksmith's and the streetcar
     turning the corner next to the butcher's.

We had the balanced perception of an inconceivable, peaceful harvest
of big fourfold, sweet tomatoes, packed
with attention and method in rectangular crates that they transported
from the countryside straight to the city markets and the bustling ports.
Huge automobiles travelled the sunny roads
like inscrutable purple hills.
                                        We stood up,
uncovered the mirrors, saw ourselves,
and were young thousands of years ago, young
thousands of years later, for time and the sun
are the same age—our own age;
and this light was in no way a reflection
but our own light filtered through from all those deaths.

And this Stranger was ours most of all. The women heated water for
     him to wash,
the men went to buy food for the table. The littlest girl of the house
brought clean towels, a sliver of pink scented soap,
a cup of hot water, the large shaving brush,
and set them down by the mirror—now fully uncovered.

The steam from the hot water little by little fogged the mirror as if to
     cover it up again
and the face of the Stranger as he began to shave,
covered with lather, faded in the upright glass,
simple, young, and sweet, like the morning moon.

ATHENS, FEBRUARY 1958

In the mythic poems, Ritsos plays variations on ancient themes. He both makes archetypal characters immediate and particular, letting us glimpse them in moments of unheroic self-revelation, and makes particular figures universal, as when his deliberate anachronisms and other strategies of synchronicity turn Agamemnon, Philoctetes, Phaedra into timeless representatives of all men and women caught in the nets of the human predicament. An understanding of the basic outlines of each character's ancient legend is essential. Ritsos assumes it in his readers, and it is as important to be attentive to what the characters do not say as to what they do. In the notes that follow, we have, inter alia, provided a synthesized standard version of each legend referred to, giving variants where Ritsos seems to draw on them. For ease of exposition we write throughout as if the speakers or other characters in the poems were identifiable with their mythic prototypes, though of course this is never simply the case.

THE WINDOW

11   *St. Basil's hill* — Ritsos carefully avoids specificity of place in these poems, but the scene of "The Window" clearly matches Piraeus, and St. Basil's hill there overlooks the harbor of Pasalimani.

CHRONICLE

27   *not Samos* — Ritsos mischievously assures us that this is not the location and then goes on to detail the "one complete Ionic column, huge and towering", which (with other details, such as the reference to Pythagoras) unmistakably points to Samos as the scene of the poem. The column stands, a lone survivor, amid the ruins of the temple of Hera.

Hera — Greek goddess, sister and wife of Zeus, and deity of marriage and the life of women. She was worshiped on Samos from very early times.

Athena — Greek goddess, daughter of Zeus and patron goddess of Athens. There are no remains of a temple of Athena on Samos.

Herm — A monument consisting of a four-sided pillar, bearing a head or bust of Hermes on top and sometimes having an erect phallus below.

Apollo — Greek god of music, medicine, and the care of flocks and herds.

28　*Helen* — In ancient mythology, daughter of Zeus and Leda (whom Zeus approached in the form of a swan) and wife of the Spartan king Menelaus. Helen was carried off to Troy by the Trojan prince Paris; her abduction was the cause of the Trojan War. The expedition to win back Menelaus's wife was led by his brother Agamemnon.

Pythagoras — Greek philosopher, born on Samos but emigrated about 531 B.C. to Croton in Italy, where he founded a religious society that later ruled the city. Said to have discovered the numerical ratios determining the principal intervals of the musical scale, upon which he based an interpretation of the whole cosmos through numbers. In the wake of a revolution, retired from Croton to Metapontum, where he died. Had a theory of metempsychosis, which may be hinted at by the modern characters with ancient names in "Chronicle" (Helen, Menelaus, Penelope, Eurydice).

Ares — Greek god of war.

29　*Ploutos* (more commonly Pluto) — Greek god of the underworld, the "Rich One."

Chronos — Time, but Ritsos may also have in mind the Greek god Kronos, youngest son of Heaven and Earth, leader of the Titans and father of the Olympian gods (Zeus, Hera, Hestia, Demeter, Hades, and Poseidon).

Venetian evenings — The Venetians held Samos from 1124 to 1125, in 1172, and from 1204 to 1226.

31　*"Graziella"* — In 1844 Lamartine wrote a prose romance of this name in memory of a woman, Antoniella, whom he had met in Naples in 1812, but who died three years later.

Eurydice — The best known mythical character of this name was the wife of Orpheus, who, after her death, tried to rescue her from the underworld. His prayers to the chthonian deities were granted, but only on condition that Orpheus lead the way up from Hades without looking back to see if she was following. He looked back, and lost her.

32　*Penelope* — Wife of Odysseus. During his ten-year journey home from the Trojan War, she kept importunate suitors at bay by weaving, saying she would marry when her weaving was done, but secretly at night undoing each day's work.

MOONLIGHT SONATA

40　*the Odeion* — The Odeion (theater) of Herodes Atticus, on the south side of the Acropolis, built about A.D. 150 for Herodes' wife Regilla. Today, partially restored, it is used for musical and dramatic performances.

41　*St. Nicholas* — As we have said, Ritsos is deliberately vague about identifications of this sort, but there is in fact a church of this name in the Plaka, in Athens. If you stand at the top of its steps, you find yourself looking out over the modern city—"concrete and airy" as the poem says—with the Acropolis directly at your back. It is a spot where the layers of Athenian history seem to converge, as if the steps could move you through the fourth dimension as well as the spatial three.

AGAMEMNON

The story of the House of Atreus is the background for "Agamemnon", "Orestes", "The Dead House", "The Return of Iphigenia", "Under the Shadow of the Mountain", and "Chrysothemis". Atreus quarreled with his brother Thyestes. At a banquet of pretended reconciliation, Atreus served Thyestes with the flesh of the latter's own children. Atreus had two sons: Agamemnon, king of Mycenae, and Menelaus, king of Sparta. After the abduction of Menelaus's wife Helen by the Trojan Paris, Agamemnon became leader of the expedition to Troy. Agamemnon and his wife Clytemnestra had four children: Orestes, Electra, Iphigenia, and Chrysothemis. The Greek ships assembled at Aulis on the way to Troy, but were becalmed. Under the pretext that she was to be married to Achilles, Iphigenia was sent to Aulis, where Agamemnon sacrificed her to Artemis to ensure a favorable wind for his ships. (In some versions of the story, Artemis substituted a deer at the last moment, and Iphigenia was saved and taken to the Tauric Chersonese [Crimea].) Shortly after Agamemnon's return to Mycenae, which this poem describes, he was entangled in nets and murdered in his bath by Clytemnestra and her lover Aegisthus, a surviving son of Thyestes, born of the latter's incest with his daughter Pelopia. Clytemnestra and Aegisthus were in turn killed by Orestes and Electra. The best-known ancient treatments of the myth are Aeschylus' *Oresteia*, Sophocles' *Electra*, and the *Orestes*, *Electra*, and *Iphigenia at Aulis* of Euripides, on all of which Ritsos draws.

49   *prophetic cries of a crazed woman* — Cassandra, daughter of Priam, ruler of Troy. Apollo gave her the gift of prophecy to win her love, but when she cheated him he turned the gift to a curse by causing her always to be disbelieved. Brought as war booty to Mycenae by Agamemnon, in some versions of the Atreid story she is killed by Clytemnestra.

51   *Ithaca* — Greek island in the Ionian Sea, home of Odysseus.

     Achilles — Son of Peleus and Thetis. Greek hero in the Trojan War. Agamemnon's demand that Achilles hand over the captive woman Briseis to Agamemnon so angered Achilles that he refused to fight. This "wrath of Achilles" is the theme of Homer's *Iliad*. Achilles' death at the hands of Paris and Apollo is foretold in the *Iliad*.

     Patroclus — Companion to Achilles, who led Achilles' troops in battle after Achilles had refused to fight (*Iliad* 16). Patroclus' death in battle forced Achilles to return to the fighting, where he slew the Trojan Hector.

54   *Balius and Xanthus* — Two immortal horses of Achilles (*Iliad* 19.400ff.).

56   *Philemon* — There is no Philemon mentioned in the *Iliad*, and the only Phi-
lemon familiar from Greek mythology is the Phrygian countryman who
entertains Zeus and Hermes. The name was perhaps chosen at random.

Antilochus — Son of Nestor and a close friend of Achilles. Mentioned sev-
eral times in the *Iliad* as a brave Greek warrior.

Lekythos — A tall jar with a narrow neck used for oil or unguents and
offerings to the dead.

57   *Erotes* — Representations of Eros, the Greek god of love, as a winged
putto.

58   *Lachesis* — One of the three fates, all daughters of Zeus and Themis: Clo-
tho ("The Spinner"), Lachesis ("Getting-by-lot"), and Atropos ("Un-
avoidable").

Trojan Horse — A huge, hollow wooden horse, left by the Greeks in front
of Troy after their purported withdrawal from the siege. The Trojans, in-
duced to believe the horse was a sacrifice to Athena, opened their gates and
took the horse into their city. The horse was filled with Greek soldiers who
opened the gates of Troy to the Greek army, which conquered the city.

59   *Ion* — Again, the name does not occur in the *Iliad*, and was perhaps chosen
at random. (We are hardly to suppose him the eponymous ancestor of the
Ionians.)

ORESTES

Orestes was the son of Agamemnon and Clytemnestra. He avenged his
father's murder by killing Clytemnestra and her lover Aegisthus. In some
versions of the story (Aeschylus' *The Libation Bearers*, for example) his
sister Electra welcomes Orestes but does not actively participate in the mur-
der. In Euripides' *Orestes* she is almost monomaniac from hatred and helps
to kill Clytemnestra. Orestes gains entry to the palace with a messenger
bringing news of his own purported death. As in "Agamemnon", the setting
is the palace of Mycenae, with its Lion Gate.

65   *A woman's lamentation* — The voice is Electra's.

Pylades — Son of Strophius of Phocis, to whom in some versions of the
story Orestes was sent after the murder of his father Agamemnon by Cly-
temnestra and Aegisthus. Pylades is a friend to Orestes.

66   *I don't want to cut my hair* — Cutting one's hair was a traditional part of
the ritual of lamentation for the dead.

the two marble lions — A subtle distortion. The lions above the great lintel
of the Lion Gate at Mycenae are of limestone.

68   *Zara* — One of the two mountains that tower over Mycenae. Mt. Zara is
to the south. To the north is Mt. Ayios Ilias.

69   *hydromel* — Mixture of honey and water offered as a libation to the powers of the underworld.

    teeth of the dead . . . are white seeds — Perhaps an allusion to the story of Cadmus' founding of Thebes. Cadmus was told by the oracle at Delphi to found a city where a cow, which he would find outside the temple, lay down. The cow led him to the site of Thebes. To get water for the city, he killed a dragon, guardian of the spring of Ares. At Athena's instigation, he sowed the dragon's teeth and a field full of armed men sprang up. Most of the armed men killed one another in battle, but five survived to become ancestors of the Theban ruling class, the Spartoi ("sown men"). The blending of Theban and Mycenean mythology is deliberate (cf. the introduction to "The Dead House": "She imagined that their house had been moved to somewhere in ancient Thebes, or, rather, Argos . . .").

79   *the cow was a symbol in some ancient religion* — The obvious religion is Hinduism, in which the cow was, and remains, sacred; but another possibility is the Egyptian cow goddess Hathor.

THE DEAD HOUSE

The speaker is Electra. The sister shuffling about offstage is Chrysothemis. Their uncle is Menelaus.

85   *Thebes* — Ancient Greek city in Boeotia, setting for the legend of Oedipus.

    Argos — Ancient Greek city in the northeastern Peloponnesus. General name for Agamemnon's domain.

86   *the younger one's blond ringlets* — There is no younger brother in the story of the House of Atreus. This brother represents a fusion of the myth of the House of Atreus with Ritsos' own family history.

89   *a slender slaughtered woman* — An allusion, though not exclusively, to Iphigenia.

90   *a blind man . . . with a lyre on his knees* — An allusion to Homer, though again perhaps not exclusively.

93   *the brilliant victory* — The sack of Troy.

98   *Knossos* — Site of the largest Minoan palace in Crete, and the scene of numerous Cretan myths including those of Minos, Ariadne, Pasiphaë, Daedalus, and the Minotaur.

THE RETURN OF IPHIGENIA

Iphigenia was sacrificed to Artemis at Aulis by her father Agamemnon to ensure a favorable wind for the Greek ships sailing to Troy. In one version of the story (followed by Euripides in his *Iphigenia among the Taurians*), Artemis snatched Iphigenia away at the last moment, substituting a deer for the young woman and taking Iphigenia to the Tauric Chersonese (Crimea), where she became a priestess of Artemis. There is also a legend at Brauron (on the coast of Attica southeast of Athens, site of a sanctuary of Artemis) that the purported sacrifice took place there, and that a bear, rather than a deer, was substituted. In "The Return of Iphigenia", the brother is Orestes, with his friend Pylades. The two sisters are Electra and Chrysothemis. The scene is Mycenae.

105 *a charred log* — This is the primitive wooden image (*xoanon*) of the goddess that Iphigenia has removed from its shrine in the Crimea and will take with her to Brauron.

Under the Shadow of the Mountain

The speaker is Electra. The scene, again, is Mycenae (although here in particular it must be noted that Ritsos' own childhood home in Monemvasia, in the Peloponnesus, was even more nearly in the "shadow of the mountain", the huge rocky offshore promontory for which Monemvasia has been aptly described as the Gibraltar of Greece).

138 *the two decapitated lions* — The two lions of the Lion Gate at Mycenae.

the gold and proper obol between the corpse's teeth for the ferry fare — The Greeks put an obol into the mouths of the dead as payment for the ferryman Charon to ferry them across the River Styx in the underworld, but this coin was copper, not gold.

144 *Pelasgian* — A generic term in antiquity used to describe the earliest inhabitants of Greece and their supposed remains (walls, etc.).

Epidaurus — City on a peninsula in the Saronic Gulf with a temple of Asclepius.

Delphi — Site on the southern slope of Mt. Parnassus, above the Gulf of Corinth, and home of the most prestigious oracle of Greece, presided over by Apollo.

Chrysothemis

Chrysothemis is the daughter of Agamemnon and Clytemnestra and sister to Orestes, Electra, and Iphigenia.

150 *this gate . . . one slaughtered girl* — The Lion Gate of Mycenae. The slaughtered girl is Iphigenia.

160 *dogged . . . by the Furies* — The Furies, or Erinyes, are spirits of punishment, avenging wrongs, especially the murder of kindred. Orestes fled Mycenae pursued by the Furies after the murder of Clytemnestra and Aegisthus (see Aschylus' *The Libation Bearers*).

163 *hens . . . laying red eggs* — Red eggs are traditionally prepared at Greek Easter.

PERSEPHONE

Persephone (also known as Korē, "the Maiden") was the daughter of Zeus and Demeter, goddess of grain. She was abducted by Ploutos, ruler of the underworld, to be his queen. Ploutos was Demeter's brother and Persephone's uncle. The grieving Demeter sought her daughter far and wide. At last Zeus ordered Ploutos to return the girl to earth. Ploutos gave Persephone the seeds of a pomegranate to eat, thus compelling her to remain thenceforth for part of each year in the underworld, since the Greeks believed those who had eaten food in the land of the dead could no longer return to the land of the living.

177   *Cyane* — A water nymph who accompanied Persephone on her last, fatal flower-gathering expedition and who unsuccessfully tried to keep Ploutos from taking Persephone to the underworld from the Sicilian meadows of Enna.

178   *three rivers* — Three of the rivers of the underworld—Styx, Acheron, and Lethe—were all believed to flow from a central rock.

      cupping glasses — Heated glasses applied to the body, creating a partial vacuum, to relieve internal congestion. Also used with scarification to draw blood.

181   *his two black horses* — The scene of the abduction, showing Hades-Ploutos with Persephone in his chariot and the cowering nymph Cyane, is the subject of a splendid fourth-century B.C. mural found in 1977 in a royal Macedonian tomb.

182   *poplars, cypresses, sterile willows, wild mint, pomegranates* — All either symbolic of death or in some other way associated with Persephone in Hades. Persephone changed the body of one of her rivals for Ploutos' affection into a bed of mint (see Ovid's *Met.* 10.719).

183   *Serapis* — A Hellenistic deity from Ptolemaic Egypt, combining the attributes of Osiris (king and judge of the dead) and Apis (a sacred bull originally identified with Ptah).

      Bryaxis the Athenian — The famous statue of Serapis by Bryaxis (perhaps in fact not the Athenian but another fourth- to third-century sculptor of that name) is described in detail by Clement of Alexandria (*Protreptikos pros Hellenas* 4.48.1–3), and it is clearly this description, with its reference to gold, silver, bronze, lead, and tin on the surface, that Ritsos has in mind here.

184   *an ugly dog* — Cerberus, a mythical watchdog often represented as having three heads, guardian of the underworld.

187   *the three women always there* — Probably the three fates, but also perhaps the three Marys of Christian tradition.

Because of a prophecy that he would kill his father, the child Oedipus, son of Laius, king of Thebes, and Jocasta, was given to a shepherd to be exposed but was instead raised to manhood. After a quarrel at a crossroad, Oedipus killed Laius, having no notion of his identity. Jocasta's brother Creon became ruler of Thebes and offered Jocasta and the kingdom to anyone who could rid Thebes of the Sphinx, a creature half woman, half lion who menaced the city by posing a riddle and carrying off Theban young men as long as the riddle remained unanswered. Oedipus solved the riddle, which concerned the three ages of man, and married Jocasta his mother, by whom he had four children: Eteocles, Polyneices, Antigone, and Ismene. When the blind seer Tiresias revealed to Oedipus what he had done, Oedipus blinded himself and left Thebes. His sons Eteocles and Polyneices agreed to rule the city in alternate years, Eteocles the elder taking the first year. At the end of the year, Eteocles refused to give up the throne. Polyneices raised a coalition against the city (the famous "Seven against Thebes") and the two brothers killed each other in the fighting. Creon forbade the burial of Polyneices, but Antigone defied the ban, buried her brother, and was herself put to death as a result. Antigone's fiancé Haemon, son of Creon, killed himself in grief at Antigone's death. Haemon's mother, Creon's wife Eurydice, killed herself in grief at Haemon's death. This version is, in essence, that followed (and partially created) by Sophocles in *Oedipus the King, Antigone,* and *Oedipus at Colonus,* and Ritsos adheres to it closely. Sophocles portrays Ismene as an average, unheroic, conformist woman (in sharp contrast to Antigone), anxious not to offend or overstep the bounds of social decorum. Ritsos takes her for his narrator and lets her make her own apologia.

198   *unwept, unbefriended, . . . unwedded* — From Sophocles' *Antigone* (line 876). Such direct borrowings from ancient sources are extremely rare in Ritsos and thus carry added significance.

203   *Argives* — Polyneices went from Thebes to Argos after Eteocles' refusal to give him the throne. The Seven against Thebes were led by the Argive Adrastus. While the list of the seven varies, most were Argives.

212   *dusty all over* — Antigone gave her brother ritual burial, in a dry, windy dawn, by scattering dust over the decaying corpse (Soph. *Ant.* 246ff., 408ff.). When Ismene sees her, she has just come from doing this, which is why she is "marked by fate," fated as she is to die for her defiance of Creon's order.

AJAX

Ajax was the son of Telamon, king of Salamis. In the *Iliad*, Ajax is portrayed as a huge man, the "bulwark of the Achaeans", whose straightforward strength contrasts with Odysseus' cunning. His characteristic weapon is a huge shield. After Achilles' death, Achilles' arms, which should have gone to Ajax, went by trickery to Odysseus instead. Ajax went mad with anger and grief. (Once again, Ritsos draws heavily on Sophocles' version. In the latter's *Ajax*, as in Ritsos' poem, we first see Ajax surrounded by animals he has tormented and slaughtered in his madness.) In a final gesture of despair, Ajax killed himself by falling upon his sword, leaving his Phrygian wife Tecmessa and his son Eurysaces. Teucer, Ajax's half-brother, was absent at the time of Ajax's suicide but returned in time to take a leading part in the struggle to secure him an honorable burial. In some versions of the story, the wild iris sprang from the blood that flowed at Ajax's death.

219   *Ida* — An extensive mountain range in northwest Asia Minor. The highest peak, Gargaros (4,650 ft.) offers an extensive view over the Hellespont, while a lower spur forms a crescent around the territory of Troy.

pallid lofty icons — A characteristic conflation of mythical and Christian imagery, including St. George and the dragon ("a huge snake"), the Cyclops ("one great solitary eye"), Androcles and the lion, and John the Baptist ("a severed head on a tray").

220   *tied under the belly of my horse* — A reminiscence here of Odysseus' escape from the Cyclops' cave, clinging under the belly of a ram.

223   *threw into the helmet . . . hand-to-hand combat against the enemy* — See *Iliad* 7.170–272.

Hector was charging furiously over the trenches — See *Iliad* 16.114–23. Hector was the son of Priam, king of Troy.

227   *Mother* — Ajax's mother was the Athenian Eriboea or Periboea, daughter of Alcathoös. Telamon married her after the death of his first wife, Glauce, daughter of King Cychreos of Salamis.

PHILOCTETES

On the expedition to Troy, Philoctetes was the leader of seven ships from Methone, Thaumakie, Olizon, and Meliboia. Methone is in Macedonian Pieria. The other towns are in Magnesia, in Thessaly. On the way to Troy, the ships stopped at Tenedos, where Philoctetes stumbled into the sacred shrine or precinct of a god and was bitten by a snake. On the advice of Odysseus, he was left by the Greeks on the island of Lemnos because of the stench of his suppurating wound and his agonized cries of pain. Philoctetes had received magic weapons from Heracles (often a bow and poisoned arrows, but in Ritsos' account spears and a shield) as a reward for lighting Heracles' funeral pyre on Mt. Oeta. According to an oracle, Troy could not be taken without these weapons, so Neoptolemos, Achilles' son by Deidameia, was sent by Odysseus to get the weapons, by trickery if necessary, and take them to Troy. The plot of Sophocles' *Philoctetes* (on which Ritsos draws) turns on Neoptolemos' moral struggle over his obligations to Philoctetes. In Ritsos' monologue he is the (unnamed) narrator. Philoctetes was finally persuaded to return to Troy, where his wound was healed and he killed Paris. Neoptolemos was one of the Greeks in the Trojan Horse.

231   *labors of Heracles* — Heracles was the son of Zeus and Alcmene. He performed twelve famous labors while in servitude to his cousin Eurystheus of Argos, after which he was promised immortality by the Delphic Oracle.

235   *Patroclus* — See note to "Agamemnon".

       Mother — Deidameia was the daughter of Lycomedes, king of Scyros. When the Trojan War began, knowing Achilles was destined to die at Troy, his mother Thetis hid him on Scyros, dressed as a girl. There he met Deidameia and fathered Neoptolemos. When Calchas the prophet told the Greeks that Troy could not be taken without Achilles, Odysseus and other Greeks went to find him and discovered him on Scyros, after which Achilles went willingly to Troy. There is no ancient testimony that Deidameia was hanged.

237   *called up with my class* — As Achilles' son, Neoptolemos would be called up to do his military training in Thessaly, here described.

239   *Oeta* — Mt. Oeta, a 7,000-foot range in the south of Thessaly, forms the main barrier between northern and central Greece.

245   *the Seven-headed one* — The Lernaean hydra, a swamp creature that ravaged the countryside around Lerna in the Argolid. Killing the hdyra was Heracles' second labor. The hydra is usually given nine heads (one of them immortal), but the number of heads varies from seven, as in Ritsos, to the hundred given the creature by Ovid. In some versions, for every one head cut off, two grew back.

       who killed the guard of Hades — Cerberus was a fierce three-headed dog who guarded the underworld. Heracles' twelfth labor was the fetching of Cerberus from the underworld. In most versions, however, Heracles brought him up, then took him back again, but did not kill him.

HELEN

       Helen was the daughter of Zeus and Leda, whom Zeus visited in the form of a swan. She was the wife of the Spartan king Menelaus, brother of Agamemnon. Helen's abduction by the Trojan Paris was the cause of the Trojan War. Her visitor in Ritsos' monologue has no certain identity, nor does he need one: he is any Trojan War survivor, almost Everyman.

253   *Aphrodite* — Greek goddess of love and beauty.

256   *Proteus* — King of Egypt. In some versions of the story (most notably that of Stesichorus, followed by Euripides in his *Helen*), Paris took a phantom Helen, fashioned from clouds, to Troy, while the real Helen was stolen by Hermes, at Zeus' direction, and taken to Proteus to guard in Egypt. Ritsos does not follow this variant, but he is very conscious of it and of the moral

it poses—that the war was all for nothing. It is interesting that Ritsos has Helen mention Proteus, Theoclymenus, and the Dioscuri, all prominent in Euripides' *Helen*, though her own narrative makes it clear that she was indeed at Troy. The effect is to produce a dreamlike universality of place.

Theoclymenus — Son of King Proteus and a leading character in Euripides' *Helen*.

Castor and Polydeuces ("Pollux") — The Dioscuri, twin sons of Zeus (or Tyndareus) and Leda and brothers of Helen. Famous for their fraternal affection, they were also regarded as protectors of persons at sea. They became the two brightest stars in the constellation Gemini. In Euripides' *Helen*, they function as a joint deus ex machina.

Theseus — Son of Aegeus (or in some versions of Poseidon) and national hero of Athens. As a ruler of Athens, Theseus is supposed to have brought about the union of the various communities of Attica into one state. Helen recalls him because he carried her off when she was very young, and as a result Attica was invaded by her brothers Castor and Polydeuces.

Peirithoüs — Son of Ixion. Peirithoüs made a compact with Theseus that they would both marry daughters of Zeus and helped Theseus carry Helen off from Sparta. Theseus and Peirithoüs then went to the underworld to try to win Persephone for Peirithoüs. Peirithoüs was caught and had to remain in the underworld, but Heracles rescued Theseus and brought him back to the surface of the earth.

Andromache — Wife to Hector, and after his and Achilles' deaths the booty of Neoptolemos. Euripides made her the subject of one of his lesser plays.

258 *E and Θ* — Epsilon and Theta, first letters of the Greek words Ἔρως (*eros*) and Θάνατος (*thanatos*), love and death.

262 *Eurotas* — A river near Sparta, flowing the entire length of the valley and plain between the Taygetos and Parnon ranges.

263 *Corinth* — Greek city just west of the isthmus between north Greece and the Peloponnesus.

Sicyon — Greek coastal city thirteen miles west of Corinth, on the Corinthian Gulf.

266 *I climbed alone to the top of the high walls* — See *Iliad* 3.121–461, in which Helen climbs the Trojan wall with the Trojan king Priam, identifies the Greek leaders for the king, and watches Paris and Menelaus engage in single combat. Aphrodite ended the combat by cutting Paris' helmet strap and spiriting him safely away from the field.

269 *Anadyomenes* — Plural of Anadyomene, an epithet for Aphrodite derived from the verb ἀναδύομαι (*anaduomai*), to come up or rise, especially from the sea. "Aphrodite" or "Venus Anadyomene", and later "anadyomene"

tout court, came to signify a painting by Apelles depicting Aphrodite rising from the waves. It had many imitators.

eagles and Ganymedes — Ganymede was a Trojan youth who was abducted by Zeus in the form of an eagle and taken to Olympus, where he was made cupbearer to the gods and became immortal. Again, the episode was a favorite subject for artists (e.g., Leochares).

270 *Taygetos* — A mountain range overlooking the plain of Sparta.

Mistra — The Byzantine capital of the Morea (Peloponnesus), on the foothills of Taygetus, a few miles west of Sparta. It was built under the great castle erected in 1249 by William II of Villehardouin, the prince of Achaea. It fell to the Ottoman Turks in 1460 and was finally destroyed by Ibrahim Pasha during the Greek War of Independence. This is one of Ritsos' more subtle anachronisms.

Odysseus — King of Ithaca and hero of the Trojan War, noted for his cunning. His ten-year wandering journey home from Troy and his destruction of the suitors who laid siege in his absence to his wife Penelope is the subject of Homer's *Odyssey*.

Circe — Daughter of the sun and an enchantress who turned Odysseus' men into swine and kept Odysseus himself with her as her lover for a full year. (See *Odyssey* 10.133–574.)

Nausicaä — Daughter of Alcinoüs, king of the Phaeacians. Nausicaä found Odysseus washed up on shore and took him to her father, who sheltered him. Books 9–12 of the *Odyssey* are told as a traveller's tale in Alcinoüs' palace. Alcinoüs sent Odysseus with gifts and an escort safely home to Ithaca. In retaliation for this aid to Odysseus, Poseidon turned the Phaeacian ship to stone as it arrived back home, and set a ring of mountains around the city to cut it off from the sea.

Symplegades — The Clashing Rocks, usually located at the entrance to the Black Sea, and said to crush anything that tried to pass between them — until the Argo sailed safely through with the help of Hera (see Apollonius Rhodius 2.561ff.), after which, in accordance with a prophecy, the rocks fused together and clashed no more. Homer seems to identify the Symplegades with the Wandering Rocks (Planktai) or Drifters encountered by Odysseus (see *Odyssey* 12.59–72), although these latter are often located in the Straits of Messina.

PHAEDRA

Phaedra was the daughter of Minos, king of Crete, and Pasiphaë, daughter of the Sun. Minos was the son of Zeus and Europa, whom Zeus carried off in the form of a bull. To settle the question whether he or another should rule Crete, Minos prayed to Poseidon to send him a bull from the sea that he could sacrifice to the god. Poseidon did so, but Minos substituted another bull for the sacrifice. In retaliation, Poseidon made Pasiphaë fall in love with the bull Minos had kept. Daedalus helped Pasiphaë to disguise herself as a cow. She coupled with the bull and bore the Minotaur ("Minos Bull"), a creature half man, half bull. Daedalus constructed a maze, the labyrinth, in which to hide it.

Attica was required to send to Crete a yearly tribute of young men and women for the Minotaur. Theseus, son of Aegeus or Poseidon (see note to "Helen"), volunteered to be one of the youths sent to Crete, where he killed the Minotaur with the help of Ariadne, daughter of Minos and Pasiphaë, who gave him a thread by means of which he could find his way out of the labyrinth. Theseus took Ariadne to Naxos, where he left her (or where she was taken from him by Dionysus).

Theseus joined Heracles in an expedition against the Amazons and carried off the Amazon Antiope (in some versions called Hippolyte or Melanippe), by whom he had a son, Hippolytus. Theseus later married Phaedra. In some versions of the story, Antiope appeared at their wedding, where she was slain. Phaedra fell in love with her stepson Hippolytus, who repulsed her (whether from honor, modesty, latent homosexuality, or simple antisexuality is uncertain). She hanged herself, leaving a letter in which she accused Hippolytus of rape. Theseus believed the accusation and prayed to Poseidon that his son might perish. When Hippolytus was driving his chariot on the shore, Poseidon sent a bull from the sea to frighten the horses. Hippolytus was thrown from his chariot and dragged to his death. The myth is treated at length in Euripides' *Hippolytus*, on the psychology of which Ritsos plays some of his subtlest variations.

273   *Yannis Tsarouchis* — Modern Greek artist (d. 1989).

276   *March ring* — A ring made of woven hair, worn according to Greek country superstition as a protection against sunburn.

277   *deer — the favored beasts of your Goddess* — Artemis, goddess of wild animals and the hunt, "lady of wild things". Her special animal was the deer. Hippolytus, an avid hunter, professed a particular veneration for her, rejecting her fellow goddess Aphrodite, to his own ultimate destruction.

279   *when you first came to Athens for the festival at Eleusis* — After his marriage to Phaedra, Theseus sent Hippolytus to live with his grandfather Pittheus at Troezen. Theseus hoped that when Pittheus died Hippolytus could rule Troezen, while Theseus' children by Phaedra could follow his own rule in Athens. Hippolytus was sent to Athens to be initiated into the Eleusinian mysteries. It was on that visit that Phaedra fell in love with him.

284   *Academy, University, Stadium, Aeolus streets* — Streets in modern-day central Athens.

294   *Aphrodite and Artemis* — Euripides' *Hippolytus* is framed by a prologue, spoken by Aphrodite, goddess of love, and an epilogue, spoken by Artemis. This is a similar reminder that the story must be seen, in part, as a tale of rivalry among the gods, played out with mortals as pawns.

The scene is set in a house of mourning (hence the covered mirrors).

309   *Venetians, Franks, Turks* — The Venetians occupied much of Greece in the twelfth and thirteenth centuries, in part as a bulwark against the Moslem powers to the east. Frankish (German, Italian, French, and English) rulers also claimed parts of Greece, notably after the Fourth Crusade of 1204. Even when in 1261 the Byzantines destroyed this "Latin Empire" many areas (including Athens) remained in Frankish hands until long after the Turkish conquest. By the close of the fourteenth century, the Turks had occupied Macedonia and Thessaly; Constantinople fell to them in 1453 and Mistra (see note to "Helen") in 1460. The Venetians held some territory in the Aegean until the seventeenth century, but by that time most of Greece had become part of the Ottoman Empire, where it remained until the War of Independence in 1825–30 (although even then parts of Greece did not gain independence until later—Crete, for example, which became independent only in 1912).